Tamarind City

Bishwanath Ghosh was born on 26 December 1970 in Kanpur, Uttar Pradesh, where he began his career as a journalist before moving to New Delhi to work with the Press Trust of India and *The Asian Age*. In 2001 he relocated to Chennai where he spent seven years at *The New Sunday Express* and three at *The Times of India*. He is currently a deputy editor with *The Hindu*. In 2009 he wrote the bestselling travel book, *Chai, Chai: Travels in Places Where You Stop But Never Get Off*, also published by Tranquebar.

BISHWANATH GHOSH

Tamarind City

WHERE MODERN INDIA BEGAN

First published by Tranquebar, an imprint of westland ltd in 2012

Published by Tranquebar, an imprint of Westland Books, a division of Nasadiya Technologies Private Limited in 2023

No. 269/2B, First Floor, 'Irai Arul', Vimalraj Street, Nethaji Nagar, Alapakkam Main Road, Maduravoyal, Chennai 600095

Westland, the Westland logo, Tranquebar and the Tranquebar logo are the trademarks of Nasadiya Technologies Private Limited, or its affiliates.

Copyright © Bishwanath Ghosh, 2012

Bishwanath Ghosh asserts the moral right to be identified as the author of this work.

ISBN: 9789357767774

10 9 8 7 6 5 4 3 2 1

The views and opinions expressed in this work are the author's own and the facts are as reported by him, and the publisher is in no way liable for the same.

All rights reserved

Typeset by Arun Bisht for FourWords Inc
Printed at Saurabh Printers Pvt. Ltd.

No part of this book may be reproduced, or stored in a retrieval system, or transmitted in any form or by any means, electronic, mechanical, photocopying, recording, or otherwise, without express written permission of the publisher.

For two women in my life:
My mother Karabi,
who did not live to see this book,
and my wife Shuvashree,
who saw me through it.

CONTENTS

Author's Note viii

Prologue: The Train to a New Identity ix

CHAPTER 1
Company Comes Calling 1

CHAPTER 2
North of South 25

CHAPTER 3
Do You Believe in God? 59

CHAPTER 4
A Sacred Sunday   101

CHAPTER 5
Sex and the City   136

CHAPTER 6
The Rich Girl and the King of Romance   170

CHAPTER 7
Chandamama and Madras Miscellany   195

CHAPTER 8
A Seaside Story   231

CHAPTER 9
Come December   258

CHAPTER 10
All Roads Lead to Chennai   279

CHAPTER 11
My Street   298

Acknowledgements   314

AUTHOR'S NOTE

When writing about a city you are still living in, you don't have the luxury of looking back at it from a distance, with a boxful of notes and memories to draw from. You live your subject each day, and one of the biggest challenges is to sift through your daily life to collect material that may be used to paint a portrait.

This book, however, does not pretend to be an exhaustive or authoritative study of Chennai or of Tamil culture. It is born purely out of my desire to understand a city I've called home for over a decade now.

B.G.

PROLOGUE: THE TRAIN TO A NEW IDENTITY

At times, even a minor act of nature can decide things of great significance to some of us—such as the title of this book.

One morning around six o'clock, when the roads of Chennai are stirring awake, wife and I were driving home after dropping a friend off at the railway station. Rarely do you find yourself driving at a leisurely speed in your own city at that hour; usually it is a dash to catch a plane or train, when the eyes are glued to the watch and blind to the blossoming of a new day.

We were on Commander-in-Chief Road, gliding towards Mount Road, when something fell from a tree straight onto my lap. Taking it to be a large insect, I instinctively shook it off. As the tiny intruder lay near my feet, I examined it from a distance and then picked it up with glee.

'What's that?' my wife, who was driving, asked.

'A piece of tamarind.'

'But why are you smiling?'

'Because that settles it.'

'Settles what?'

I had just signed the contract for this book, intended to be a portrait of Chennai, which I proposed to call *Tamarind City*. The title was based on my childhood impression of the city. However, when I bounced it off my well-wishers in Chennai, they all, quite expectedly, raised the same argument: 'But tamarind is not unique to Chennai, it is commonly used all over south India.' That set me thinking: should I be fastidious about such technical accuracy—even though Chennai has traditionally been representative of the whole of the south and therefore qualifies as Tamarind City—or celebrate the image that was sown in me as a child?

For weeks, I see-sawed between *Tamarind City* and the various names that came to mind at odd times of the day. I visualised these titles on the spine of an imaginary book, but none of them was convincing enough to make me say—this is it!

Then, that morning, the balance was tilted by a weightless piece of dry tamarind that fell straight from the tree onto my lap. I knew this was it.

■ ■ ■

I was thirty, single and commitment-phobic when I moved to Chennai in 2001. I was hoping to spend a few carefree

Prologue: The Train to a New Identity

years in the city before returning to Delhi to settle down. But Chennai turned out to be a rocking chair. Swinging to its gentle rhythm, the balmy sea breeze always apologising on behalf of the heat, I didn't realise how quickly the last two digits of that year got interchanged.

Today I am forty, married, and leading a fairly comfortable existence as an honorary Madrasi. Yet, as I look into the mirror every morning, stroking the new grey sprouting on my chin, I often find myself asking: But wasn't it only the other day I took the train to Chennai?

I had almost missed the train.

Delhi lay under a thick blanket of fog on the night of 13 January 2001, when I arrived at the railway station to board the Tamil Nadu Express. I was to travel 2,157 km in the next one-and-a-half days to reach Chennai. A small party of friends, including my girlfriend, had come along to see me off. They engaged me in humorous banter as we stood in a circle on the platform. Much of the ribbing was forced, just to break the awkward silences that we kept slipping into. They were aware, as was I, that for all the years we had spent together, I would be past tense once the train pulled out of the station.

The train's departure was scheduled for 10.30 pm, but there was no sign of the train even at ten o'clock, which was unusual. Trains originating from a station usually park themselves at the designated platform way ahead of the departure time. Finally, the recorded female voice, the nightingale of Indian Railways, announced a delay—first by thirty minutes and then by an hour.

The delay, presumably due to the fog, was robbing my departure of drama. I could see my friends growing weary of waiting. The banter was now too artificial for comfort. A farewell is most effective when short and sweet; the longer it drags, the more you wish the person left sooner.

To make matters worse, a male voice—live and not automated—came on the public-address system to announce that the departure of Tamil Nadu Express had been postponed indefinitely due to the dense fog engulfing north India, and that passengers must wait until further announcement.

I could see the smiles vanish from the faces of my friends. They were friends alright, but why should they stand indefinitely in the bone-chilling cold to wave goodbye to someone they might never see again? They bullied me into going back to my girlfriend's place, which was very close to the railway station, and advised me to keep checking the train's departure time over phone. The girlfriend was delighted. She had earned a few more hours with me. She perhaps knew the relationship was eventually going to be devoured by distance. As soon as my friends dumped me back at her place and left after giving me farewell hugs, having fulfilled their responsibility of seeing me off, I called up the station. To my horror, I was told that the Tamil Nadu Express was leaving in thirty minutes.

As I ran across the empty platform, weighed down by a heavy bag containing my lifetime's collection of music cassettes, and dragging with numb fingers a large suitcase that had all my clothes and a few books, I desperately looked for a coolie to not only carry my luggage but also guide me to the air-conditioned coaches. The AC coaches are clubbed at one end of the train, and if you happen to be unwittingly walking towards the opposite end, you are only walking into deep trouble. But none of the coolies, who otherwise accost you at the very entrance of a station, was in sight. They were not required on that platform anymore because all the passengers had already boarded the train, except me. Finally I spotted one and called out to him. He turned out to be a fellow passenger—wearing a bright red shirt—standing outside his coach. I said sorry to him and ran in search of mine. I had barely got past the door, after pushing the giant suitcase in, when the train gave a jerk and began to move.

By the next afternoon, I had left north India and its freezing cold way behind. The sun now shone brightly on green fields. I stood by the door and watched the train roll on furiously from the land of parathas and puris to the land of idlis and dosas, from the land of Kavitas and Savitas to the land of Kavithas and Savithas, from the land of Hindi to a land where someone like me would now be speaking only English.

I was, however, accorded one last chance to speak in Hindi. As I stood by the door, smoking, I noticed a young Sikh emerging from the lavatory, wiping his hands. He stood next to me. I remembered seeing him the night before and what had struck me about him was the permanent smile pasted on his face. He was smiling even now as he wiped his hands and put the handkerchief back in his pocket.

'Do you live in Chennai?' I asked him. It had been hours since I had spoken to anyone.

He recoiled in mock horror at my question. Then, slapping his palms together, burst out laughing.

'*Chennai main rehkar marna hai kya?*' he asked. 'Do you think I'm crazy to be living in a place like Chennai?'

His body was still shaking with mirth.

Why did I choose Chennai? Why did I want to leave Delhi in the first place—the place to *be* if you are a journalist? That's because I was bored and tired. Bored of chasing politicians, and tired of trying to extract a sentence or two out of them in order to produce a 450-word story. I wanted to break free from the routine; from the constant fear that I might someday lose my job if I did not chase people hard enough for so-called exclusives.

But why did I not choose Mumbai or, for that matter, Kolkata, considering that I am a Kanpur-bred Bengali who had never had the chance to live in Bengal? A job-hop to Kolkata could have reconciled me to my roots.

I guess it had something to do with my memories of childhood. My parents had lived in Chennai at different times and they always spoke highly of Madras, as the city was known then. Much of my mother's childhood was spent in and around Madras, and that is why idli and dosa were often the Sunday brunch special during my growing-up years in Kanpur. And when I was about six years old, my father was sent to IIT-Madras for three months on a training programme. He came back with a lot of toys (purchased from Moore Market, which was soon to be destroyed in a fire) and tales. I have long forgotten the tales, but my first impression of Madras, formed on the basis of his accounts, was that it was a city of tamarind trees. No other detail registered because of my inborn love for the taste of tamarind. For the first few months after coming here, whenever I went out in search of lunch, I would ask only for tamarind rice.

At times, walking the streets of Chennai, I wonder if I am walking over footprints left behind by my father way back in 1976. I also wonder about one more thing: how did a family manage back then, with the husband living in

Madras for three months and the wife alone in Kanpur, looking after two small kids? Did they not worry to death about each other, considering one had no idea what was happening with the other until a long-awaited letter arrived? I guess they did not. That was the time when one assumed all was well until bad news, if there was any, arrived. They did not have the device to worry. The device came in the form of the mobile phone. On one hand, it allows you to stay in touch, but on the other, if a close member of one's family does not answer repeated calls or if the phone turns out to be switched off, you panic.

Long before mobile phones became commonplace, satellite TV had entered our homes. It was in 1993, when I still lived in Kanpur, that I found myself being swept off by the high-energy choreography of Tamil songs. Songs that did not have choreography had scenery. Till then, in movies, I had only seen the streets of Bombay or the hills of Kashmir and—occasionally—Switzerland. I must have seen picturesque south Indian locations too, masqueraded as pretty north Indian villages in Hindi films, but there was no way my untrained eye could have distinguished them as south India. But the Tamil songs I now got to watch, thanks to satellite TV, presented the beauty of the south in its purest form. The greenery, the beaches, the backwaters: pristine and strikingly fresh to the eye of a north Indian.

It was not as if I was completely oblivious to the beauty of south India as shown in films. During my college days, I had watched, in seedy theatres located in squalid neighbourhoods of Kanpur, dozens of soft-porn movies that were invariably shot in Kerala, some of them in its dense jungles—can it get more picturesque than that? But at the time, you were so eagerly waiting for the female characters to take off their clothes that the background scenery was completely irrelevant. The natural beauty of Kerala came to be acknowledged by the rest of the country only in 1998, when the then prime minister, Atal Behari Vajpayee, spent his year-end vacation in the backwaters of Kumarakom. By then, I had already become a diehard fan of present-day south Indian songs and choreography. I remember waiting for hours for one particular high-energy dance number, *Kalluri Salai*, one of the early compositions of A.R. Rahman, in a film called *Kadhal Desam*. Even today, I get goosebumps watching the song.

What eventually pulled the trigger for me was Rajeev Menon's *Kandukondain Kandukondain*, which was an adaptation of Jane Austen's *Sense and Sensibility* and which I watched, with the help of subtitles, in a theatre in Delhi. I still remember the automated female voice correctly pronouncing the words, *Kandukondain Kandukondain*, when I called up the theatre to find out about the availability of tickets. My friends thought I was mad to be interested in watching a Tamil film. Needless to say, I watched it alone. Tears trickled down my eyes during the final scene.

What made *Kandukondain Kandukondain* eminently appealing to me was the interesting mix of stars: Tabu and Aishwarya Rai, two actresses north India loved; Mammootty, the highly-acclaimed Malayalam actor; and Ajith Kumar and Abbas, two reigning heart-throbs of Tamil cinema of the time who demolished the notion that heroes had to sport double chins, pot-bellies and thick moustaches.

One of the most sublime moments of the film is a scene where Abbas, who plays a sophisticated young tycoon, lies lazily on a raft that is drifting on the blue-green waters. Facing the overcast sky, eyes shut in reverie, he is softly singing the verses of the revered poet Subramania Bharati. It begins to rain, but Abbas continues singing and then deliberately rolls over and plunges into the water, wanting to soak in the sensuality of the moment. It was a case of the present fondly embracing the past, the urban merging with the rural, of sophistication bowing before simplicity—that too in such an idyllic setting. I wanted to be there.

When I finally decided on the date to leave for Chennai, I went to the New Delhi railway station to buy a ticket. All the trains bound for Chennai were full. But there was one seat—just a single seat—available in a three-tier AC coach of the Tamil Nadu Express. I had made it just in time.

Throughout the journey, I was fascinated by the newness of everything—each new set of fellow passengers, new stations, new landscapes. I was thirty years old but had never travelled down south before—a gap in my education, an omission that I was now going to make up for. I kept looking out, trying to get a feel of the expanse of India as the train rapidly progressed from one state to another. It was dashing through Maharashtra when I had opened the conversation with the young Sikh, who laughed when I asked him if he lived in Chennai.

His body was still shaking with laughter, and he pulled out the handkerchief, which he had just put in his pocket, to wipe the tears that my question had induced. I asked him why it was such a crazy idea to be living in Chennai.

'What is there to do in Chennai? It is such a boring place. I can't ever imagine living there. I am only going there to fetch my wife. I reach there tomorrow morning and take the train back in the evening. In Delhi, there is so much life. I meet up with my friends in the evenings and have drinks, and then we go on long drives. If a policeman catches us, we give him five hundred rupees. He is happy, we are also happy. But you can't do such things in Chennai.'

I nodded as if I agreed with him.

Then he brought his face closer to mine and said in a lowered voice, '*Ek baat bataoon? South ke log hotey badey darpok hain*'—You know something, south Indians are very timid.

He burst out laughing again, slapping his palms together.

Timid. I had heard that before. It is because of their so-called timidity that people from the south are still preferred as tenants in the north. They pay the rent on time, hardly make any noise to disturb the landlord or fellow tenants, and promptly vacate whenever they are asked to. Clearly, it was the case of civility being mistaken for cowardice. But such finer qualities are often lost on north India which is still driven by the old saying, *Jiski lathi, uski bhains*—the one who wields the stick owns the buffalo.

■ ■ ■

So engrossed I was in the journey that I had completely forgotten I didn't know a soul in Chennai. I was not even sure where I was going to stay. All I had was an assurance from a certain man called Pugazhendi, who had promised to pick me up from the station and take me to the accommodation he had found for me. But Pugazhendi was a busy man, and we barely knew each other. How far could I rely on his assurance?

Pugazhendi had been a journalist with a Tamil paper till he discovered the filmmaker in himself. He had just made his first film, starring Khushboo, the actress of north-Indian origin who was once such a rage in Tamil Nadu that her fans built a temple to her. The film, if I recall correctly, was about a woman fighter of the Liberation Tigers of Tamil Eelam, or LTTE, falling in love with an Indian doctor. The film ran into trouble with the censors and Pugazhendi had to make several trips to Delhi to plead his case with the broadcasting ministry. It was during one such trip that we met at the Press Club in Delhi. He wore a white khadi shirt and a dhoti, and came across as a shy, modest man. He did not smoke or drink, and stood out like an island of virtue in the club. When I told him I was relocating to Chennai, he offered to find me a place to stay, even if as a temporary arrangement till I found one of my choice, and gave me his card.

I called him a few days later. He told me he had been very busy but that he would soon find a place for me. He asked me not to worry. Three days before taking the train, I called him again. He said he had found a mansion for me.

A mansion?

Yes, a mansion.

And how much would that cost me?

Not much, just ₹ 2,000 a month.

More good news: he said his manager would be waiting for me near the engine of the Tamil Nadu Express, holding a placard with my name on it. All this seemed too good to be true.

Around seven o'clock, on the morning of 15 January, thirty-one hours after I had left Delhi, I saw many fellow passengers pulling on trousers under their lungis. Chennai was nearing. The friendly waiter from the pantry car—I still remember his name, Krishnamoorthy—served one final round of coffee.

The first glimpse of Chennai from the train: roadside temples, yellow autorickshaws, men on bikes, young women on scooties. They all wore a purposeful look as they went about their chores, certain about their destinations. They had no idea they were being watched intently by a man who was coming to live in their city with no specific purpose, and who was not even sure where he would be heading to once the train had pulled in at the station.

Coolies invaded the train even before it could come to a halt. My huge suitcase made me a perfect catch. But even if I hired one of them, what could he do other than drop my luggage at the taxi-stand? From there, where would I go?

With hope in my heart, I dragged the suitcase in the direction of the engine. Sure enough, a young man was holding a placard with my name on it. And standing next to him was Pugazhendi, in his trademark white shirt and dhoti. I couldn't decide whether to feel important or grateful. As directed, I got into an autorickshaw along with the man who had held the placard. He was Pugazhendi's manager. Pugazhendi followed us on his Bajaj scooter. We were now heading towards the mansion.

The mansion, I discovered, is the common name for a lodge meant for bachelors and single men. I subsequently got to learn that there were scores of single men in Chennai who had attained old age living in these mansions. My mansion, however, was a newly-constructed one, located in T. Nagar, the heart of Chennai. I was given a room on the second floor, and as I climbed up, I noticed a hand-painted warning on the first landing: 'Alcohol strictly prohibited'; and on the second landing, another, 'Women visitors strictly not allowed.' Basically a place where one could exist, but not live.

In hindsight, I consider myself lucky to have checked into the mansion. I was baptised as a Chennaiite by fire.

That afternoon, when I ventured into the adjacent street in search of a mobile phone connection, I ran into a sea of people. Never before in my life had I seen such a multitude gushing into a narrow street. This was not an office crowd: it was Pongal, a holiday. They all walked leisurely, the countless families that had descended on the street. The men looked menacing with their thick moustaches. The women wore flowers in their hair and on their faces sweat-smudged talcum powder or a yellow tan left behind by turmeric paste. I had never thought the term 'rubbing shoulders' could be so literal. I began to feel giddy.

Where was the Chennai I had seen in the songs? There was no breathtaking choreography here, only suffocating crowds. I managed to find my way out of the street onto the main road, but there again, more people. They were coming in hordes, from all directions. I felt like a child lost in a village fair who was desperately trying to spot his parents.

The main road turned out to be South Usman Road, and the street branching off it, which nearly choked me, Ranganathan Street. Even during the leanest of seasons, as I was to experience subsequently, they are packed with people, mostly shoppers. South Usman Road and Ranganathan Street are home to Chennai's biggest retail stores—so big you have see them to believe. The number of employees in each store would easily outnumber the staff of a decent-sized software company. It is said, and not without reason, that you can find everything under the sun on South Usman Road and its tributaries, except a father or a mother. T. Nagar would be a desert without South Usman Road and Ranganathan Street; and what would Chennai be without T. Nagar?

Today, when I look back, I feel extremely proud that I spent my first fifteen days in the city not in the cosy home of a friend or relative living by the sea in the posh neighbourhood of Besant Nagar, but right in the centre of action where one could experience the authentic sights, sounds and smells of Chennai.

The sights: that of a woman selling flowers alongside a man selling cheap varieties of lingerie, of men wearing dhotis and women bright colourful sarees, of raw mangoes sliced like toothcombs and displayed to make mouths water. The sounds: of the nadaswaram emerging from the temple, the cacophony of the crowd, the call of the hawkers, the hissing of the batter when it is poured on the pan and spread out in a circle that eventually becomes a dosa. The smells: the sweet of the flowers and the sour of the idlis being steamed by roadside vendors. It is delightful to watch the vendor extricate hot idlis from a smoking piece of cloth. All this, thanks to Pugazhendi.

For the next ten days, Pugazhendi would come to the mansion every morning. He would read the newspaper while I bathed and got dressed, and then, astride his Bajaj scooter, we would go house-hunting in T. Nagar. He was enchanted by the calm of a certain street called Murugesan Street. 'Best for creative people, very peaceful place,' he would say. He had been a frequent visitor to that street until recently because the music director Illayaraja, who had composed the background score for his film, lives there.

We did see a house on that street, but the landlady was overbearing. She kept lecturing me about how a tenant, especially a bachelor, should conduct himself. One could choose to turn a deaf ear to her but she lived on the ground floor and would obviously be keeping an eye on me. That house was ruled out. We took our hunt to the adjoining streets, which were as quiet and leafy, but nothing worked out to my satisfaction.

Prologue: The Train to a New Identity

Meanwhile, I had also spoken to a few brokers. One morning, when Pugazhendi was held up by work, I went to see a broker who called to say that he had found a flat that suited my budget. The broker worked out of his home. Pasted on the wall behind his desk was a blown-up poster of the New York skyline, the twin towers of the World Trade Centre intact (they were to melt away in less than eight months). That morning, I realised that a broker, who is usually seen as a despicable character, was a family man too. He asked to be excused for a few minutes while he went to drop his daughter to school. His wife served me coffee and biscuits. Then, riding pillion on his bike, I went to see the flat. I liked it instantly. For once, I saw rooms painted in a pleasant shade of white and not the gaudy green that dominated most of the houses I had seen so far. Moreover, this was a flat and not an independent house, which meant that I was not going to live with the landlord. I said yes. I found it painful to fork out the brokerage, but felt immensely grateful towards the broker. As I stood in the empty flat, looking out of the window, I asked the broker, 'So where in T. Nagar are we?'

'Murugesan Street,' he replied.

Pugazhendi, when he heard the news, was most happy. He directed his manager to arrange for a fish-cart to transfer my belongings from the mansion to the flat. For one last time I rode pillion on Pugazhendi's scooter, while the manager followed us on the cart along with my luggage.

For the first few years since I became a resident of Chennai, till I got accustomed to its ways, I would begin each day feeling as if I had arrived that very morning. The city always threw up a sight or a sound that was new to me. Each morning, it would be awash with fresh colours. I would gape at the cinema posters, pasted on the walls, announcing new releases or boasting about the number of weeks a particular film had run. And the inevitable political posters, which don't fail to amuse me even now, showing either a laughing Karunanidhi or a sombre-looking Jayalalithaa. The two leaders, bitter rivals, have been taking turns in ruling Tamil Nadu. I have always wondered why Karunanidhi is always laughing in the posters, as if someone just cracked a joke. Jayalalithaa, on the other hand, wears a dignified smile, if one at all. The former actress mostly appears grim in the posters. Quite recently, I spotted the image of a laughing Karunanidhi on the hoarding of a new release: it turned out that the film had been scripted by him. Karunanidhi, whose family today has a steely grip over the Tamil film industry, stays in touch with his former profession by writing the script for the occasional film. Politics and cinema are Siamese twins in Tamil Nadu. Here, politicians can generate as much hysteria as the film stars, and most often it is the stars who go on to become politicians. If anyone is capable of causing frenzy other than them, it is God.

I clearly remember that night, a few months after I moved to Chennai. It was well past midnight and the entire neighbourhood was in deep slumber. I was in bed too, drinking rum and writing in long-hand a piece for the paper. A sudden burst of crackers jolted me out of my thoughts. Even as the crackers exploded, loud drumbeats rent the air. I rushed to the balcony to take a look. A procession of about thirty people was following an idol being carried on a hand-pulled cart. A diesel power generator placed at the rear of the cart helped illuminate the idol. The drummers and the men who burst the crackers walked at the head of the procession. Following the cart were the devotees, mostly women. Their sarees shone in the light provided by the generator. Back in the north, whenever a wedding procession passes—though never at this unearthly hour—people stand at their gates or balconies to watch. The whole idea behind making noise is to get people to watch. But that night I seemed to be the only person on the street witnessing the procession. My neighbours slept through the noise. The sound of crackers going off at odd hours was part of their life. It was to become part of mine as well—eventually.

■ ■ ■

The lay north Indian has known very little about Chennai except that it is inhabited by conservative and religious people called Madrasis who live on idli and dosa. There was no need to know more. The south, for the north, was always the back of beyond. People from the south came to the north in large numbers to work. But there was no movement in the reverse direction. Being posted to the south, in fact, was considered a punishment. While I was in Delhi, I knew of someone who, when he fell out of his boss's favour, was transferred to Chennai. The transfer order had the desired effect: he quit.

Even most Western writers, in their India-experience books, have given Madras a short shrift, confining their powers of observation to Bombay, Delhi or Calcutta. There are exceptions, though. James Cameron, the legendary British journalist who was in and out of India from the time of the 1945 Simla Conference till the 1971 Bangladesh war, spent some time in the city and found it agreeable. 'I have a sort of trust in Madras,' Cameron wrote in his 1974 book, *An Indian Summer*. 'It is an agreeable, rather boring place; it is the sort of place I would be if I were a town.' Several decades after he set foot here, multinational companies from across the globe came to discover the trust he talked about.

Today, Chennai is a throbbing manufacturing hub that is often described as the Detroit of India, and home to countless software companies, the giants as well as start-ups. It is also the country's capital for cure, the hub of medical tourism, where people from remote corners of India come for treatment and most often double as tourists, squeezing in a trip to the beach and some of the temples during their stay. Consequently, young professionals from the north are increasingly packing their bags to take up jobs in Chennai—and Bangalore and Hyderabad as well. Working in the south is no longer a punishment, but a privilege.

Till the multinational companies came, Chennai was living at its own pace. But after becoming a global city, it could no longer afford to. The change was rapid. I am glad that I lived through the change. I came in 2001, just in time to catch a glimpse of the old Chennai. Back then, it was still possible to travel a distance of five kilometres in less than fifteen minutes even during rush-hour—something impossible now unless you are driving at three in the morning. Trees were yet to be gobbled up by flyovers. People seen talking on mobile phones were few and far between, as a result of which peace prevailed in restaurants and theatres. There were no cineplexes: the very first one to come up was still in the making. Pubs were non-existent: the salaried tippler had to make do with either the 'permit room' of one of the lower-rung hotels or one of the hellholes attached to liquor shops that masqueraded as bars. When you wanted to eat out, the choice was between a regular multi-cuisine restaurant, a typical south Indian eatery or a fancy Punjabi dhaba. International brands, be they clothes or cosmetics, were still brought by relatives from abroad when they came to India on holiday. And there were just two English newspapers.

Today, just look at all that you get in Chennai. There are now four mainstream English papers. When it comes to eating out, the choices are mind-boggling: Chinese, Italian, Mexican, Lebanese, Thai, Malaysian, Korean, or how about Japanese? At the last count there were seven Japanese restaurants in the city. Pubs are a dime a dozen. As for international brands of clothes or perfumes, you name it and Chennai has it.

Yet, there is a Chennai that hasn't changed and never will. Women still wake up at the crack of dawn and draw the kolam—the rice-flour design—outside their doorstep. Men don't consider it old-fashioned to wear a dhoti, which is usually matched with a modest pair of Bata chappals. The day still begins with coffee and lunch ends with curd rice. Girls are sent to Carnatic music classes. The music festival continues to be held in the month of December. Tamarind rice is still a delicacy—and its preparation still an art form.

It's the marriage between tradition and transformation that makes Chennai unique. In a place like Delhi, you'll have to hunt for tradition. In Kolkata, you'll itch for transformation. Mumbai is only about transformation. It is Chennai alone that firmly holds its customs close to the chest, as if it were a box of priceless jewels handed down by ancestors, even as the city embraces change.

Amid all the changes racing over the city, I realised my own life had fallen into a pattern. The boundaries of Chennai, for me, had shrunk to the few stretches of roads that lay between my home and office. I dreaded becoming just another resident, so busy earning his living that he is no longer alive to his own city. I wanted to rekindle the romance for which I had travelled 2,157 km on a freezing night a decade ago.

So with a notebook in hand, I set out again.

Chapter

1

COMPANY COMES CALLING

Chennai, that charming old lady with a string of jasmine tied around her hair, is too modest to talk about herself. You may have to spend a whole afternoon in her home, looking at yellowing letters and photo albums even as you sip the filter coffee made by her, to know that many men who once mattered to the world had courted her when they were non-entities.

'A letter by Robert Clive!' you ask in astonishment. 'When did you know him?'

'I first met him in 1744. He must have been just eighteen. He was only a clerk then. Later he became Lord Clive. Very moody fellow!'

'Arthur Wellesley! You knew him too?'

'Yes, he came in 1797, or was it 1798. At the time I had no idea he was going to defeat Napoleon one day,' she smiles. You can detect a hint of pride in her eyes.

'And look who's here! Isn't that Elihu Yale?'

'Yes, that's him. They named a university in America after him. I spent many years with him.' You find her blushing.

'Unbelievable!' you gape in wonder. 'I had no idea you knew these people so well.'

'How does it matter, sir?' she smiles shyly. 'It's all past. Would you like to have some vadas?'

That's Chennai—or Madras, if you prefer—for you. She will never offer to show the albums to you. You need to be either curious or plain lucky to find them. And unlucky are those who have spent an entire lifetime drinking her coffee and eating her vadas without even knowing such precious albums exist.

Chennai's modesty shines through her citizens. The stranger sharing the table with you at the idli shop could be one of the richest men in the city but the unassuming white dhoti and shirt will give you no indication of his wealth. Even the elderly and the most distinguished will humbly address you as 'sir'.

Then there is Fort St George, the repository of Chennai's memory albums, the epitome of modesty.

To quote a self-explanatory poster inside the fort museum: 'Fort St George is a miniscule fort when compared with other impregnable forts of India. The walls are dwarfish, the moat is dry and the fort has no natural defences on any side. But it stands tall on its heritage because the seed for the transformation of a commercial enterprise incorporated in a faraway land, into a ruler of a great subcontinent, was sown here.'

Given its humble appearance and self-deprecating nature—so typically Madras—it is not surprising that the awareness of its existence is next to nil in most of India. But almost every modern institution in the country—be it education, engineering, medicine, the army, or judiciary—has its roots in Fort St George.

Modern India originated in Fort St George.

■ ■ ■

The Mughal Empire was still scaling the peak of its glory when seeds of its doom were sown in the sands of a faraway, nondescript seaside village called Madraspatnam. The year was 1640.

Shah Jahan, one of the greatest Mughals, had just founded the city of Shahjahanabad, the Old Delhi of today, making it the new capital of his mighty empire. Till then he was ruling from Agra. The emperor, forty-eight and on the throne for twelve years then, was unveiling the golden period of Mughal architecture. The construction of the Red Fort had just about begun, while the Taj Mahal was still being built in Agra. The foundation for the Jama Masjid, India's grandest mosque, was to be laid only a decade later.

That year, when the architectural masterpieces of the Mughal dynasty's most prolific and aesthetic builder were still in the making, two employees of the East India Company, Andrew Cogan and Francis Day, dropped anchor off Madraspatnam. The Company, which was into exporting locally-procured calico and muslin, was going to build a trading post on a strip of beach three miles long and a mile wide.

Until then, on the east coast, the Company was carrying out business from the port towns of Masulipatnam and

Armagon (now known as Durgarajupatnam), both located in present-day Andhra Pradesh. But there it was facing stiff competition from the Dutch. The Company knew that in order to expand trade, it must get away from the Dutch to a favourable location where they had the support of the local ruler.

So it was now shifting its operations to Madraspatnam, on a strip of beach that Francis Day had leased from the local governor of the Vijayanagar Empire the year before, in August 1639. The site was barely three miles from the Portuguese settlement of San Thome, where Day, a hard drinker and a womaniser, had found a lover during his expeditions down the coast to scout for land. Returning to Armagon after signing the lease, Day had written an emotional letter to his boss Andrew Cogan: 'Changes of time are fickle. And if you suffer this opportunity to pass over, you shall perhaps in vain afterwards pursue the same when it is fled and gone.' He had personally delivered the letter to Cogan—so keen was he on selling the idea of setting up the trading post in Madraspatnam.

The eager 'grab it or regret later' tone of the letter had the desired effect. Both Cogan and Day, after winding up business in Armagon, set sail for Madraspatnam, arriving on 20 February 1640 along with a party that included some twenty-five soldiers, a gunner, a surgeon, clerks, carpenters, smiths and a staff of servants.

The construction of the settlement, which they grandiosely called Fort St George, after their national patron saint, began on 1 March. At the same time, some 2,000 km up north, an army of workers, craftsmen, artisans and elephants was toiling to build Shahjahanabad, the new capital of the Mughal Empire.

In another 200 years the East India Company was to cover those 2,000 km and put an end to the powerful dynasty. But who would have imagined it then. Cogan and Day were mere traders seeking to beat competition and make profits—comparable in the present day to executives of a multinational company bolstering its India operations. Their employers in London, however, were not very pleased with the idea of having an independent settlement. They were alarmed by the word 'fort' and thought the entire venture to be a waste of money and an unnecessary luxury that could lead to political entanglements with the local rulers and affect business. Needless to say, Cogan and Day never got due credit for building Fort St George. What they built, though, eventually become the springboard for the British to rule India.

Madras, which grew rapidly around the fort, became India's first modern city. When Cogan and Day dropped anchor, the birth of Calcutta was still half a century away, Bombay was merely a group of islands under Portuguese control, while Delhi had only just become the capital city of a medieval-era empire.

But the names of these two men don't ring a bell in Chennai. Ideally, one would have expected a Cogan Coffee Shop here and a Day Dosa Corner there.

On the other hand, Lieutenant Jermin, the commander of the two dozen soldiers who arrived in Madraspatnam along with Day and Cogan, continues to be toasted as the first army commander of Madras. At the headquarters of the army in Chennai, the wooden plaque bearing the roll of commanders of Madras has his name right on top: *Lieut Jermin, 1640–1649*. It is a different matter that the soldiers of the East India Company in those days were decrepit men pulled out of the taverns of London. Very few had seen actual service, and those who had were old and worn out. But once you hold an army rank, at least the army remembers you.

Come to think of it, the very first man to court Chennai—that charming lady with a string of jasmine around her hair—was Francis Day, the binge-drinker and womaniser who chose her so that he would stay near the lover he had acquired in the Portuguese settlement of San Thome.

■ ■ ■

I first visited Fort St George in early 2010, when I had already lived in Chennai for nearly a decade. Once you make a city your home, you put many things on hold, at times eternally; unlike the traveller or tourist who covers as many places of historical or social interest as possible in the little time he has at his disposal. But subsequently I was to visit the Fort several times to make up for this omission.

My maiden visit took place on a very pleasant January morning, when the state government was preparing to move out of the Fort. Ever since it was built some four centuries earlier, Fort St George always remained a seat of power—first for the town of Madraspatnam; subsequently for the Madras Presidency; finally, post-Independence, for the state of Tamil Nadu—but now it was going to lose that exalted status.

That morning, broom-wielding women clad in blue sarees had virtually taken over the particular wing where the legislative assembly met and where the ministers had their offices. They went about their business with a lazy but purposeful gait, clearing every visible piece of garbage and dusting settees. Inside the assembly hall, where ruling and Opposition legislators had been sitting face to face but had not seen eye to eye in decades, a technician carried out last-minute sound checks while a male sweeper scrubbed the green carpet. They were all readying the premises for the session of the legislative assembly that was to begin the next day—the last to be convened in Fort St George. The next session, scheduled three months later, was going to be held in a brand new building, designed by a German firm, on Mount Road.

The new edifice was a product of Karunanidhi's whim. In 2007, when serving a fifth term as the chief minister, he realised he had completed fifty years as a member of the legislature. To mark the occasion, he decided to build a swanky secretariat. The Omandurar Government Estate—which was an assortment of structures both historical and fairly recent—was earmarked as the site. By mid-2008, bulldozers had flattened over a dozen of these structures. The casualty included the 250-year-old Government House, the home of the governor of the Madras Presidency right from 1752 till Independence. No one knew that Government House was going to be demolished until it had already been.

Once the site was secured, Karunanidhi ordered the new secretariat to be constructed in fifteen months. He wanted to consecrate it while he was still the chief minister; he knew if the building stood unfinished, the Opposition, when it came to power, would be too glad to put it to another use. Labourers from Bengal and Bihar toiled round the clock towards achieving his ambition. By late 2009—when he had barely a year and half for his term to end—Karunanidhi, even though eighty-six and wheelchair-bound, was visiting the site daily, at times several times a day.

In March 2010, even before it was fully ready—fifteen months turned out to be too short—the new secretariat was inaugurated by the prime minister of India. On the day of the inauguration, the oblong structure was sufficiently furnished so that nothing looked amiss to the august audience when the ribbon was cut. At the function, one speaker after the other heaped generous praise on Karunanidhi, stopping just short of equating him with a modern-day Shah Jahan.

His bitter enemy Jayalalithaa, meanwhile, made it known unequivocally that she was going to revive Fort St George as the seat of the Tamil Nadu government if she returned to power. An alarmed Karunanidhi, hoping to forestall the reinstatement, overnight turned the rosewood-panelled assembly hall at Fort St George into a library for classical Tamil literature. He, of all people, should have known Jayalalithaa better.

After she returned to power with a landslide win in the April 2011 elections, she not only took the secretariat back to Fort St George but also ordered that Karunanidhi's dream building be turned into a hospital. The Fort, once again, became the city's most important address.

■ ■ ■

Time seems to remain still in Fort St George despite the change in government and political whims every five years. Tip-toeing into St Mary's Church, which stands quietly in the Fort compound and is almost as old as the Fort itself, you can travel back three centuries. The church is the oldest existing structure in Fort St George. The Fort was built in 1640, the church in 1680. While the rest of the structures in the Fort were either rebuilt or added on much later, St Mary's Church has remained the way it stood 330 years ago.

Since a stony silence presides over this church like a venerable priest at almost all times of the day; people whose names are inked in the registers of the church—maintained since 1680 and now placed under glass cases with their first pages open—float in front of your eyes like full-fledged characters.

Robert Clive, one of the architects of British India, got married in St Mary's Church. But that was much later. The very first marriage recorded in the register, on 4 November 1680, is that of Elihu Yale with Catherine Hynmer.

Yale was the governor of the Fort from 1687 to 1692. It was during his tenure that the corporation for Madras and the post of the mayor were created, and the supreme court, which evolved over time into the present-day Madras high court, was set up. But despite an eventful stint, Yale was sacked because he used his position for private profit—he was engaged in an illegal diamond trade in Madras through an agent called Catherine Nicks.

Yet he stayed on in Madras for seven more years, having packed off his wife to England. He lived in the same house with Mrs Nicks, fathering four children with her, and a Portuguese mistress called Hieronima de Paivia, who also bore him a son. He finally returned to London in 1699, an immensely wealthy man. As he busied himself spending the money he had made in India, a cash-starved school in the American colony of Connecticut requested him for a donation.

The Yale family had lived in Connecticut for a long time before returning to England in 1652 when Elihu Yale was three years old. So when the college sought financial assistance, he shipped across nine bales of exquisite Indian textiles, 417 books and a portrait of King George I. The school kept the books and raised £562 from his other donations and, in gratitude, decided to rename itself after him. Thus was born Yale University, with the help of ill-gotten wealth amassed in Madras.

Robert Clive, unlike Elihu Yale, began as a humble clerk. He was barely eighteen when the East India Company dispatched him to Madras in 1743. The ship carrying him lost its course and found itself on the coast of Brazil. While the ship underwent repairs there, which took several months, Clive spent his time learning Portuguese—something that was going to prove useful since Portuguese had been the lingua franca of international trade in India and many natives understood the language.

Clive eventually reached Madras on 31 May 1744. A man of unpredictable moods, he loathed being confined to his desk as a book-keeper at Fort St George. The monotony of the job and the oppressive heat of Madras had driven him to such despair that he attempted suicide in his quarters at Fort St George.

Clive's gun refused to fire when he put it to his head. After two futile attempts, a fellow book-keeper happened to stop by without the faintest idea of what Clive had been up to. Clive, sitting morosely in his room, asked the visitor to fire the same gun out of the window. And lo and behold, the weapon spat out a bullet. Clive jumped up in disbelief. 'Well, I am reserved for something great!' he exclaimed. 'That pistol I have twice snapped at my own head!'

Clive became a celebrated soldier soon after the French, stationed in nearby Pondicherry, attacked Madras in 1746. The attack caught Fort St George unawares and Clive had to escape to Fort St David in Cuddalore, about a hundred miles further south, where he joined the Company's forces as a volunteer. His acts of bravery in the battle against the French came in for commendation by none other than Major Stringer Lawrence, the commander-in-chief of the Company's troops who subsequently went on to raise India's first professional regiment, the Madras Regiment.

Clive's fortunes changed. The clerk went on to be hailed back home as a 'heaven-born general'. Adulation awaited him when he sailed back to Britain in 1753, but not before he had married Margaret Maskelyne in St Mary's Church that very year.

Two years later Clive was sent back to Madras, but during this posting, destiny was to seduce him to Bengal. In 1756, when Calcutta was captured by Siraj-ud-Daulah, the nawab of Bengal, Clive was dispatched from Madras along with a large number of troops to retrieve the city from native hands. He not only recaptured Calcutta but also ignored the directive of his bosses in Madras to return to Fort St George once the task had been accomplished. He went on to fight and win the Battle of Plassey, neutralising every potential threat to the East India Company in Bengal and thus laying the foundation of British India.

But Calcutta did not even exist when Job Charnock, its soon-to-be founder, had his three daughters baptised in this Madras church. The three girls, born of a Hindu widow rescued by Charnock from a sati pyre, were baptised on 19 August 1689. (Calcutta was born only a year later, on 24 August 1690.) The granite water font in St Mary's, in which the girls were baptised, remains intact.

■ ■ ■

So who owns Fort St George today?

'It's a tricky question,' an officer of the Archaeological Survey of India, or ASI, laughs when I put the question to him. 'You can safely say it belongs to the government. When you say government, it can mean the army, it can mean the Tamil Nadu government, and it can also mean the ASI.'

As things stand, the army is generally considered to be the master of the land, and it continues to occupy most of the buildings in the Fort. But since ours is a democracy and the Fort has served as the seat of a democratically-elected government for a number of decades, the state government exerts its authority as well: some of the structures, such as the secretariat and the legislative assembly hall, are under its control. Then there is the ASI, which, since Independence, has been responsible for the protection of fourteen structures in the Fort and which has made the renovated Clive House, a three-storey building of seventeenth-century vintage, its regional headquarters.

It was in Clive House, also known as Admiralty House, that Robert Clive lived briefly with his wife in 1753, the year he got married. The building subsequently served as the Courts of Admiralty and also as the town house of the governors of Madras. One of the rooms on the ground floor has been designated as Clive's Corner, but the door seems to remain locked to the public.

During one of my earlier visits to the Fort, I had, in fact, approached the front desk of the ASI office, asking if I could see the room where Clive had tried to commit suicide. I was ignorant of the fact that Clive lived in this house only towards the end of his first stint in India when he had become a celebrated soldier, and that this was not the building where he had put a gun to his head. But the ASI staff I encountered turned out to be altogether ignorant of Clive's suicide attempt. All they were aware of were the rules, and rules prohibited people like me, the general visitor, from taking a tour of the building. It did not impress them when I said that I was a journalist who intended to write a book on Chennai.

'In that case,' one of them told me, 'please visit our website. It has all the details.'

'What about Clive's Corner?' I argued. 'Can I take a look?'

'No, sir. Please visit our website. It has all the details.'

The refusal made me even more curious about Clive's Corner. What lay behind the locked door?

In the following months, however, I not only read up more on the history of the Fort but also, quite incidentally, happen to make friends with a few army officers stationed in Chennai. So one morning, after the previous night's rain has cooled off Chennai and when the clouds are still shielding the sun, I return to the Fort with a friend in the army. Clive House, magically, is no longer out of bounds. A young man frantically runs up and down to fetch the keys.

Clive's Corner, I know by now, is a museum. But only when the man opens the door and shows us in do I realise how small the room is. From its walls hang frames that seek to encapsulate the life of Lord Clive—including facsimiles of some of his letters and also of the entry in the church book recording his marriage with Margaret Maskelyne. It puzzles me why this room should stay locked. If anything, the public should be encouraged to visit it so that they can learn that Clive began his illustrious career as a clerk of the East India Company in Madras.

My colonel friend and I then walk down to an adjacent building. It is featureless but formidable, surrounded by an even more formidable wall. The most intimidating part, however, is the gate which, when closed, could be broken open only by an army of elephants—the latch alone is likely to be heavier than an AK-47 rifle. It was meant to be impenetrable because it served as the Madras Arsenal, right from 1772 until 1931. The insignia of the Royal Engineers, who constructed the grand arsenal, is still in place at the entrance, a few feet above the forbidding door.

Today the giant gates remain open at all times. Stray dogs roam through them. As for the edifice itself, it now houses the offices of the Military Engineering Services and also serves as the embarkation headquarters, which handles movement of defence personnel and cargo. Though sturdy, it is in need of repair in places, but the army is not permitted to carry out renovation without the permission and supervision of the ASI.

'Just imagine,' an officer posted at the building tells me, his lips curving into an ironic smile, 'we are from the Military Engineering Services, whose job it is to maintain all buildings belonging to the defence ministry, but here we are not allowed to repair our own office. Even if we carry out minor repair work, the ASI slaps us with a notice.' But he must realise that this building is no ordinary defence property: it is over two centuries old and is the cradle of the modern Indian Army.

The Madras Arsenal, whose construction began in 1770, is where Writers' Building once stood. It was in a room in Writers' Building that Clive stayed when he first arrived in India and where he made that abortive bid to kill himself. Come to think of it, a faulty gun decided the destiny of modern India.

Right now, I am standing in the compound of the erstwhile Writers' Building along with three army officers who, unlike Clive, have received professional training to fight the enemy. But their immediate foe seems to be the prospect of relocating to new places after a rather cushy stint in Chennai.

Two of them have just received orders for their next posting: one is going to Rajasthan, another to Punjab. The third officer has still six months to go before he receives his order. It's a nomad's life, that of a soldier. Just when you are beginning to feel at home in a particular place, it's time to move on. Finally, after thirty or forty years, when you retire, you've forgotten where home is. You settle down either in the final place of posting or in a quiet town where real estate is cheap. The only wealth of an army officer, once he retires, is the treasure-chest containing anecdotes that he would have accumulated during the span of his service.

What's making the two officers most unhappy about leaving Chennai is they will have to pull their children out of the schools they are studying in. The quality of education in Chennai, they say, is the best in the country. But no matter which part of the country their children study in, they are eventually going to learn about Lord Clive. One, however, cannot be sure if they will ever realise that their fathers had once shared office space with Clive, although in different centuries.

■ ■ ■

Arthur Wellesley, the future Duke of Wellington, spent several months in Fort St George planning and subsequently fighting a decisive war that would consolidate British rule in south India before he went on to win the most iconic battle in British history—the battle of Waterloo in which Napoleon was defeated.

Arthur Wellesley arrived in Calcutta in 1797 when he was twenty-eight, exactly forty years after Robert Clive won the Battle of Plassey and secured Bengal for the British. The very next year, Arthur's elder brother Richard Wellesley, later Lord Mornington, also reached Calcutta as the new governor-general of India. Clive was long dead by then, finally succeeding in a suicide attempt in 1774 when he killed himself with a pen-knife in his London home.

Arthur Wellesley, who had just been promoted to colonel before being sent to India, happened to be in Madras, studying the Company's relations with Mysore, when the elder brother stopped by on his way to Calcutta to take charge as the new governor-general. The two brothers discussed the threat posed by Tipu Sultan who, after losing half his territories and surrendering his two sons as hostages to the British under the 1792 Treaty of Seringapatnam with Cornwallis, was raring to strike back. The ruler of Mysore had even got promises of assistance from the French—including Napoleon himself. The Wellesley brothers came to the conclusion that Tipu needed to be done away with. A military expedition against Mysore was ordered. Funds began to be raised in Madras for the war.

It was during this time that Lord Edward Clive—the son of the first Lord Clive, the 'heaven-born general'—arrived in Madras to take charge as the governor of Fort St George. He took office in Admiralty House, where his parents once lived and which is today occupied by the Archaeological Survey of India. Edward Clive relieved Lt Gen. George Harris, the commander-in-chief of the Company forces in Madras who was holding additional charge as the governor and who was now going to lead the war against Tipu Sultan.

On 31 December 1798, days before Company troops set out to fight the war, Richard Wellesley returned to Madras after having assumed office as the governor-general in Calcutta. He wanted to stay near the scene of action so that there was no delay in communication and in settlement of post-war issues. Moreover, his younger brother was going to be in the battlefield.

Arthur Wellesley, being the younger brother of the governor-general, remained the blue-eyed officer of Lt Gen. Harris during the war. But he did prove his mettle as a military leader with meticulous logistic planning that eventually punched holes in Tipu's defences. Tipu Sultan was found with a bullet through his head and given a dignified funeral. Lt Gen. Harris installed Arthur Wellesley as the governor of Mysore and Seringapatnam, and returned to Madras. Arthur Wellesley subsequently went on to defeat the Marathas and further expand British rule in south India. He was only thirty. A greater success now awaited the future Duke of Wellington in Waterloo.

The news of Seringapatnam's fall reached Fort St George on 4 May 1799, and for many years Madras celebrated the day. During his stay in Madras, when the expedition against Tipu Sultan was planned, Arthur Wellesley lived in a palatial house in Fort St George, right next to the Madras Arsenal. The house subsequently came to be known as Wellesley House. On the other hand, Richard Wellesley, in keeping with his position as the governor-general, stayed in the Admiralty House. Edward Clive, the governor, had to temporarily move out to a garden house in the city to let his superior stay there.

Lord Edward Clive was succeeded in 1803 by Lord William Bentinck, who went on to become governor-general of India twenty-five years later and who is today best remembered for outlawing gruesome Indian customs such as sati. In 1854, George Harris, the grandson of Lt Gen. Harris who had led the war against Tipu, became the governor of Madras; and when the mutiny broke out in 1857, the younger Harris despatched a strong force from Madras to Kanpur and Lucknow to quell the mutineers.

So, British India was effectively built on the discipline and resilience of troops from Madras—first the victory at Plassey, then the end of Tipu Sultan, which was followed by the defeat of the Marathas, and finally the crushing of the mutiny.

Today, one wing of Wellesley House serves as the offices and depot of the Army Service Corps, the department that is responsible for the supply of provisions to soldiers and their families. It is still a handsome building. The ground floor seems to have served as an arsenal once upon a time because the walls, pillars and the ceiling are extra thick, as if designed to absorb an explosion. You no longer find gunpowder stocked there, only sacks of rice and tins of cooking oil neatly stacked up.

A broad staircase leads to a large hall on the first floor where air-conditioned wooden cabins stand like islands. Air-conditioning is not really required in any of the British-built structures in Fort St George because they were designed specifically to beat the Madras heat. The walls are all exceptionally thick and the ceilings extraordinarily high, with ample ventilation and natural lighting. But the requirements of the twenty-first century have necessitated the construction of cabins within brick walls and therefore the need for air-conditioning.

The officer who is in charge of the depot, a tall Sikh colonel with the physique of an athlete, offers us coffee in his cabin. He has just been transferred to Chennai. 'When I first inspected the godown (he is talking about the ground floor where the sacks of rice are stacked), one of my men kept clapping his hands as we walked. I asked him what he was doing. He told me, "Saab, there are a lot of snakes here. They go away when we clap." This is a very old building, you see. Over two hundred years old,' he says. 'Come, I will show you around.'

He leads us out of the hall into the other rooms of Wellesley House, warning us from time to time, 'Please walk on the sides because the floor might just cave in.' When a seasoned army man warns you, you listen. So in the places he indicates, we walk in single file, staying as close to the wall as possible.

Most of the rooms are in a state of abandonment, used only to pile up jute sacks and empty tins of edible oil. One of them, though, is used for stocking uniforms for men in the Army Service Corps. It is a rectangular room, occupied by racks on which the uniforms are arranged neatly, just the way clothes are displayed in garment shops. But about a century or two ago, this room had clearly been used for a different purpose. Hoisted on two of its facing walls is a cage each, big enough to hold a human.

'These are most likely to have been used to punish disobedient soldiers,' the Sikh colonel tells us, pointing up at the cages. Installed in each cage is a crossbar that arches up into a metal ring, resembling a dog collar. Looking at them, it is very easy to imagine a man, his hands tied behind him, straddled on the crossbar and his head sticking out of the immobile metal collar. And since the cages are fixed high up on the walls, it is obvious that the idea was to make an example out of the prisoners—imagine the sight of two men confined up there, for hours or perhaps days, frozen in the posture of a dog on a leash.

Another wing of Wellesley House has long fallen prey to neglect and is in total ruins, its skeletal walls now providing home to wild shrubs and snakes. The second floor of this wing collapsed in 1980, leaving a solitary wall on the edge of the roof standing precariously ever since. The army wants to pull down the wall because it may come crashing down any time and hurt the men. But the ASI does not want the army to touch it, and at the same time seems to have done precious little either about the wall or about the several other houses in the vicinity of Wellesley House that now stand like skeletons with huge trees growing out of them.

It is quite possible that Warren Hastings lived in one of these houses before the East India Company sent him to Calcutta as India's first governor-general—if not exactly in one of these houses, then at least in a house that must have existed before on the spot, because records say that Hastings lived south of St Mary's Church during his tenure in Madras as the export warehouse-keeper from September 1769 to February 1772.

Like Robert Clive, Warren Hastings too had joined the Company as a clerk at the age of eighteen. As soon as he joined service in 1750, he was sent to Calcutta. When Siraj-ud-Daulah, the nawab of Bengal, captured Calcutta in 1756, Hastings found himself imprisoned in Murshidabad, the nawab's capital. He was freed when Clive arrived to recapture Calcutta. After the Battle of Plassey was won, Clive appointed Hastings as the administrator of Murshidabad.

In 1764 Warren Hastings returned to England, but in 1769 was sent back, this time to Madras as the export warehouse-keeper. The designation might sound lowly, but today the post would be called vice-president (exports).

As an administrator of Madras, he played a key role in developing the resources of the city. He also reformed the system of procuring textiles from weavers by abolishing the institution of company merchants, who used the services of brokers to get the cloth from the weavers. Hastings instead appointed agents who would roam the country and personally procure cloth from the looms. And it was he who first suggested that Madras port should have a pier. In 1770, he wrote to his brother-in-law John Woodman:

> My dear Brother, I have occasion to address you again upon a subject in which I hope to meet with assistance from you rather than from any other of my correspondents. It is this. The surf rises so high continually upon this Shore as to make the Landing always troublesome and often dangerous. Now, I have conceived it possible to carry out a Causeway or pier into the Sea beyond the Surf, to which boats might come and land their goods or passengers without being exposed to the Surf.

The brother-in-law wrote back a detailed letter as to how a pier should be built. But Hasting's idea could not take off because shortly after, in February 1772, he had to sail to Calcutta to take charge as India's first governor-general. Madras port got its first pier only in the middle of the nineteenth century.

There seems to be something charmed about the soil of Fort St George. Many clerks and soldiers and administrators who came to serve in Madras as non-entities were catapulted to unbelievably high positions—high enough not only to decide the destiny of India but also of Britain. During the eighteenth and nineteenth centuries, a number of illustrious Britons, including prime ministers, commanders-in-chief, governors-general, members of Parliament and bureaucrats had one thing in common—the Madras connection.

Present-day Madras, that is Chennai, is somehow shy of celebrating this connection. It would make far more sense to have the entire Fort vacated so that it could be restored and turned into a museum that would welcome visitors with the signboard, 'Modern India began here.'

■ ■ ■

To get an idea of social life in eighteenth-century Madras, which was centred in the Fort, you only have to look at the advertisements placed in the *Madras Courier*, the first newspaper to be started in the city.

The *Courier*, a weekly, began in October 1785 and ran for thirty-six years. A number of the advertisements carried by it find place in Henry Davidson Love's *Vestiges of Old Madras*, published in 1913, which is by far the most authentic and comprehensive record available of the city's colonial history until the year 1800.

Drinking was serious business back then and alcohol was never in short supply. Madeira wine, produced in the Portuguese island of the same name, was the favourite drink of Madras. Other varieties of alcohol were available too:

> 23rd March, 1791 – MESSRS BEGGLE AND HEEFKE have for sale at their Godown, the last nearest the Exchange in Bandicoot Alley, Fort St. George, Coniac Brandy of a superior quality, in Casks from 50 to 60 Gallons each...

The Exchange, which Messrs Beggle and Heefke gave as a landmark so that customers could easily locate their godown, is today the Fort Museum. The Exchange building came up in 1790 and it housed, among other things, the first bank of Madras and also the first public library. It was also the place where—to use twenty-first century parlance—the nightlife of Fort St George thrived. On the first floor, where portraits of stiff-upper-lipped colonial masters hang today, the merchants of the Company met to gossip and conduct business over drinks. It was the place to head to after work.

Apart from the Exchange, there were a number of taverns in and around Fort St George that catered to the European population. Each of the taverns had a loyal clientele—as is mostly the case with watering-holes—and whenever they happened to shift from one place to another, they utilised the services of the *Courier* to inform their patrons about the change in address:

> 12th January, 1792—FORT TAVERN, COURT HOUSE STREET. John Card begs leave to acquaint his friends and the public in general that he is removed from the London Tavern in Black Town to the Tavern in Fort St. George, and he humbly solicits the continuance of that encouragement he has hitherto experienced.
>
>   N.B. Soups every morning, and dinners dres'd on the shortest Notice—and the very best Wine.

It is difficult to tell whether Madras had a deadline for nightlife as it does today, when all drinking dens must shut by eleven o' clock. But parties held at the homes of Europeans are known to have lasted till two in the morning.

■ ■ ■

The fishing village where Francis Day chose a strip of land to build Fort St George was already known as

Madraspatnam. Black Town, the adjoining settlement that was constructed along with the Fort, was called Chennapatnam by the natives.

The East India Company continued to call the new city they founded Madraspatnam, later shortened to Madras; while the natives stuck to the name Chennapatnam. The exact origins of these two names remain shrouded in uncertainty.

About Madraspatnam, the most plausible theory is that the name derives from the wealthy Madeiros family that lived in the nearby Portuguese settlement of San Thome. Chennapatnam, on the other hand, is widely believed to have taken its name from Chennappa—the father of Damarla Venkatappa, the local governor of the Vijayanagar Empire who had granted the strip of land to Francis Day to build Fort St George. Venkatappa was supposedly keen that the new settlement be named after his father.

In 1800, Captain Colin Mackenzie—who fought in the war against Tipu Sultan and went on to become the surveyor-general of India and was hailed as 'the man who mapped India'—prepared a genealogical list of the Damarla family. In that list, he entered Chennappa's name as 'Damuel Comar Chinapa Nairdu', who 'founded the Village of Chinaikupom, now called Chinapatnam or Madras.'

If that be the case, then the capital of Tamil Nadu—officially rechristened Chennai from Madras in 1996 by the government of Karunanidhi—is actually named after a Telugu-speaking Naidu.

Chapter 2

NORTH OF SOUTH

But, where are the people?

The question strikes you instantly when you look at photographs of Madras taken about a hundred years ago. There appears to be hardly anyone around. The barrenness of the roads draws your eye as much as the landmarks the photographs portray. In a picture of the famous Kapaleeswarar temple in Mylapore, shot in 1906 from the North Mada Street, there are precisely four human beings in the frame. Today you will need divine intervention to be able to park on the street.

Even First Line Beach, the most vital road of Madras in the early colonial era, with the harbour on one side and the all-important public buildings on the other, appears deserted in a 1910 photograph. As if it is under curfew. Today the same road, renamed Rajaji Salai, is as much a nightmare for the motorist as the pedestrian. If any place in the city remains as unpopulated as it was a century ago, it is perhaps the sea.

To look at such pictures is an escape, a temporary relief. You wish for a few moments that you lived in that era and then return to reality with a thud. Today Chennai is bursting at its seams. Its vehicle population has grown by 300 per cent in the past fifteen years alone. Nearly 1,000 new vehicles are hitting the roads every day. Most of the roads, however, remain as narrow or wide as they were a century ago.

Part of the blame can be laid at the door of the British. Madras may have been the first Indian city to be founded by them, but a couple of centuries later, when they were in the position to write India's destiny, they were concentrating their energies on building Calcutta and subsequently Delhi and Bombay. Madras was relegated to the back of beyond.

This perhaps explains why none of Chennai's colonial structures are as imposing or intimidating as those you find in the three other cities. You don't have anything the size or the grandeur of Rashtrapati Bhawan or Victoria Memorial here. The city's colonial history lies mostly hidden in the lanes and back alleys of Black Town, or George Town, in north Madras.

Today north Madras is considered the boondocks. It is a highly congested commercial district, housing a number of wholesale establishments dating back to the eighteenth and nineteenth centuries, which has remained untouched by development. As the city grew southward, it took prosperity along with it. South Chennai is now posh, while the north is neglected, crime-infested and deprived of development. From being the starting point of the city, it has now been left way behind to qualify as backward when it comes to infrastructure and the social profile of its inhabitants.

During the ten years that I have lived in the city I have not known a soul residing in north Chennai—the only exception being a young man I had hired as a driver several years ago. I am, of course, not counting certain community-specific neighbourhoods such as Sowcarpet, where the prosperous Marwari community lives, or Perambur, which is a railway settlement. But if you ask around, you will find quite a number of people who, even though they have lived in the city all their lives, have not paid a single visit to north Chennai.

When Madras was born, Black Town adjoined the Fort. But during the intermittent French attacks between 1746 and 1759, engineer John Call pointed out that since the houses in Black Town were within 200 yards of the northern wall of the Fort, the enemy could easily take cover in them and mount a direct attack, and recommended immediate demolition of all structures within 400 yards of the Fort's wall.

Based on his recommendation, made in October 1757, a part of the Black Town was immediately ordered to be pulled down. An esplanade was created. To prevent encroachments, six obelisks, each fifteen feet high, were erected along the esplanade in 1773 to mark its boundary. Of the six obelisks, only one survives today. The esplanade subsequently became China Bazaar Road, renamed post-Independence as Netaji Subhas Chandra Bose Road or, simply, NSC Bose Road.

It's six in the morning and I am standing on NSC Bose Road, at the parking lot outside the high court. In another half-an-hour or so, I shall be part of a small group to be taken on a heritage tour of Broadway, once upon a time the main commercial thoroughfare of not only George Town but the whole of Madras. I am the early bird because I did not sleep at all. I have been up all night, like I always am whenever I have an early-morning engagement or a flight to catch. In the crisp morning air, I feel as alert and refreshed as one can be.

Across the road is Black Town, or George Town. I try imagining the scene it must have presented in its heyday. John Matheson, a Glasgow businessman who wrote *England to Delhi* after visiting India in 1862, describes it thus:

> (The) centre of social life, called the Black Town, is separated from the Fort by a wide esplanade, and contains the principal shops and bazaars, the large storehouses of European firms, together with a crowd of native dwellings built of brick and bamboo. Here, through a close huddle of streets, deep laid in dust, moves a busy throng of passengers, bullocks and creaking vehicles, raising stifling clouds, together with a great babble of sound. Palanquins are in spare use in Madras as compared with Calcutta and Bombay. The bazaar shops are filled with the various productions of the country, some of them exhibiting a fine display of hand-loom muslins and cloth of gold. There are boxes of lace and artificial flowers from Pondicherry; talc pictures, in glaring colours, from Trichinopoly; specimens of tamarind-wood found in the sands; gold and silver ornaments; articles in coral and amber; moco stones, garnets and many other characteristic wares.

From the close, crowded precincts of the Black Town it is a refreshing transition to the adjoining esplanade, whither, as in Bombay, European ladies drive every afternoon to meet their husbands and accompany them home.

You don't see European ladies anymore, only thick crowds; and those creaking bullock-carts have been replaced by a river of mechanised vehicles that emit clouds of the poisonous kind. But at this magical hour, George Town doesn't look too different from the time of Matheson's visit, holding against her bosom the history of Madras's social life like a precious piece of memory. It is because of the history that men like Sriram keep returning to her.

Venkatakrishnan Sriram, who is forty-five, wears many hats. He is an engineer by qualification and runs his family business in the fields of hydraulics and software, but Carnatic music and heritage are his two passions. When delivering lectures on these subjects—which he is called upon to do often—Sriram never consults a prepared text: it's all stored in his head. Every August, when Chennai celebrates its founding day—it was on 22 August 1639 that the lease for the land on which Fort St George stands was believed to have been signed, Sriram takes time off his business to give lectures and lead heritage walks.

Soon they begin to arrive, in one car after another, the well-to-do people of Chennai who have come to discover the old Madras that is very new to them. At six-thirty sharp, Sriram arrives. He has a portable amplifier strapped to his waist. After a headcount, we all get into a van.

'Every brick and street corner of George Town has been witness to several interesting incidents,' Sriram tells me as the van goes past shuttered shops on NSC Bose Road—Paris Cool Home, Dolphin Print Centre, The Bharathi Mart (P) Ltd, Bollywood Fashion Mela—and enters Broadway. 'You name any aspect of life—music, dance, politics, economics, warfare, religion, medicine, business, crime—George Town is a treasure-house of stories.'

People in the van are eagerly looking out the windows. Most of them live less than twenty kilometres from George Town, but in terms of architectural ambience, they are travelling some two centuries back in time. They are tourists in their own city.

'In any other country,' Sriram tells me, 'most typically any city in Europe, this would have been declared a heritage quarter where people could go about, mingle with hawkers, see the old buildings and generally absorb the atmosphere of the place. But that is not likely to happen here in the near future. There is complete ignorance on such possibilities. None of the heritage buildings here has any documentation on site so that tourists can read and know.' Sriram is doing his bit to make up for this lapse.

Broadway, despite the real-estate activity sweeping through the city, remains largely untouched. At this hour, the road pretty much resembles a late statesman's bungalow that has been turned into a public museum—the objects in the rooms frozen at the very spot he had last seen or used them. And as Sriram begins to tell the stories behind the buildings, Broadway comes alive.

We see Bharathi Women's College, which had been the site of the jail in Madras—right from the late seventeenth century until Independence. We see Beehive Buildings, where Oakes and Co., the biggest retail merchants of their time, started business in 1843. 'Short of a wife and a housekeeper, you could buy everything from them—from an apron to steel beams for the construction of a building,' Sriram tells us. We see a dilapidated building in which ran Mrs Klug's Bioscope, Madras's first permanent cinema theatre started in April 1911; though no one is sure who Mrs Klug was, where she came from, and where she went after shutting down the theatre within six months. We see an ornate Indo-Saracenic building of nineteenth-century vintage, now abandoned and locked up, where the legendary movie mogul S.S. Vasan ran the *Ananda Vikatan* magazine for several years with the help of names such as 'Kalki' Krishnamurthy and Sadasivam.

But it's the story of Broadway itself that is most fascinating. The road was built in the 1780s. By then Black Town had expanded and new areas, such as Muthialpet and Peddanaikpet, were added to the map of Madras. Peddanaikpet was by and large inhabited by people belonging to the 'right-hand' caste, while Muthialpet was home mostly to people of the 'left-hand' caste.

No one knows today on what basis the people were divided into right-hand and left-hand castes, because both groupings seemed to have a mix of upper as well as lower castes. The right-hand caste, which claimed superiority, comprised mainly landed cultivators, herdsmen, grain traders, potters, field labourers and peasants. The left-hand caste, which challenged the superiority, included merchants, artisans, leather workers and tanners. Caste riots, breaking out mostly due to disputes over religious rituals, were a common feature in Black Town in the seventeenth and eighteenth centuries, and a constant headache for the administrators at Fort St George.

In between Peddanaikpet and Muthialpet ran a drain, which was purchased in 1779 by a seemingly eccentric lawyer from Calcutta called Stephen Popham. Popham was secretary to Sir John Day, the advocate-general of Bengal, and he had sailed to Madras the year before in connection with a case. Following a nasty argument with his boss, he decided to stay on in Madras and took great initiative in the development of Black Town and its drainage system. Though, being a wily lawyer, he always made sure he stood to gain personally from the plans he sold to the government of Madras.

Once he decided to stay on in Madras, Popham took residence, from what is apparent from records, in Peddanaikpet. But he found that his house was situated opposite a stinking piece of marshy land. With plans of levelling it and making Black Town cleaner, he promptly bought that piece of land and subsequently also purchased the remainder of the malodorous stretch extending southwards right up to the boundary of the esplanade (today's NSC Bose Road). He was allowed to buy the lands on the condition that no building coming up along the drain should overlook Fort St George.

At the time, Tipu Sultan's father Hyder Ali posed a big threat to Madras, and an attack by the French was always a possibility. The administrators at Fort St George were toying with the idea of flattening Hoghill, an elevated piece of land opposite Chennai Central station where the government general hospital stands today, lest it became vantage point for the enemy.

The hill, in fact, had been marked as the site for a new fort in case Fort St George ever got washed away by the sea. But at this time, Hyder Ali and the French posed a greater threat to the East India Company than the waves of the Bay of Bengal.

There was a huge obstacle, though: how to vacate the people living on Hoghill? Popham, astute lawyer that he was, suggested that the government exercise martial law in view of Hyder Ali's 'threatening attitude' and remove the residents. Hoghill was flattened without delay. The soil recovered from it, instead of being consigned to the sea as had been considered initially, was used to fill up Popham's drain. The drain became Popham's Broadway. Unfortunately, he didn't live long to enjoy his creation. He died, on the same road, in 1795, fatally injuring himself in a fall from his curricle. He was fifty-three.

Popham was the plan man. Throughout his stay in Madras, he kept presenting plans to the government at Fort St George for the improvement of Black Town. It was he who introduced modern policing in Madras. In one of the plans, he suggested, 'Every street should be named, its name marked in English and the Country Languages; its Inhabitants registered with their Trades, &c ... Every Birth and Burial to be noticed in a Book ... with an Account of the arrival and departure of Strangers...'

Popham was clearly way ahead of his times.

Popham's Broadway is today Prakasam Road. Why it was renamed so, Sriram tells the story. The story goes back to 3 February 1928, when the much-hated Simon Commission arrived in Bombay. Protests broke out all over the country including in Madras, where a peaceful procession marched through Broadway. As soon as the marchers poured out to China Bazaar Road, now called the NSC Bose Road, one policeman from the contingent posted at the spot panicked and opened fire. The bullet hit a man called Parthasarathy and he dropped dead on the spot. The remaining protestors, startled by the gunshot, instinctively recoiled into Broadway. The police, who had now overcome their initial nervousness and become aggressive, announced that anyone stepping forward to claim the body of Parthasarathy would meet the same fate. Upon which, a fifty-six-year-old lawyer-cum-journalist called Tanguturi Prakasam bared his chest and dared the police to shoot him even as he dragged the body of his comrade back to the crowd of protestors. Prakasam later became the chief minister of Madras state and subsequently of Andhra state.

Many shops, though, continue to identify the road variously as Broadway, Popham's Broadway and Broadway Road.

■ ■ ■

I return to north Chennai days after, in the company of a friend called Murali Krishnan, a percussionist who runs a drums school. Murali and I go back a long way. I first met him almost a decade ago, when he was in his early twenties. During my initial years in Chennai, when both of us were bachelors, we had spent countless evenings together. I would hold him captive in my home and subject him to my kind of music, the Hindi film music of the 1970s and '80s, asking him to identify the various percussion instruments being played in a particular song. In between songs, we would discuss women who caught our fancy.

The plus point with Murali was that he did not drink, which meant I did not have to worry about the alcohol falling short, as would often happen when other friends came over. For dinner, he occasionally took me to a Gujarati eatery on Broadway, where they served unlimited home-evocative food for a paltry sum. After a heavy meal at the mess, we would go for a walk on the Marina.

Murali, a resident of south Chennai, has had a connection with the north since childhood. His grandfather lived in Perambur, the railway settlement, and the girl he was to fall in love with in adolescence lived there too. Their relationship was built on the numerous bicycle trips he made, as a schoolboy, through the roads and streets of north Chennai.

He once took me on a guided tour of north Chennai on his motorcycle. But at the time I must have been only a couple of years old in the city and had no knowledge whatsoever of its history, so I was far from fascinated as we ploughed through the crowds and congestion.

I distinctly remember the fishing harbour, where Murali drove into the semi-circular pier. I thought we would drive leisurely through the semi-circle and emerge out of the other end. But my heart stopped for a few moments when, midway, Murali suddenly applied the brakes: the pier had ended! A few feet more and we would have plunged straight into the black waters of the sea. The remainder of the pier began only about a hundred metres away. In fact they are two separate piers forming a near-arc, but from a distance appear to be one semi-circle. Murali, who knew this, burst out laughing. He had wanted to scare me. But I saw something even scarier: pairs of young lovers sitting on the edge of the piers with their legs dangling. They had nothing to hold on to except each other, and even a minor imbalance could have sent them both hurtling right down into the menacing depths below. But they were laughing and chatting, as if sitting in a park. They seemed to be too deeply in love to love their own lives.

On our way out of the fishing harbour, Murali drew my attention to a number of young men who had either a hand or a leg missing. They were most likely victims of sickle fights that often take place between gangs of rowdies. Elsewhere in the world, the word 'rowdy' is most likely to bring to mind the image of a mischievous schoolboy. But in Chennai, a rowdy means a goonda, a hardened criminal, who thinks nothing of slashing an opponent's throat in full public view.

North Chennai is infested with rowdies. A rowdy in Chennai is not taken seriously, by the police or the public, unless he earns a sobriquet that makes him stand out from the rest and gives a fearful ring to his name: Bomb Selvam, Welding Kumar, Gate Rajendran, Punk Kumar, Blade Mani.

On the way back home, manoeuvring our way between gigantic container-lorries that ferry cargo to and from the port, we crossed a dilapidated building that stood with its bricks exposed, much of the plaster having worn away. It wore a halo of history.

'You see that?' Murali had pointed at the structure. 'That's Royapuram railway station, the very first station to be built in Madras.'

I had half a mind to ask him to stop there. Railways stations are always fascinating; the smaller the station the better. But I had had enough of north Chennai and was eager to get back home. My white handkerchief turned black when I wiped my face at a roadside stall where we had stopped to have coffee.

As the years rolled on, Murali and I began to meet less frequently, marking our presence in each other's lives only on occasions such as our birthdays or weddings of people we both knew. We attended each other's weddings as well. Today, if at all we meet, we do so in the company of our spouses, when we make small talk and split after a couple of drinks. No one has the time; each has something to do or somewhere to go later in the evening or early next morning. And it was only the other day when Murali and I would spend hours together every so often, listening to the same set of songs over and over again, devouring Gujarati food, and then strolling on the Marina—as if we were the idlest souls in Chennai.

Ever since I started working on this book, I have been meaning to go back with Murali to north Chennai, especially Royapuram railway station. So, one evening, when he calls to invite me to one of his shows, I plead with him to take me to Royapuram. Gone are the days when I could just ask him. Murali is now much older and prosperous; one has to plead.

'How about tomorrow morning?' he asks.

I am pleased as well as surprised.

Next morning we take off around eleven. As we reach the fag-end of Mount Road and are about to get into the congestion of George Town, Murali asks me, 'Shall we stop by at the Kalikambal temple?'

'Is it an old temple?'

'You might want to see it. Shivaji had visited the temple.'

'Shivaji?'

'Yes, Chhatrapati Shivaji. Shivaji of the Shiv Sena.' He bursts out laughing. Murali's laughter is as big as him: he is six foot plus and has a girth that complements the height.

Soon we find ourselves stranded on a narrow lane leading to the temple. The planners of George Town had obviously not foreseen the invention of the motor car, leave alone two cars crossing each other on any of its streets. Our path is blocked by an assortment of approaching vehicles: a red car, two autorickshaws, fish carts, motorcycles, bicycles. Behind us, too, a medley of vehicles—each driver impatient and honking away, as if honking would dissolve the jam. Murali's driving and glib-talking skills are put to the ultimate test. He gets out of the car and assumes the role of a traffic cop, politely persuading smaller vehicles to clear the way and then squeezing the car through the little space available.

Thambu Chetty Street, where the south Indian-style temple stands, presents a bigger challenge: where to park the car? When we park in front of a shop whose shutters seem to have been down for decades, a woman comes running. She is carrying a bunch of pink coupons in her hand and seems to be a parking attendant. She shoos us away and asks us to park further down the road, but once we find a new location, she comes there too to chase us away and ask us to park elsewhere. Traffic on Thambu Chetty Street comes to a halt several times as we manoeuvre the car around. Finally, we park at the very spot where we had parked first, but this time the woman does not seem to have a problem at all. She hands us a pink parking coupon and even asks us to hurry up since the temple would soon close for the afternoon.

We remove our footwear in the car and walk barefoot to the temple. An elderly, kind-looking priest also asks us to hurry up if we want to have a glimpse of the goddess. We stand in silence for a few minutes in front of the deity. There is no crowd pushing us from behind, no pot-bellied priests asking us to keep moving. After circumambulating the shrine, we saunter into the temple office.

Since it is almost lunchtime, the office is empty save a lone office-bearer. He tells us about the powers of the goddess and how the who's who of Chennai visits the temple regularly. He names actors and actresses, all very popular. He mentions that some members of Karunanidhi's family also come often. 'But please don't mention their names, sir,' he pleads.

Atheism is one of the founding principles of the party that Karunanidhi heads; therefore his family's ties with God, even though an open secret, can only be discussed in hushed tones by the general citizenry. We ask the office-bearer about the most important visitor the temple has ever had, and he points us to a plaque on the wall. It reads:

CHENNAI SRI KALIKAMBAL DEVASTHANAM
NO. 212, THAMBU CHETTY STREET, MADRAS – 1
ON THIS DAY OF 3RD OCTOBER 1677
CHATRPATHI SIVAJI MAHARAJ
VISITED THIS SHRINE AND WORSHIPPED
SRI KALIKAMBAL

Shivaji's visit to the temple, including the date of his visit, appears to be a historical fact, because when I got back home that evening and looked up history, I found that he was indeed in the vicinity of Madraspatnam in the later part of 1677. He had even sent word to Fort St George that he was in need of British engineers. But the East India Company, deeply suspicious of his intentions and not wanting to anger his powerful enemies, politely turned down his request.

On the lanes branching off Thambu Chetty Street, I came to know from Sriram later, was practised the world's oldest profession once upon a time. Sailors would emerge from the harbour and stroll into George Town, to be beseeched by women waiting on the dark lanes. This was in the late nineteenth and early twentieth centuries. But in orthodox Madras, prostitution could never become an organised business to find home in a particular location. That is why unlike other big Indian cities, Madras doesn't have a red-light area.

This is not to say that people from that era did not stray out of their homes in pursuit of pleasure. A few minutes' walk from Thambu Chetty Street stood the devadasi quarter once upon a time.

■ ■ ■

The 6 September 1856 issue of *The Illustrated London News* reported an event that had taken place two months earlier in faraway Madras. It carried a sketch by Captain Barnett Fort of the Madras Army, depicting in detail the inauguration of the Royapuram railway station on 28 June, and a report on the inaugural ride that lasted up to Ambur, near Vellore:

> As the train proceeded across the arid plain of the Carnatic, it brought to view the countless number who thronged the route. The train dashed by the masses of colours, here clustered by a bridge, there collected under the deep shade of a tope, crowded round a station house, or fringing the edges of a cutting, cheering loudly as the train flew by them. Now and then too, a hearty laugh broke forth when in passing some pasture ground, the lazy cattle, startled by the rushing shriek of a train, flew frantically away, sometimes followed by the scared herdsman himself, who, thinking that the fiery-fiend whom he saw approaching might crush him also, took to his heels with all his speed.

At Ambur, the passengers—about 300 Europeans led by Madras governor Harris, who was to send troops to crush the mutiny that broke out in north India a year later— were treated to a sumptuous dinner. On the same day, a select crowd of natives too experienced the joy of a train ride, but in a separate train that travelled a shorter distance to Tiruvallur.

Like every other modern institution in India, railways too originated in Madras, in the sense that the Madras Railway Company was formed way back in 1845, when the first-ever train ride in India, from Bombay to Thane, had not even been thought of. But the Great Indian Peninsula Company, set up much later, beat Madras by opening the Bombay-Thane line in 1853. Since the original structures of Bombay and Thane stations no longer exist, Royapuram station, declared open in 1856, is today the oldest railway station in the entire subcontinent.

Captain Fort's sketch depicting its inauguration shows a large crowd of elegantly-attired Europeans gathered on the low-lying platform of the station. The eagerness to board the train is palpable. The platform looks strikingly grand because of its Corinthian pillars. From above the tall pillars hang large flags that add to the regal air. Two tracks run in front of the platform: a train waiting on each of them. The train farther from the platform, carrying the natives, already has the steam-spewing locomotive attached to it. They are witnessing the inauguration ceremony from the train; while the Europeans, gathered on the platform, are part of the ceremony.

This afternoon, however, Murali and I find neither the crowds nor any train as we drive into the Royapuram station, which is now painted in deep red and its Corinthian pillars in white. Murali parks the car right under the porch of the historic station, as if he owns the place. No one stops us: there is hardly a soul around anyway. In the hall described in *The Illustrated London News* as 'very elegant and most superbly furnished with handsome punkahs & c.', a couple of dogs are sleeping.

Given Chennai's notorious neglect of its heritage, Royapuram station had nearly gone to the dogs. When I saw it outside during my first trip to north Chennai with Murali, it was a crumbling building, left to fall on its own. But good sense eventually prevailed upon the railways which restored the station in 2005.

In the hall, there are pictures of the station before and after restoration. Inside the ticket window, a lone clerk is marking time. The train services may have increased since the restoration, but this does not seem to be a busy station, even though it was Madras's main railway terminus until 1907. All I can hear is the chirping of birds.

Standing on the main platform, I try to visualise the scene of the station's inauguration in 1856. The few Corinthian pillars that remain unmistakably belong to Captain Fort's sketch. So it was here that the journey of railways in south India began. A railway employee, who has been watching Murali and me looking around and taking pictures, comes over. He tells us that some of the old pillars had to be broken to facilitate electrification of the line, and that how it had been nearly impossible to bring them down—so strong they had been. He also tells us that the Burma teak furnishings in the hall were stolen during the restoration. Our conversation is cut short when a passenger train suddenly whizzes past, startling both Murali and me.

Since this platform has no shade and the sun is beating down mercilessly, we too get back to the hall and emerge on the platform on the other side of the building, which is shaded by what appears to be a fibreglass roof, red which has faded into patches of yellow. The slanting roof is held up by antique cantilevers. The platform is clean and empty and bears a historic look.

While Murali takes pictures I sit on the lone wooden bench whose backrest has 'M.S.M.R' engraved on it. M.S.M.R stands for Madras and Southern Mahratta Railway, which came into being in 1908 following the merger of the Madras Railway Company and the Southern Mahratta Railway. The company had its headquarters in Royapuram until 1922, when it shifted to the Central station. The bench, therefore, is about a hundred years old. If only it could speak. It must have seated countless genteel Europeans and distinguished Indians, and countless vagabonds and rowdies in the dark decades before its restoration.

The harbour is in close view: I can see the cranes and containers. At some distance is the Royapuram bridge, which we had taken to get here; the sound of the traffic on it is now no louder than the buzzing of flies. Right in front of me are three pairs of rail tracks, covered in places by vegetation. A dog is sleeping close to my feet. If you want to spend a quiet day with a book, this bench is the place to be.

The door to the station master's office is right next to the bench, and all this while, perhaps because of the silence, we've assumed that he must not be in. But he has been on his seat all along. He looks up from the paperwork and smiles nervously at us when we step in. He is puzzled that two strange men should be barging into his room and asking him questions related to his work. Murali, with his gift of the gab, puts him at ease by explaining to him, in Tamil, the purpose of our visit.

The station master tells us that at present, twenty-seven pairs of local trains pass through Royapuram station each day, apart from the occasional goods train; and that there is one train which still originates from Royapuram station—a goods train—and goes straight to Delhi.

As he talks, my eyes travel around his office. On the wall is a large diagram of the station, down to the minute detail which only a railway man can decipher. There are homilies too, in English, about the dangers of drinking and driving—a train, that is. In a corner of the room, on an antiquated table, lies an assortment of iron equipment related to rail tracks. To my untrained eye, most of the iron pieces appear to be fishplates. I also spot a piece of childhood fascination—the signalman's lantern!

I lift it with great excitement and call out to Murali to take a look. The station master smiles at us. We are still examining the lantern when we hear a rattling sound on the tracks outside and soon find a goods train passing by. We rush out to the platform with the lantern. I hold it up pretending to be the signalman, with the moving train in the backdrop, as Murali takes pictures. Then we quickly exchange positions. We put the lantern back in place and thank the station master for his time.

Only much later, when we are back in the bustle of the traffic, does it strike me that I had forgotten to ask the station master something pertinent: how does it feel it to be presiding over the country's oldest surviving railway station?

■ ■ ■

Not very far from the Royapuram station is Robinson Park. Here was born, just two years after India's Independence, a powerful movement that was to alter, irreversibly, the political landscape of Tamil Nadu. The park is our final stop for the day before Murali and I return to the Chennai we are familiar with.

In the late 1930s, as the struggle for freedom was peaking across the country, down south a man almost as elderly as Gandhi was leading a spirited movement against the domination of Brahmins over the Dravidian society and the imposition of Hindi in schools. He was E.V. Ramaswami Naicker, known to followers as Periyar, the Great One.

Periyar was born in a wealthy, deeply religious and upper-caste—but not Brahmin—family of Kannada-speaking merchants settled in Erode. He denounced God and became a bitter enemy of the Brahmins at the age of twenty-five when, arriving in Benaras as a hungry soul, he was denied entry to a Brahmins-only lodging where food was being served free to pilgrims.

He subsequently joined the Congress, as every self-respecting Indian did those days, but quit soon after, claiming that the party was in the stranglehold of Brahmins. In 1925, at the age of forty-five, he started his self-respect movement, aimed at breaking the hold of Brahmins on Dravidians. He called it the real freedom movement.

In 1938, Periyar was invited to head the Justice Party, which had been founded two decades earlier by two influential citizens of Madras, Sir P. Theagaroya Chetty and Dr T.M. Nair, to demand greater representation for non-Brahmins in the administration of Madras presidency. The Justice Party came to power in the presidency in 1920 when elections to the Madras legislative council began to be held, and stayed in power for a total of thirteen years. T. Nagar, which was until then a large tank, was developed by the Justice Party administration and many of its roads and landmarks were named after its leaders—Panagal Park, Usman Road, Dr Nair Road, Thanickachalam Road, to cite a few.

T. Nagar itself stands for Theagaroya Nagar—or Thyagaraya Nagar, as it is spelt today—Theagaroya Chetty being one of the founders of the party.

In 1937, however, the party suffered a crushing defeat at the hands of the Congress, which was riding the popularity wave in the freedom movement. The new Congress government under Rajagopalachari made Hindi compulsory in schools. To fight the move and also to revive its electoral prospects, the Justice Party aligned with Periyar's self-respect movement and made him the president of the party.

But Periyar, who was keen on social transformation rather than political change, withdrew the Justice Party from electoral politics in 1944 and renamed it the Dravida Kazhagam, which was meant to be a social reform organisation. His protégé, C.N. Annadurai, a journalist and a scriptwriter, became the general secretary of the new organisation.

Annadurai differed with his mentor on various issues. He did not support Periyar's call to celebrate Independence Day as a day of mourning (Periyar had wanted the British to stay and the Brahmins to go). Annadurai was against Brahminism and not the Brahmins. He, like many others in the organisation, was also not comfortable with the idea of staying away from electoral politics. The differences between the two reached a flashpoint in 1949 when Periyar, a widower for sixteen years, got married a second time at the ripe age of seventy, to his secretary who was only thirty. It was clear that he wanted to groom her as his successor.

On the morning of 17 September 1949, Annadurai and many other senior members of the Dravida Kazhagam met at a house on Coral Merchant Street in George Town and decided to break away from their mentor and launch the Dravida Munnetra Kazhagam, or the DMK. The next day, a Sunday, they held a rally in Robinson Park to announce to the public the birth of the new party.

It was only in 1967 that the DMK could win elections, with Annadurai becoming the chief minister, and since then no non-Dravidian party has been able to come to power in Tamil Nadu. Annadurai could rule only for two years—he died of cancer in 1969—but to date no political leader in the state has been able to match his stature.

If Periyar awakened the dignity of the Dravidians, it was Annadurai who showed them that they too could become political masters. As a scriptwriter who sent political messages to the masses through theatre and cinema, Annadurai was also the creator of the everlasting bond between cinema and politics in Tamil Nadu.

Far more places in Chennai are named after him than any other leader or actor: you have Anna Salai, Anna Flyover, Anna Square, Anna Nagar, Anna University, Anna Library, Anna Zoo and Anna what-not. Even when M.G. Ramachandran, the charismatic face of the DMK, formed a new party after a fall-out with Karunanidhi, he named it the Anna DMK, which later became the All India Anna DMK.

At two-thirty in the afternoon, harsh rays of the sun are bouncing off the vast barrenness of Robinson Park, making us squint. The park is all clay; it's more like a school playground. There are football goalposts and a basketball court, but boys, like anywhere else in the country, are playing cricket with tennis balls. Against one of the boundary walls stands a brick-and-cement podium. Whether this was the podium where Annadurai stood sixty-two years ago to announce the formation of the DMK, one can't be sure.

In a corner of the park lies a drunken man in a lungi—so drunk that he is unable to sit up. He is shouting curses at the boys because every now and then a ball hits him.

The boys who come to retrieve the ball, however, are unfazed by his slurry outbursts.

In another corner, which is shaded by trees, reflectors have been set up and a camera positioned. There is a small crowd of onlookers too. From a distance I can hear someone shout: 'Ready? Ready? Action!'

Murali and I walk towards the reflectors. The fact that they are shooting in a park in Royapuram, that too with such a small crowd of onlookers, I presume they must be shooting for a small-budget TV serial. But as Murali finds out, they are shooting a movie. The scene is like this: The hero is sitting on the ground in the park, looking forlorn, when someone approaches him and says something nasty. The hero looks up, talks back, and while still talking, gets up from the ground and dusts off his posterior and assumes a confrontationist posture. The actor who is supposed to approach the forlorn hero in the park is not around today. So a unit hand is holding a piece of paper at a height where the actor's face would have been, to help the hero look up at the correct angle. In the ten minutes that we spend there, the hero, who I am sure looks gloomy in real life too, is required to do six takes of emoting to a piece of paper, getting up each time and patting the dust off his bottom.

On the way back, we climb the Royapuram bridge, from where we can see the Royapuram station. Murali slows down. We can spot the bench where we had been sitting just about an hour ago. Murali wants to take pictures. But I feel we might hold up traffic if we stop the car.

'We'll come back some other day,' I tell him.

Murali relents and drives on. 'Some other day,' he says, 'some other days never come'.

If Francis Day was able to get the land from the local governor of the Vijayanagar Empire to build Fort St George, it was only because of the good offices of a god-fearing and prosperous Telugu merchant called Beri Thimmappa, who sold dyes to the East India Company and also served as Day's dubash.

A dubash—the word derives from *do bhasha*, or two languages—was the native interpreter who could speak the language of the foreign traders. As Madras began to grow, dubashes became the most influential lot of natives, amassing immense wealth and property by acting as middlemen on behalf of the foreign rulers and traders.

Thimmappa, who hailed from a town called Palacole in West Godavari district of present-day Andhra Pradesh, had no male heir, only a daughter. When Day and Cogan came to build the settlement, he too migrated to Madraspatnam along with his grandson, Ketty Narayanappah Naidu, to assist the two Englishmen in their mission. They became the first family to settle in the town of Madraspatnam.

Thimmappa and his grandson not only supplied men and material for the construction of the Fort but were also instrumental in the building of Black Town, the native settlement that came up right next to it. Thimmappa, the pious Vaishnavite that he was, also built the Chennai Kesava Perumal temple in the brand new settlement. In 1648, he gifted the temple to the grandson:

> Whereas at Chennai Puttanem I have built the Chennai Casava Permaul Covil ... which all I do (hereby) transfer to you, and which you are to (hold and) enjoy, from son to grandson, as long as the duration of (both) the Sun and Moon; performing the divine Services to their

utmost extent. Should anyone act prejudicially towards the charity, he would incur the guilt of having massacred a black cow on the banks of the Ganges.

But the temple was demolished exactly a century later, when a part of Black Town was flattened during the French attacks so that the British had a clear view of the approaching enemy. The bricks of the demolished structures were used to fortify the northern front of the Fort. As compensation, land was granted to the Hindus a little away from the original location to rebuild it; and on that land came up two temples instead of one—Chennai Kesava Perumal and Chennai Mallikeswarar—and they are still in existence. On the spot where Beri Thimmappa's temple stood now stands the Madras high court.

Apart from this, not much is known today about Thimmappa and his immediate descendants, except that they were extremely religious, prosperous and charitable businessmen. But from the sixth generation onwards, the life of Chennai's oldest family has been an open book.

The two great-grandsons of Narayanappah Naidu, Thimmappa's grandson, were well-known merchants of Madras—Ketty Bashyam Naidu and Ketty Narayanappah Naidu. Bashyam was barely two years old and Narayanappah not even born when their father passed away. The brothers were brought up by their maternal uncle, Parthasarathy Naidu, and under his guidance, they set up Appah & Co. in 1894. It began as a provision store and then turned into a wholesale commission agency, trading mainly in chillies, coriander seeds, turmeric, groundnuts and foodgrains. They would receive the produce from Guntur and Nellore and stock them in their godown in George Town, from where other agents would buy them in large quantities and ship them abroad.

Bashyam had four sons and three daughters, while Narayanappah had three sons and a daughter. In 1928, four young men—two sons each of Bashyam and Narayanappah—got together and formed yet another Appah & Co., the chemists and druggists. Those were good times for the extended Naidu family—the first family of Chennai—which now lived in Appah Gardens, a palatial house sitting like a majestic island in the middle of fifty grounds of lawns on Taylors Road in Kilpauk, one ground being equal to 2,400 sq ft.

As the icing on the cake, Bashyam's eldest son, Ketty Venkataswami Naidu, had launched himself into a successful career in politics, becoming the mayor of Madras in 1938 and subsequently a minister in the Madras state government headed by Rajagopalachari in 1952-'54. Appah Gardens had become an important address in Madras.

Bashyam did not live to see any of his sons doing well. He died at forty-two. His bust today overlooks a small neatly-kept park in Kilpauk, a couple-of-minutes' walk from Appah Gardens. It was his younger brother Narayanappah who continued to be the family patriarch till the ripe old age of ninety.

Today I am at the home of one of Bashyam's grandsons, Ketty Aravamudu. His father, Bashyam's third son Ketty Alavandar Naidu, was instrumental in setting up Appah & Co., the chemists and druggists. Aravamudu is sixty-five, soft-spoken and genial. Five years ago, he retired as regional sales manager in the pharmaceutical division of Glaxo, and now leads a quiet life with his wife on a quiet street in Anna Nagar. His son and daughter, both married, live in America. He hopes they will return someday, for good. What keeps him mostly occupied these days is the family tree. He happens to be one of the six trustees of Appah Charities—which keeps the family's centuries-old commitment to the upkeep of certain temples in and around the city. He is also one of the seventy-two designated legal heirs of the Appah family, which still owns vast properties in old Madras.

'I may be sixty-five,' smiles Aravamudu as his wife brings us coffee and biscuits, 'but I am still a young member of the family. Many of my cousins are much older, and many of them are no more.'

In all, the family has nearly 250 members today, including the grandchildren, spread across six continents. It consists of some thirty doctors, as many engineers, a pilot, an advocate, a chartered accountant and nearly half-a-dozen artistes.

'The days when you boasted about the first doctor or the first engineer in the family are way, way behind us. Today we have lost count,' laughs Aravamudu.

In December 2009, he organised a family get-together at Harrison Hotel in Nungambakkam. About 150 members, from all over the world, were able to make it. The chief guest on the occasion was the chronicler S. Muthiah, who is considered the last word when it comes to the knowledge of Chennai's colonial history. Though many members of the family had been getting together during festivals and religious occasions, this was the first time they were meeting as Chennai's first family—the new-found identity being driven home by Muthiah who, through his popular column in *The Hindu*, had been reiterating to the lay Chennaiite about the role Thimmappa played in founding Madras.

Aravamudu, who belongs to the eighth generation of the Thimmappa family, is dressed in a cream shirt tucked into a pair of dark trousers when I meet him at his house. In that attire, he bears hardly any resemblance to the dhoti-clad men of his preceding generation. In the black-and-white pictures that he shows me of them, all the seven brothers—the four sons of Bashyam and the three of Narayanappah—look strikingly alike. The individual facial features that might have distinguished one Naidu brother from the other are all hidden by the mandatory turban, thick moustache and the Vaishnavite caste-mark on the forehead. Aravamudu sports a moustache too, a greying one, but not the turban or the caste-mark. He is, after all, a Glaxo man.

Why Aravamudu chose to work in Glaxo and not in Appah & Co., the pharmacy started by his father, and why he lives in Anna Nagar and not in Appah Gardens—tell the story of the disintegration of Chennai's first family and the demise of its prosperous businesses.

The two Appah & Co.s, the wholesale commission agency as well as the pharmacy, were legends in Madras. In 1954, when the commission agency was celebrating its diamond jubilee and the pharmacy, quite coincidentally, its silver jubilee, the family brought out a souvenir to showcase its success story.

Aravamudu shows me one of the few surviving copies. The black-and-white pictures of the lavish tea parties being held on the sprawling lawns of Appah Gardens leave you in no doubt about the kind of life the family once led, and the range of personalities who sent congratulatory messages to the two companies on the twin occasions speak volumes about the respect it commanded. The entire who's who of Madras, right from the governor and the chief minister down to prominent merchants and pharmaceutical companies, had sent their best wishes—all duly compiled in the yellowing souvenir that is now held together by strips of cellophane.

On 5 September that year, the employees of the two Appah & Co.s were treated to lunch and given a month's salary as bonus to commemorate the occasion. The same evening, a party was organised on the lawns of Appah Gardens. As many as 1,000 people, including the elite of Madras, attended. The Madras Corporation band was in attendance. Those who made speeches on the occasion included Sri Prakasa, the governor of Madras state, and Sir A. Lakshmanaswami Mudaliar, the vice-chancellor of Madras University. Proposing the vote of thanks, Venkataswami Naidu, who had been the mayor and a minister, especially lauded Appah & Co., the chemists and druggists, for pulling through the Second World War when medicines were in short supply. He also promised to continue the tradition the parent firm had upheld for the past sixty years. The garden party wound up with the national anthem played by the Madras Corporation band.

The two Appah & Co.s might have survived a war that changed the destinies of millions of families across the world, but they were unable to survive the tugs within the seven brothers. Barely two decades after the famous garden party, they both shut down.

Aravamudu was about ten years old when the diamond jubilee of the company set up by his grandfather coincided with the silver jubilee of the one started by his father. They all lived in Appah Gardens then—the 100-member-strong family of the seven brothers. Bashyam, of course, had died long ago. Narayanappah, the patriarch, was now eighty-one and confined to home because of a paralytic attack. But, it was one big, happy family.

'I grew up with my cousins. We used to go to school together in cars. The family had seven cars, all Austin A-40s. Getting into a train or a bus was a novelty for us. All our friends happened to be our own cousins; we never had friends from outside. The elder cousins used to take care of us. Wherever we went, people would look up to us as a big family, rich people. In school we were given greater attention than others. We had our own cricket team, our own football team,' recalls Aravamudu.

He switches on his laptop and takes me on a virtual tour of the Appah Gardens of his boyhood. It had been quite a task, he says, to trace the pictures and put them in order for the family reunion. 'Here, this was the entrance. This was the porch. This was the garden. Here, see the fountain. And look at this well, such a huge well. See the car sheds. As I told you, we used to have seven cars. This was the pooja room. This is an annaprasanam ceremony, when a baby is fed with solids for the first time. See this small boy being brought in a big procession? He is going to write the letters of the alphabet for the first time. And this girl, she has just attained puberty, so the family is celebrating it. This is the wedding between two toys, which used to take place before a real wedding. See this, a separate tent erected for non-vegetarians during a function. These are things we want to pass on to our children—our heritage. When they saw the pictures, my own children could not believe I once lived in such a big house.'

By the time Aravamudu stepped into his teens, Appah Gardens had become too small to accommodate the individual ambitions and needs of the seven brothers, each of whom had several growing-up children. So in the sprawling gardens that were once the venue for famous tea parties, seven new houses came up. Seven houses for seven brothers.

Then, they fell like ninepins.

'I had just joined college when the difficult times began. My uncle (Venkataswami Naidu, who had been the mayor and a minister) had to spend a lot of money in politics. The money came from the family businesses. Not to be left behind, the other brothers also started drawing money from the businesses. Soon, the two firms were in the doldrums. Those were the dark days. First the businesses had to be sold off; then the houses went, one after the other.

'My father moved into a rented house in Anna Nagar. We were now travelling in buses. I completed my studies and joined Glaxo. We had been dealers for the company, so getting a job with them was not a problem. My mother was very upset with the way things had turned out, but my father took it all in his stride. He said whatever the situation, we would have to face it. He was a practical man and highly religious.

'Even during the most difficult of times the family did not touch the money that had been put aside for generations for religious commitments. That corpus remained intact. We all worked hard, my brothers and I, and we pulled our families through the bad patch. Our cousins, who we grew up with, also worked very hard and became successful. From a joint business family, we became a family of professionals.'

Of Aravamudu's two elder brothers, one became an electronics engineer and another a chartered accountant. Of the younger two, one had a successful career in marketing and the other is a doctor who now runs a well-known diagnostic centre in Chennai. Each of the brothers, Aravamudu included, today owns two houses each.

Aravamudu narrates his family's history in a matter-of-fact manner that is embellished by humour. He can afford to laugh today because he and his siblings and cousins went on to do well in life and were not the direct recipients of the humiliation that his father and uncles had to suffer while going from riches to nearly rags. Even his once-powerful uncle, the former mayor and the minister, travelled in buses in his old age because the cars were long gone.

The building that housed Appah & Co., the commission agents, on Audiappah Street in north Chennai, not very far from Fort St George, has long been demolished. Appah & Co., the pharmacy, on Netaji Subhas Chandra Bose Road, formerly known as China Bazaar Road, is today a hotel by the name of Rolex.

As for Appah Gardens, it is now the name of a street off Taylors Road in Kilpauk. In its heyday, the street used to be the driveway leading to one of Madras's most famous addresses, dotted by the seven bungalows belonging to the seven brothers. Today it is yet another street looked after by the Chennai Corporation, and is flanked by brand-new houses and multi-storeyed flats that have come up in place of those bungalows.

According to Aravamudu, two of those bungalows still remain with the family, though I spot only one as I drive through Appah Gardens—the street—immediately after my meeting with him. Considering the colourful high-rises that have come up on the street, it is highly possible that one of them escaped my attention. But the one that I spot is a white, handsome building: not very old but very neglected, as if waiting for a realtor who would be glad pull it down and build luxurious flats for seven well-to-do families on that single piece of land.

Even today the family is sitting on a real-estate goldmine, still owning 450 grounds of land in old Madras, but the mining rights are locked up in documents that remain in the names of Bashyam and Narayanappah. 'According to the deed, the land is ours but the superstructure belongs to other parties. If we sell the land, we can only sell it to the owners of the superstructures, or else we will have to buy the superstructures from them in order to fully own the land. It is all very complicated. But still, we have properties here and there, and whenever a sale happens, the money is divided between the seventy-two legal heirs,' says Aravamudu.

When I ask him whether all the seventy-two, considering that they are so spread out and busy and well-to-do today, are always aware about their due share whenever a piece of land comes up for sale, I expect an mournful answer on the lines of how painful it was to get all them together for a certain transaction. But his reply is prompt. 'When it comes to property, you don't need to remind people about their share.' He laughs.

'But you see, the sale of properties, festivals, religious ceremonies—these are occasions when the family gets together. The customs, the traditions, they have kept us together. That's the great thing about Hinduism. It may not be possible for us to stay as a joint family because as the numbers grow, you need to have your own space. But it is always good to think of the old days.'

Chapter 3

DO YOU BELIEVE IN GOD?

*T*radition is daywear in Chennai. While in other big cities it stays mothballed in trunks, taken out only during festivals and weddings, here tradition is worn round the year—like uniform.

There is a plump woman I run into every afternoon. She must be in her late twenties. She carries a miniature jewellery store on her person—from chunky gold earrings to necklaces and bangles. Here eyes are always kohl-lined and she sports a sparkling bindi on her forehead. She wears loose-fitting salwar-kurta, the dupatta always firmly in place, and a bunch of fresh jasmine hangs from her jet-black hair.

You usually see women dressed up as traditionally as this either in a temple or at a wedding or, in the case of Chennai, even at workplaces. But I see her every afternoon at the gym, where everybody else comes prepared to release copious amounts of sweat. Her sole obsession, during whatever little workouts she is put through, is to not let her dupatta move from its position even by a fraction of an inch. The dupatta is pinned to her shoulder all right, but any vigorous movement would have it flapping around. So she tries to be as dainty as possible when it comes to lifting her hands or twisting her torso. On the treadmill, she walks like a toddler practising its first steps. The jasmine retains its freshness, she her weight.

There are times when I am tempted to tell the woman that she is only wasting her time and should instead consider investing in a treadmill at home. But it is none of my business. Maybe she is particular about exercising in a gym, wearing what she pleases. That's her uniform—the flower and the jewellery and the dupatta—without which she would lose her identity. Why should she enter the gym dressed like someone else? Apart from me, no one, not even her trainer, seems to find her attire or attitude out of place. Just as no one in the workplace finds it odd when a male colleague, bound for pilgrimage to Sabarimala, shows up barefoot and wearing a beard and a black dhoti. The pilgrimage attracts about a million devotees annually to the shrine of Lord Ayyappa at Sabarimala in the Western Ghats of Kerala. Legend has it that Ayyappa was born out of a union between the two male gods, Shiva and Vishnu. One day, the two happened to be together in the forests when Shiva asked to see Vishnu's female form Mohini, the divine enchantress. Vishnu, the wise one, knew what it could lead to. He refused. But Shiva wasn't one to give up.

Vishnu eventually relented and transformed into Mohini. Ayyappa was born from the inevitable union that followed. But for pilgrims, a trip to Sabarimala must be preceded by forty-one days of voluntary abstinence from all sources of pleasure, inherent as well as acquired. Grooming is prohibited, so is meat-eating, smoking, alcohol and sex. Such a prolonged sacrifice, in fact, earns the Sabarimala-bound employee the respect of his colleagues—far from anyone sneering at him because he is sitting at his desk barefoot, wearing an unkempt beard and a black dhoti around his waist.

This is Chennai.

Even today, it is common to see Brahmin men, no matter where they work or what positions they hold, wearing the caste-mark on their foreheads—the general exceptions being those who have had a liberal upbringing outside Tamil Nadu or have grown up in Anglicised homes.

It's not just the Brahmins. Chennai, as a society, worships tradition. You can expect to be jolted by a sudden burst of crackers at any time of the day. If they go off during the day, it means a funeral procession is passing by; if during the dead of night, it has to be a procession being taken out from a neighbourhood temple. But no one gets startled out of bed or opens the window to see what is going on. No one ever berates people for setting off crackers at two in the night. It would be sacrilege to interrupt them because they are only doing their job of being faithful to tradition.

The bursting of crackers for reasons of mourning or religion is a Dravidian practice. Yet, when you shut your eyes and think of traditional Chennai, it is invariably a Brahmin motif that springs to your mind. Even though Brahmins form a miniscule part of its population—not even five per cent—their distinct appearance and strict adherence to customs make them the most visible community in the city.

There are two sects of Tamil Brahmins, the Iyengars and the Iyers. The feud between them dates back to time immemorial. Iyengars are Vaishnavites, the followers of Vishnu, the protector of the universe. They are subdivided into two sects, the Vadagalais and the Thengalais. The Vadagalais paint a white elongated 'U' on their foreheads; while the Thengalais wear the 'Y' mark—a white line descends from the 'U' to cover the bridge of the nose, making it resemble the alphabet. There is a running feud between them as well.

Iyers, on the other hand, are Shaivites, the followers of Shiva, the god of destruction. In accordance with the appearance of their god, as portrayed in the images, they smear ash horizontally on their foreheads. While the ash that Shiva wears is supposed to have come from funeral pyres, the ash that an Iyer applies usually comes from burnt cow dung.

These days not many wear caste-marks that are elaborately drawn to a T; most office-going men make do with abbreviated versions—a thin vertical red line in the case of the Iyengars and a small horizontal smear of ash for the Iyers. Similarly, the row between the Iyengars and the Iyers, or between the two sects of Iyengars, is no longer as pronounced as before. It still exists, but more like a rivalry between two sisters-in-law living under the same roof.

Their visibility made them an easy target when Periyar launched his campaign against Brahmins in 1925. Periyar was born into a wealthy family of upper-caste Hindus who were staunch Vaishnavites. A picture of Periyar's father shows him wearing the 'U' mark on his forehead, with a streak of red running in the middle of the 'U'. Periyar grew up listening to religious discourses at home, though he was habituated to picking holes in the mythological stories, much to the irritation of his family. But he was not against God.

Then something happened in 1904, which not only changed his personality but also triggered the transformation of Tamil society. Periyar, who was then twenty-five and married, slipped out of home one day wanting to be a renunciate. Wandering through various towns—along the way he gave away all his belongings and jewellery except for a solitary ring—he finally arrived in Benaras, hungry and penniless. He found his way to a choultry, a Brahmins-only inn where they are fed for free, but was stopped at the gate. He sported a moustache, which Brahmins do not. The gatekeeper rudely pushed him back to the street. Periyar, it is said, was so hungry that he ate the leftovers dumped outside the choultry.

While reading about the episode, a story I had heard in my boyhood sprung to my mind. It's a true story. Back home in Kanpur, we had a Bengali Brahmin family living in the neighbourhood. They had a son, who went to the same school as I but who was much older. He was an athlete, rugged and sunburnt. He once happened to visit Haridwar, where he went to an ashram run by Bengalis. The ashram was started by a holy woman his family revered. It was lunchtime when he reached the ashram and food was about to be served. Who minds free lunch? So he sat down, cross-legged, joining dozens of other men seated in rows. But when it was his turn to be served, the volunteer who was scooping out steaming rice onto leaf-plates held back his ladle and asked the young man to show his sacred thread. Imagine this: a hungry young man, who is now doubly hungry because the aroma of food has already hit the air and he has caught a glimpse of the dishes being served. And just when he can't wait any longer to eat, the volunteer chokes his salivary glands. The young man, my neighbour, pulled the sacred thread out of his collar, held it up and got up to leave. Ignoring the volunteer who was now begging for forgiveness, he marched out and ate in a hotel. He had kept his self-respect intact, something that Periyar could not afford to at the time.

Periyar was neither a Brahmin nor had any money to buy food. Yet in order to survive he took up the job of assisting a local priest. The job entailed bathing in the chilling waters of the river at four in the morning and helping his boss set up shop before pilgrims started arriving. The longer he stayed in Benaras, the more he saw the corrupt side of it. He was by now thoroughly disillusioned and angry with the injustice of the Brahminical order. Periyar sold the solitary ring he had saved to pay for his return journey. Back home, he took his sweet revenge—and how.

Within decades of his being thrown out by the gatekeeper, the entire Tamil society had turned upside down. The Brahmin, whose looming presence evoked reverence and fear among the general population for centuries, had lost his predominance. It all began with Periyar eating the leftover food, during which he noticed an inscription on the wall of the choultry. The choultry, it turned out, was built by a rich Dravidian like his father who saw Brahmins as emissaries of god. And yet he—the son of a wealthy Vishnu-worshipping Dravidian—was insulted by the very men his father patronised back home. Why should Brahmins, belonging to the Indo-Aryan race, lord over native Dravidians? The question became the war-cry of his Self-Respect Movement.

Periyar died in 1973, at the age of ninety-four. A UNESCO citation, conferred shortly before his death, hailed him as the 'prophet of the new age, the Socrates of South-East Asia, father of the social reform movement and arch-enemy of ignorance, superstition, meaningless customs and base manners.' He was still alive when his protégés took political power. Since 1967, only Dravidian parties have ruled Tamil Nadu. Today, their leaders evoke the same reverence and fear as the Brahmin once did.

The Tamil Brahmin is now pretty much like the British monarch, all regalia and no power. He remains the metaphor of Madras, keeping his traditions alive in the confines of his palaces. He remains as visible, is envied and respected, and still wields considerable influence on society. But he no longer has a say except, maybe, within his own community.

One Sunday morning, in late 2009, I found myself attending a Brahmin swayamvaram. The swayamvaram, as most of us know, was the ancient tradition of a Hindu princess choosing her groom from a row of princes by placing a garland around the neck of the man she thought was right for her. But this swayamvaram was the human equivalent of a matrimonial page from *The Hindu*: nearly 250 families crammed the auditorium of the Sanskrit College in Mylapore. When I arrived at the college that morning, I was imagining young men lined up in rows and young women, in turns, going past them with a garland and choosing their groom on the spot. I knew very well that this wouldn't be the case, but what was the harm in weaving visuals in your mind if that serves to kill some time while negotiating Chennai traffic. It so happened there was not much traffic to be dealt with on a Sunday morning and it was not long before reality greeted me in the form of the combined smells of jasmine, talcum powder and sweat as I squeezed my way into the jam-packed auditorium.

Not many young men were to be seen around. And the young women I could spot were few and far between: they could well have been the sisters or sisters-in-law of prospective grooms or brides. The swayamvaram was basically an interface for the elders, who had come armed with the bio-data and horoscopes of their sons and daughters, hoping to find a match for them before the sun went down. The parents walked up to the dais one after the other and rattled off the education qualifications of their marriageable children and specified the kind of 'alliance' they were looking for. Those incoherent or inaudible were berated by Swaminatha Sharma, the loud and zealous master of ceremonies who repeated the qualifications and the requirements for the benefit of the audience. The most sought-after attributes were 'good family' and 'minimum graduate'.

'Super idea, sir! Super idea! Brahmins for Brahmins,' an elderly woman, who had come in search of a daughter-in-law, gushed when I asked her what she thought of the swayamvaram. Her only son, who was twenty-three years old and pursuing his masters in computer applications, told me, 'I am already earning ₹ 30,000 per month because I rent out my vehicles to some big companies. I am also a classical dancer. I am looking for a middle-class girl, nineteen or twenty, who has pleasing tendency,' he told me. Pleasing tendency? 'Someone who is nice to my mother,' he clarified.

A fifty-something woman now went up to the dais and, in fluent English, read out her daughter's bio-data. It was a very impressive one. I could see eyes lighting up. But there was a hitch. 'She is based in Mumbai and can't get a transfer,' the woman broke the news as well as many hearts. 'Is there someone who is working in Mumbai or around?'

Immediately a hand shot up. It belonged to a bespectacled, studious-looking man who must have been in his late twenties. Swaminatha Sharma, the emcee, asked him, 'Are you ready to take a transfer to Mumbai?' The bespectacled man nodded. Sharma told the woman, 'There you are, go talk to them.' The audience clapped.

My eyes followed the fifty-something woman who was now wading through the crowd in the direction of the young man. I went after her. I wanted to eavesdrop. A female relative of the man—I later came to know she was his cousin and a lawyer—greeted the fifty-something woman. They decided to move out of the hall for a chat. I followed them.

While the two women launched into a discussion, the young man hovered around in the background, wearing a shy smile. They spoke in Tamil, which I don't understand too well, so I had to make do with reading their faces. Even though they exchanged phone numbers, neither of the women seemed to be too pleased with the direction in which the conversation was headed. I soon got to know why.

'The thing is,' the bespectacled man's cousin told me, 'her daughter earns ₹ 60,000 whereas my cousin brother earns only ₹ 30,000. So the girl has to come down to the level of ₹ 30,000, or else the marriage will only end up in divorce. Money is not the only criterion for a happy marriage, am I right or not?' The Mumbai girl's mother was not the only one they had met since the morning. 'We met another family. They are a poor family, but a good family. They didn't have any demands. Usually, the girl's side has so many demands,' the lawyer said.

It goes without saying that the Mumbai girl's mother was also not entirely pleased with the idea of her daughter marrying a man who earned half her salary. Such an alliance was out of the question. The shy smile on the face of the bespectacled man, who had flown down from Pune to attend the swayamvaram, had disappeared.

I too was forced to do the disappearing act soon after. I happened to make the grave mistake of asking one of the volunteers if I could speak to Swaminatha Sharma once the swayamvaram was over. He either misunderstood my question or misheard me, because I could see him making his way through the crowd and heading straight to the dais. The volunteer interrupted Sharma and pointing at me, whispered something. The microphone picked up every word and I could hear the name of the newspaper I represented. Sharma, pleased that Press was in attendance, smiled generously at me and motioned me to come to the dais. He loudly called out, '*Vaanga,* sir! *Vaanga,* sir!'

Suddenly there was silence. Every single pair of eyes in the hall was on me now. From the distance, I tried indicating in sign language that I would see him later. I don't know if he understood, but I was now headed to the nearest exit. I had barely stepped out of the door when the din resumed in the hall.

■ ■ ■

Ever since Dravidian parties began to rule Tamil Nadu in 1967, the Brahmins have been reminded time and again that they should fend for themselves and not expect anything from the government. The Brahmin, who was never rich nor had the muscle power, fell back on his traditional wealth and weapon: knowledge.

Today, Brahmins constitute the majority of Chennai's intellectual class and much of the highly-educated middle-class, most of whom have a son or daughter either studying or living in America. Abroad is the place to be because back home, government-run professional colleges and institutions have almost shut their doors on them, leaving only a narrow gap for Brahmin candidates to enter. For those not flying abroad to train as engineers or doctors, chartered accountancy is a respectable option back home that remains untouched by the quota system. I have a colleague whose family boasts of ten chartered accountants—all living together under an extended roof.

Yet there are a large number of Brahmin families who do not have the money or the merit to thumb their noses at the government. Many of them scrape together a living, their caste hanging around their necks like an albatross. There are some among them, though, who trudge on, unmindful of the altered social dynamics, and chart their own course.

Srimathy was born in an Iyengar family in 1969, the year Karunanidhi first became chief minister. He had succeeded Annadurai, who died within two years of inaugurating Dravidian rule in Tamil Nadu. Periyar, the Dravidian Gandhi, was alive.

Srimathy was born in Madras. She was a late child. She was only five when her father, who worked with the railways, retired and the family moved to their native town of Kumbakonam. By now her sister, twenty years older and married, was settled in Madras.

Life in Kumbakonam was as small-town and old-time as it could get. Srimathy's day would begin with a bath in the river followed by the drawing of the kolam at the doorstep. After which she went to school. In her spare time, she would play with her friends in the neighbourhood or master the art of stringing flowers together. The town would be asleep by seven o' clock.

About twice a month, she would visit her sister in Madras, who lived in Triplicane. 'From her house it was one straight road to Marina. We would prepare snacks at home and carry them to the beach in the evenings. There we would buy knick-knacks made out of shells. It was like a picnic. This is one memory of Madras from my childhood. Another memory is taking the bus to the Egmore station. On the way, there was this theatre that was showing *Neeya* (the too-familiar story of a female snake assuming human form to avenge the death of her beloved). The film ran for many months and each time we passed the theatre, I would grab my sister's hand because the huge poster scared me,' recalls Srimathy.

Srimathy today teaches ashtanga yoga in a calm, upmarket neighbourhood near Mylapore. In spite of having the looks and the figure of a glamorous yoga instructor, she is a picture of simplicity. She charges a measly sum for teaching this most dynamic and challenging form of yoga, known in the West as power yoga. Instructors there make a fortune, but Srimathy is clear she isn't doing it for the money.

I was her student for a brief period and back then, I would reach for my classes well before time. But this afternoon I am horribly late, by almost an hour, for the meeting with Srimathy. If she is irritated, she does not show it. The rigorous training, under none other than Pattabhi Jois, the Mysore-based exponent of ashtanga yoga, seems to have taught her to keep her cool. Years of practice also shows on her appearance. I am quite surprised when I learn she is actually a couple of years older than me. I had always believed she was in her early thirties. As a student you don't ask teachers their age or personal details; you only make guesses from an inquisitive corner of your eye. But when you have a notebook and a pen in your hand, you are entitled to ask questions.

Srimathy, growing up in Kumbakonam, was not put through the rigours of a conservative Iyengar upbringing. 'My father was not an orthodox man. He would visit Shiva temples, even Sai Baba temples, something Iyengars usually don't do. I was never asked to do any chores at home,' says Srimathy.

She was thirteen when her father passed away, and she and her mother moved to Madras to live with the married sister, whose husband had now built a house in the outskirts of the city, in Tambaram. The sister's father-in-law, a strict Vaishnavite from Kancheepuram, also happened to be living with them. So it was at the age of thirteen that Srimathy, an Iyengar, had the taste of life in a traditional Iyengar household. The carefree days of Kumbakonam, under the indulgence of her broad-minded father, were now a thing of the past.

Worse, Srimathy had just attained puberty. During the three days of menstruation, she would be confined to the verandah of her sister's house in Tambaram. She would eat and sleep there, as if she suffered from a contagious disease that could spread by the very presence of a patient. 'I had to get up before everybody else did, go round behind the house and wash my clothes under the tap in the backyard. Then I would take a bath and come back to the verandah. I could not eat before my sister's father-in-law had eaten. He would eat only after he had performed his puja, which never happened before eight-thirty. In fact, I was not even supposed to watch him eating during those four days. So I would have the leftover rice from the previous day, soaked in water, and run to school. Eating leftover rice does not break the rules. Only, you should not eat freshly-cooked food before the elders in the house have eaten. So my mother or sister would put the previous day's rice on a plate and leave it for me on the verandah. There would be a separate plate for me,' recalls Srimathy.

She was too young to mind all this, but old enough to feel embarrassed when boys, especially her age, came visiting. 'I would not know where to look. The worst part is they would know why I was living on the verandah,' she laughs. She would spend time in the verandah studying, stitching or mending pillow covers, or reading Lakshmi and Ramani Chandran, two popular Tamil novelists. 'The women described in their novels were always beautiful. I would imagine myself to be them.'

Srimathy was now growing up to be a beautiful woman, but the old man was always around to make her feel like an obedient child instead of a dreamy teenager. 'My sister's son and I are almost the same age. In the evenings, we would take turns watering the plants. After that, my sister's father-in-law would make both of us sit in front of him and have us chanting shlokas. We were expected to repeat the words after him, that too loudly, pronouncing each syllable correctly. Nearby, there was an open-air gym, where neighbourhood boys would be working out, and our chants would attract their attention. From the corner of my eye I could see them staring at us. We would be so embarrassed, but we had no choice except to sit there, spines straight, and keep chanting.'

Srimathy began to venture out of home on her own once she joined college; she had enrolled for afternoon classes. Even then, she was confined mostly to an all-girls classrooms and the ladies compartment of the local train. Being seen with a man would have spelt doom. 'Word would have reached home faster than the train,' she says with a laugh. 'Even those who had boyfriends made sure the boys never came anywhere near the ladies compartment. The government employees who would travel with us were very shrewd women. They would always watch what the college girls were up to.'

Nevertheless, travelling in the ladies compartment was fun. The journey would take about an hour each way. 'We had a great group of friends, women of all ages, who took the same train. We would sing bhajans, Carnatic music, film songs. It was in the train that I discovered my singing talents. We would also have garland-stringing competitions among us. A woman sold flowers in the compartment, so much of flowers (she held her palms apart to indicate the quantity) for just five rupees.' The fun continued even when Srimathy, at the age of twenty, passed out of college and joined a private firm in Egmore as a stenographer.

Then she fell in love with a colleague. He was a year older than her. As in most Indian love stories, there was a hitch. The man was an Iyer, and there was no way her family was going to accept such a marriage. But, when she broke the news at home, it was the sister's father-in-law who turned out to be the coolest. He had no objections. Over time he had become a friend: each evening, when she returned home from college or work, he would pull up a chair next to her and enquire after her day. Though there was no escape from spending those three days of the month confined to the verandah till the time Srimathy got married and moved out.

The one person who was strongly against her marrying an Iyer man was her mother. She had other plans. She wanted to move in with the younger daughter whenever she got married, and for this purpose she was keen that Srimathy marry a relation. Her chances of living with the daughter would be bleak if she married outside the family, that too an Iyer. The mother, who saw a question mark hanging over her own future, put her foot down. But Srimathy, having shown the courage to fall in love in the first place, that too with an Iyer, was not one to back out. The mother and daughter would have frequent quarrels over this.

Decisive support for Srimathy came, once again, from an unexpected quarter: the sister's husband. Srimathy had always found him overbearing and they were prone to getting into arguments. She would avoid him. But then, he was the breadwinner and called the shots at home. He worked with the electricity board and was a leader of the workers' union. Srimathy's mother could not defy him. One Sunday, the brother-in-law took along another male relative to visit the family of Srimathy's boyfriend. That settled the matter.

Srimathy was twenty-one when she got married. The next year, she had a son. Her sister's father-in-law came to see the child. But he did not eat anything that had been touched or cooked by Srimathy. She was, after all, an Iyer now. He stuck to a glass of milk and some fruits. The old man had done the balancing act: he demonstrated his affection for Srimathy by coming to see her child but at the same time kept his Iyengar identity intact.

If things grew difficult for Srimathy after she got married, it had nothing to do with caste. Her son, as soon as he turned a year old, began having seizures. The convulsions kept returning in spite of medication. Her husband, a firm believer in alternative medicine, suggested that the child be put through yoga. The boy was four when Srimathy enrolled him—and herself—at the Krishnamacharya Yoga Mandiram.

Much of the yoga that is taught across the world today originates from Krishnamacharya, who spent many years with a guru in Tibet before beginning to teach in Mysore at the instance of the local maharaja. In Mysore he had two outstanding disciples, B.K.S. Iyengar, who was his brother-in-law, and Pattabhi Jois. Iyengar eventually moved to Pune, while Jois stayed on in Mysore; soon the West was to come to their feet. Krishnamacharya, meanwhile, relocated to Madras. He died in 1989, at the age of 101, active till the final moments. Pattabhi Jois died in 2009 at ninety-four, teaching till the end, while Iyengar, at ninety-two, is still going strong. Their longevity is the ultimate evidence of the power of yoga.

It had been my burning desire to train under Pattabhi Jois: all I needed to do was save up some money, take three months' leave and catch the Shatabdi Express to Mysore. But, alas, I am not a Westerner who can afford to throw everything up to pursue a passion. I am an Indian man, who needs to keep his job and the kitchen fires burning.

But Srimathy was fortunate enough to learn directly from Pattabhi Jois. After spending nine years at the Krishnamacharya Yoga Mandiram, learning and then teaching yoga, she went to Mysore. By then, her son had been cured. Today, the son is studying engineering. Having scored ninety-five per cent in the twelfth standard, he breezed his way into an engineering college in Chennai.

'There is nothing more I can ask from life. I am happy. Even though I don't visit temples often, I have to say God is great,' says Srimathy. Her smile lights up the empty hall we are sitting in. Soon, students will be trooping in and she will be guiding them through sun salutations. It strikes me: here is a life, that of Srimathy, that played to its own script, completely untouched by the changes in the social order brought about by the Dravidian movement.

■ ■ ■

Periyar was born only ten years after Gandhi. That makes them contemporaries, though Periyar seems to be a recent phenomenon because he died only in 1973, socially active till the last day. By then, ABBA was already a year old and Amitabh Bachchan, with the release of *Zanjeer*, had just stepped onto the ladder of superstardom. Gandhi, on the other hand, died right after Independence: my father was barely four years old and my mother yet to be born when the assassin pumped the bullets into him. So Gandhi seems remote, older by many generations. But the fact remains that the two men, both born to merchant families, set off on their political careers almost at the same time, and the similarities between the courses of their journeys is striking.

Gandhi was a loyal subject of the Empire before he decided to overthrow the British, while Periyar was a devout Hindu before he denounced God. Their revolutions were born out of humiliations—Gandhi had been thrown out of a rail carriage in South Africa, while Periyar was rudely pushed out of a choultry in Benaras. Both lived to see the fruition of their long struggle, and neither was happy with what he had lived on to see: Gandhi didn't want the country partitioned, while Periyar had to put up with the partition of his party.

As personalities, however, Gandhi and Periyar were poles apart. Gandhi was lean, Periyar stocky. Gandhi was a small eater, subsisting on goat milk and a frugal vegetarian diet, while Periyar had a huge appetite and loved meat. Gandhi, after being married for twenty-three years, became a celibate at the age of thirty-six; Periyar married for a second time at the age of seventy. Gandhi, in his ripe old age, coaxed young women to sleep naked with him only to test his powers of abstinence; while Periyar, travelling to Europe in 1931, at the age of fifty-two, gladly went to a striptease club in Berlin. Periyar never claimed to be a saint, though he looked like one, a well-fed one, with his flowing silver beard. He was direct and in-your-face. It was Gandhi who was saint-like and preachy, always advocating control over the senses.

Today, what unites Gandhi and Periyar is their near irrelevance in the very societies they once stirred.

One sunny morning, I walked out of my street, onto the main road, and flagged down an autorickshaw.

'Periyar Thidal?' I asked the khaki-clad driver.

He hadn't heard of Periyar Thidal—Periyar Grounds—the memorial of the great Dravidian leader. He asked me where it was, and when I told him, he said he was not going in that direction and sped away. It is not for nothing that autorickshaw drivers in Chennai are a despised lot.

I hailed another passing autorickshaw. This driver, too, hadn't heard of Periyar Thidal. When I told him it was somewhere near the offices of *Dina Thanthi*, the largest-selling Tamil daily, he asked me where the *Dina Thanthi* offices were. When I told him they were in Vepery, one of the older settlements of Chennai and very close to the Central station, he thought for a moment or two and quoted an obscenely steep fare. I waved him away.

Yet another autorickshaw flagged down.

'Periyar Thidal?'

'*Enga saar?*'

'*Dina Thanthi* office?'
'*Enga saar?*'
'Vepery?'
'Oh, Vepery...' The driver pondered over the destination as he took his spectacles off and wiped them, and then, rather reluctantly, said, 'Okay, *vaanga.*'
Thank God for small mercies.

There is no god
There is no god
There is no god at all
He who invented god is a fool
He who propagates god is a scoundrel
He who worships god is a barbarian

– THANTHAI PERIYAR

The inscription on the black stone pedestal, on which Periyar's statue stands at the memorial, is unequivocal about his stand on God. The statue greets you as soon as you enter Periyar Thidal, an open space dotted by about two dozen small buildings that form the Periyar kingdom. There is a Periyar Institute of Soft Skills, Periyar Legal Aid Centre, Periyar Self-Respect Marriage Bureau, Periyar Self-Respect Propaganda Institution, Periyar Library, Periyar Museum, Periyar Maniammai Institute of Science and Technology, Periyar Web Vision, Periyar Urban Family Welfare Centre and so on—even a Periyar Canteen. Only that the tiny kingdom is hardly visible from the main road and is likely to be missed by the lay Chennaiite unless one is aware of its specific location: the unassuming entrance is sandwiched between the imposing *Dina Thanthi* offices and a row of shops. Inside the compound, there is also a modern, well-furnished hall called—what else—Periyar

Centre, which is let out for public functions and wedding receptions. That morning I found a welcome arch erected at the entrance of the hall, announcing the wedding of a certain Balraj to one Anitha. Their families had also erected a congratulatory hoarding near the hall that showed a suited Balraj standing alongside a demure, decked-up Anitha, strings of jasmine hanging prominently from her hair. Sharing space on the hoarding with the newly-wed couple was an image of Mary and infant Jesus. Fortunately for him, Periyar, standing on the pedestal, had his back to the hoarding.

There is an enclosure, a sort of garden, at Periyar Thidal, where a path leads to a monument—a giant hand holding aloft a flaming torch. The path is lined with granite slabs, and inscribed on each of them is a saying of Periyar. I jotted them all down, and as I did so, one of them struck me as particularly ironical:

> The temples are not built for gods. They have come up for the livelihood of the Brahmins and to degrade and exploit the common people.

How Chennai begs to differ! Nearly every street corner has a temple, big or small, of the Brahmin and the non-Brahmin kind. On the roadside, sunburnt palmists—men as well as women—wait patiently for business. Almost every door bears a symbol that is either considered to be auspicious or warding off the evil eye. This is the same city where, not too long ago, Periyar publicly slippered the images of Hindu gods and smashed their idols. But today his acts of defiance, to the lay Dravidian, are as good as grandmother's fairytales: too remote to be relevant.

They have become remote even for Dravidian rulers. In September 2010, the Chennai edition of *The Economic Times* front-paged a lengthy report that began:

> CHENNAI: Tamil Nadu's Dravidian movement, built on the foundations of atheism and rationalism, is beginning to shake at its roots with founding member and chief minister Muthuvel Karunanidhi lavishing funds on temple renovation in a way not seen in at least a century.
>
> The movement—reformist for the untouchables and ruinous for the Brahmins—has come full circle from the days of breaking idols of Hindu deities, especially the ubiquitous Ganapathy, to spending hundreds of crores renovating temples and encouraging its members to participate in them.

The report went on to quote the minister for Hindu religious and charitable endowments, K.R. Periakaruppan, as saying, 'Till date (ever since the DMK returned to power in 2006), we have spent ₹ 420 crore on temple renovation and this is a clear evidence to show the amount of interest that Kalaignar has shown in promoting temples in the state.' Karunanidhi, who wrote some powerful Tamil film scripts before joining politics, is called Kalaignar—the honourable artiste—by his people. The report, seeking to explain Karunanidhi's change of heart, said it could be either a strategy to get votes or 'a genuine desire on the part of someone in the evening of his life and worried about his legacy to connect with God'.

To suggest that Karunanidhi might have been trying to connect with God in the autumn of his life would be presumptive. Even though MGR and Jayalalithaa—the only two people other than Karunanidhi who have ruled Tamil Nadu since 1969—also sprouted out of Periyar's ideals, they never projected themselves as atheists and rationalists. Jayalalithaa, whose charisma melts Tamil Nadu's electoral heart every alternate poll, is anything but an atheist or a rationalist. On the advice of her astrologer she added an extra 'a' to her name and, after storming back to power in 2001, donated an elephant to the Guruvayur temple in Kerala. But Karunanidhi has always kept up his agnostic image.

And yet, his government pumped in ₹ 420 crore in five years towards renovating temples dedicated to Hindu gods. According to the *Economic Times* report, the amount was three times more than what the preceding government, headed by believer Jayalalithaa, had spent on the upkeep of temples during its five-year tenure. What, then, could be the reason behind Karunanidhi's generosity?

He was obviously not out to please the Brahmin—the representative of the Aryan culture and the principle enemy of the Dravidian movement. Karunanidhi remains a Brahmin-baiter, and Brahmins in any case are too small a population to decide an election. So the largesse, going by mathematical logic, is aimed at the multitude of Dravidian worshippers who throng the temples. After all, not all Dravidians became atheists and rationalists just because Periyar asked them to do so. Even members of Karunanidhi's own family are known to be believers, but in order to protect their patriarch's atheist image, don't profess their faith publicly.

In 2007, godman Sathya Sai Baba paid a visit to Karunanidhi's residence, where members of the chief minister's family sought his blessings. Sai Baba even performed his trademark miracle of producing rings out of thin air. He gave one ring to Karunanidhi's grandnephew Dayanidhi Maran, and another to Durai Murugan, a senior minister in Karunanidhi's government. Murugan, it was reported, requested the godman to produce another ring for Karunanidhi. But Sai Baba, aware that it might cause embarrassment to the Dravidian leader, simply smiled, 'I have given him a place in my heart, while he has given me a place in his heart.'

The day after, at a mammoth public meeting called to thank Sai Baba for repairing a canal that brought water from river Krishna in Andhra Pradesh to thirsty Chennai, Karunanidhi equated him to God.

So, in the end, God is great. Periyar remains the great one only in name.

Periyar succeeded in alienating the Brahmins and getting the Dravidians political power, but he failed to uproot God from daily Dravidian life which he had wanted to. In spite of the smashing of idols, God gets more attention in Chennai than any other city in India. The statues of Periyar, on the other hand, serve as traffic landmarks.

■ ■ ■

Even though Brahmins, the traditional tormentors of the Dalits, have long been sidelined, the plight of the Dalits continues to be the same, if not worse. Dravidians with money or muscle are the new Brahmins, especially in the villages, where they don't allow Dalits to come out of the stagnating pond of subjugation and humiliation. Each time a Dalit seeks to raise his head, they dunk him back into the pond and enjoy the fruits of the Dravidian government's anti-Brahmin policies all by themselves.

Tea-stalls in many small towns and villages of Tamil Nadu still follow the two-tumbler system—one set of tumblers is meant for the Dalit customer and another for the non-Dalit, who would feel violated if he discovered that a Dalit had placed his lips on the same glass he was now sipping tea or coffee from. And in a small place, where everybody knows everybody, it is not difficult at all for the tea-seller to tell a Dalit from a non-Dalit. It is almost impossible for a Dalit to cross the line: if he does, whether inadvertently or defiantly, the consequences can be severe.

For newspapers based in big cities, an atrocity committed against Dalits in a remote place is no longer big news. If a Dalit happens to be living in a village that has a mixed population, he is bound to face atrocities: it is a given. Just like in Kashmir, where it is common for half-a-dozen people to die under gunfire in a day—you can't slot such news on the front page evening after evening.

But when a young woman—who happens to be urbane, photogenic, an accomplished poet and a writer with strong opinions, widely travelled and much interviewed—highlights the news of atrocities on Dalits on her Facebook page, people connected to her online sit up and take notice.

Meena Kandasamy has close to 5,000 'friends' on Facebook—that's the maximum number the social networking site permits you to have—and nearly 1,500 people following her on Twitter. Even though Meena is only twenty-five per cent Dalit—it was her father's father who happened to be a Dalit—she is the chic Dalit voice emanating from Chennai who uses her wordsmithery to spread the message or drive home a point.

'I would like to describe myself as a woman writer obsessed with revolutionary Dr Ambedkar's message of caste annihilation,' she describes herself on her blog. The blog not only speaks up for the oppressed castes but also features interviews she gives to various journals from time to time. In one such interview, she calls herself an angry young woman. 'The world has not seen enough of our kind, while we have had plenty of angry young men,' she tells the interviewer. 'Angry young men working among the people are killed early; angry young men becoming artistes spend a lifetime in anonymity; and savvy angry young men turn into politicians and all the revolution inside them simply fizzles out. However, society will not let angry young women exist, we will be labelled hysterics. As women, we are indoctrinated merely to accept our situation and be grateful for all the things we have. As women, we are told that it is bad behaviour to be angry, we are told that we have to change ourselves because we cannot change the system. Those of us who refuse to comply are the shrews whom everyone loves to hate.'

Meena is just twenty-six.

On my way to meet her late one morning in the sprawling campus of the Anna University, where she teaches English, I wade through her dizzyingly-long bio-data. I learn, among many other things, that she has been a writer-in-residence at the University of Iowa, and that she has published a collection of poems and is awaiting the publication of another; and that she featured in a jazz poetry concert held in Pittsburgh recently. I look forward to meeting her.

Anna University in Guindy was once known as the College of Engineering, whose origins date back to 1794. Today, engineering studies is huge business in Tamil Nadu: there were nearly 500 colleges in the state at the last count, of which about 150 were in and around Chennai. Drive out of the city in any direction and you will spot a number of engineering colleges on its periphery, standing like palaces amid vast empty land. The average Tamil boy's dream is to be an engineer—the city will easily have more engineers today than any other variety of white-collared professionals, and journalists, when they write features about social trends, invariably quote a 'software engineer' or two. Aspiring engineers, when they pass out of school, must apply to Anna University, which places them in the various government and private engineering colleges across the state—the reputation of the college they seek admission to being directly proportional to the marks they scored in school. During the counselling season each year, agents of the private colleges descend on the university campus to hardsell their institutions. Stalls are set up and glossy pamphlets are distributed. The aggressive canvassing lends the campus the look of polling day.

The sidewalks leading to the main gate of Anna University are strewn with pamphlets this morning when I arrive to meet Meena Kandasamy. I find my way through the crowd of anxious admission-seekers to find her at the pre-decided spot. We move to a quieter part of the campus and occupy a bench under a tree.

Meena turns out to be more petite than I have imagined her to be, but she is orally as articulate as she is with the written word. We begin with small talk, and I tell her about the woman in the gym who comes to work out with a bunch of flowers in her hair. Meena laughs and asks me if I know why women wear jasmine.

'Why?' I ask her.

'It has got to do with sex. Well, this is what somebody once told me, though I don't know how true it is. I was told that when a man is eager to have sex, he brings his wife jasmine that evening. Likewise, if a woman wants to have sex, she indicates her desire to the husband by asking him to bring some jasmine for her.'

I try to imagine the woman in the gym doing that.

'But as I said,' Meena interrupts my thoughts, 'this is what someone once told me. There might not be any truth to it at all.'

No one can tell you for sure how a bunch of flowers came to be a part of the daily attire of Tamil women, though commonsense suggests that the string of jasmine is more ornamental than a medium of communicating desire. By the time a practice evolves into a tradition, the purpose behind it often becomes as indistinguishable—and irrelevant—as an individual speck of sand in an hourglass. You can only make guesses or go by hearsay.

Meena, however, is fighting a tradition whose origins are pretty well-defined. And she has chosen to fight it with political poetry due to—in her words—the 'pressing responsibility to ensure that language is not at the mercy of the oppressors since it is the first site for all subjugation'.

The story of her crusade has its origins in Ramanathapuram in southern Tamil Nadu, where, once upon a time, a ravishing young high-caste woman hailing from the family of the court poet falls in love with a fortune-teller, an untouchable man twice her age. Since they are determined to get married, they have no choice but to elope since society will not permit them to live together. They run away from Ramanathapuram and come to live in Pudukottai, where they have a son. The son, Kandasamy, is barely six years old when his father, the fortune-teller, abandons his family to live with another woman.

Kandasamy grows up in an orphanage, becomes a Tamil scholar and is advised by his Brahmin teacher to go to Madras to seek employment. He comes to Madras and becomes a pracharak of the Rashtriya Swayamsevak Sangh and joins its mouthpiece, *Thyagabhoomi*, as a sub-editor. During the Emergency, when Indira Gandhi cracks down on political opponents, he, like many others, is sent to jail for six months. The stay in prison not only alters his political views drastically but also kindles the desire to settle down with a woman, unlike the committed RSS pracharak who is required to be a bachelor.

Kandasamy is twenty-nine when he comes out of jail—too old by conventional standards to find a suitable bride, that too as the son of a Dalit father. It's a different matter that the fortune-teller father had abandoned the son when he was barely six, but he had indelibly stamped his caste on the child. Fortunately for Kandasamy, he meets Vasantha, one of the six daughters of a well-to-do and educated family of Vellalars, the land-owning community. Vasantha's two elder sisters are feminists and spinsters, and Vasantha, who is also twenty-nine and a PhD holder now, is all set to go their way when she meets Kandasamy through friends. Her parents are more than happy that at least one of their daughters has decided to get married, even if to a Dalit schoolteacher who may be poorly-paid but is at least an intellectual. The couple get married and they have a daughter, Meena.

I ask Meena if there were conflicts at home due to the disparate backgrounds of her parents. 'My mother came from a family which spoke only English. They saw Tamil as the language of scavengers. They never sat on the floor. My father was totally the opposite. He came from a village and until he came to Madras, he did not even know the difference between tea and coffee. Back in the village he would be given some drink which had no distinct taste. So, off and on there would be personality clashes at home, and many of the clashes still continue. For example, even now whenever my father takes my mother to a friend's place, he expects her to join the friend's wife in the kitchen. She grumbles that he does not treat her like a doctorate but an ordinary housewife,' laughs Meena.

Meena was born in 1984, months after the anti-Tamil riot broke out in neighbouring Sri Lanka. At the time, her parents were living in Chepauk, near the University of Madras, where her mother was an assistant professor. Her father, the poorly-paid teacher, taught at a nearby Marwari-run school. The university was abuzz with political activity and anti-Sinhala sentiments ran high in Madras. Their modest home in Chepauk welcomed angry young Tamils who wanted to vent their anger. One morning, her father led a group of his students, mostly Marwari boys, in protest and burnt a jeep outside the Sri Lankan consulate.

'Imagine a Tamil teacher leading Marwari students to burn a jeep. He lost his job. I was exactly eighteen days old when he got thrown out of the school. The activist in him reformed and he went on to study further and even completed his PhD, but he never held a permanent job after that. Now he is too old for a job. So it was my mother who always supported us. She was the father figure,' says Meena.

When Meena was about four, her mother landed a job with the Indian Institute of Technology as an assistant professor in the mathematics department and the family moved into the IIT-Madras campus. The activist in her father had sobered and he was now teaching at the University of Madras, but only on an ad hoc basis, which meant he was assigned a certain number of lectures in a year. It was now the mother's turn to become the activist.

According to Meena, as soon as her mother joined IIT, she found the administration to be heavily lopsided in favour of the Brahmins. The mother felt discriminated against and went on to file a series of litigations to seek legal remedy. Meena was only a child then, but old enough to understand that her mother was fighting a battle that had something to do with caste. 'I was ten or eleven when the process of litigations started. My mother is a heart patient, so she could not travel to the lawyers all the time. It was me and my father who used to go to the lawyers. That was the time I realised there is a section of people called Brahmins. That's when I became aware of the caste system, when I was running around with the legal papers,' says Meena.

Thus, another activist in the family was born. 'When I finished school, I decided not to study further. On one hand, I had spent most of my years running to lawyers' offices, which is not a pleasant thing to do, fighting for my mother who could not get anywhere in her career just because she was not a Brahmin. On the other hand, when I was in the final year of school, my father too got thrown out of the university because he and his students had started composing election songs for the Dalit Panthers of India. I did not see the point in going to college. I started writing. I told my parents I could take up a correspondence course or join a college later if required. They agreed,' says Meena.

Meena's first piece appeared in 2001 on the website postcolonialweb.org, funded by the National University of Singapore. In the article, titled *Casteist. Communalist. Racist. And Now, A Nobel Laureate*, she wondered if V.S. Naipaul had been given the Nobel post 9/11 because he was 'anti-Islamic'. (I find the article still online, and its author has been identified as 'Meena Kandasamy, Indian Institute of Technology, Chennai, India', giving the impression to readers that she is probably an IIT academician who harbours hatred against Naipaul.) The article was noticed by a Dalit organisation, which until then ran a Tamil magazine and was looking to diversify into publishing in English. They hired Meena as the editor of the new English bi-monthly, *The Dalit*.

She subsequently went on to translate the writings of Periyar and the Dalit thinker Ayodhya Das, and of Sri Lankan Tamil poets such as Cheran, Jayapalan and Kasi Anandan. Somewhere along the way she also fell in love with a Dalit leader living in Chennai. Meena's father, even though himself born to a Dalit fortune-teller called Karuppiah (which means the black one), strongly disapproved of the relationship. Like any middle-class Indian father, he did not want his daughter to be romantically involved with a politician, that too a dark-skinned one. He put Meena under house arrest and seized her phones. At home, the boyfriend would be referred to as *karuppan*—the black one. Eventually, the father did come round, but by then Meena had outgrown her crush. Her poem had won a nationwide contest and she realised that she had a much brighter future as a poet-activist than as a politician's partner.

'I started writing poetry in 2002. They were just random poems. I started taking myself seriously only a couple of years later, when the Indian Council for Cultural Relations announced a contest, inviting poems in English from Indian women below the age of thirty. I sent them the few poems I had written, but I did not get any reply for the next two or three months.

'Then I told myself, "Look Meena, the number of people in India who know English is only two per cent, and the number of such women would be only one per cent. The number of women below thirty would be even less, and the number of such women writing poetry far less. There was one first prize, two second prizes, three third prizes and ten consolation prizes, and you did not get even one of them. It's time for a reality check. You can cheat people by telling them you are a writer, but you can't cheat yourself. This is the end of the road for you."

'Then one afternoon I get this letter, saying that one of my poems has won the first prize, and I told myself, "Okay, so somebody thinks I write well." I realised that my poems work. I wrote more and sent a couple to *The Little Magazine*, which published them, following which a friend showed my collection to Kamala Suraiyya (the late writer, formerly known as Kamala Das). She was very excited. She called me to say that I should publish the collection, and even offered to write the foreword.'

The collection, *Touch*, came out in 2006. These days, however, poetry alone does not put you in the reckoning, but packaging does. Meena, who now was an officially published poet, began writing in mainstream newspapers; she started teaching at the Anna University apart from pursuing a PhD; opened a blog to champion the cause of not only Dalits but also Tamils living in Sri Lanka—each pursuit lending credibility to the other. People began to take notice; her name began to ring a bell.

Ms Militancy, her second collection of poems, published a few months after I met Meena that morning, not only managed to attract eyeballs but also raise eyebrows and has possibly secured her a place in Dalit—or should it be feminist?—literature. The poems break the shackles of traditional female coyness and symbolically set free the oppressed, women included, from Brahminical domination.

The collection got reviewed in two Chennai papers, *The Hindu* and *The New Sunday Express*—while the former lauded her, the *Express* reviewer tore the collection to shreds, calling it a work of 'designer feminism' that is out of date by several decades. The first few lines of the opening poem, *A Cunning Stunt*:

> bound in bed and blindfolded
> I hear the man of words come to me.
>
> burying his face between my thighs
> he says a cunt by another name
> would smell as complicated
>
> and then, sniffling in sanskrit,
> he christens it *yoni*, the womb,
> uterus, vulva, vagina, the female
> organs of generation...

I couldn't help wondering how the Tamil-speaking fans of Meena, who admire her for taking up the cause of Dalits and Tamils, would react if these deliberately explicit lines were to be composed in Tamil. Would they still toast her, or tut-tut at her for using words and imageries that are unbecoming of a Tamil woman? The question, however, is purely hypothetical because Meena, even though she can read Tamil well enough to be able to translate, writes only in English.

■ ■ ■

When I took leave of Meena that morning, she had suggested that I meet the family of Muthukumar, a young man who had immolated himself in Chennai only months before in support of the Tamil population in Sri Lanka facing the onslaught of the army that was sweeping through the areas hitherto controlled by the Liberation Tigers of Tamil Eelam, or LTTE. Muthukumar, who worked as a typist in a women's magazine, was hailed as a martyr by Tamil nationalist leaders in Chennai. Karunanidhi's government gave his family a compensation of two lakh rupees. He had become the poster boy for oppressed Tamils.

Initially, it had seemed to be a good idea to find out what the aged parents made of their son's 'sacrifice': after all, political jingoism is one thing, parental love quite another. But the more I thought about it, the more I felt weary. I realised I had no desire to probe yet another case of suicide by fire and quietly gave up the idea. As a newspaper man, a part of my job is to rewrite copies turned in by the reporters, and the number of self-immolation stories I come across every week is not funny. Funny at times, when you look at the reasons for which a large number of people set themselves on fire. After battling with such stories, when I am on my way home in the silence of the night, the acts of self-immolation play in my head. I imagine myself to be the spouse or the child of the person setting himself or herself on fire, and then the stories are no longer funny. Till 10.28 pm, your house is as normal as any other in the neighbourhood, but at 10.30 pm you smell kerosene burning and hear screams from the kitchen. And then, within a matter of minutes, with neighbours watching from their windows, you are rushing that person—till recently the most familiar person in your life but now unrecognisably charred—to the hospital, only to be told that he or she is dead.

Death does not shock me anymore, though it might sadden me; but death due to suicide, especially by self-immolation, does not even sadden me. It only makes me angry. End of the day, such people become mere statistics—yet another addition to the police records—but if you zoom in closer on their respective addresses, you will find entire homes irreparably shattered, mostly over trivial reasons.

A bank manager returns home from work late in the evening and asks his wife what there is for dinner. When the wife tells him the menu, the man is so disappointed that he goes to bed without eating. The wife, even more disappointed by his behaviour, goes to the kitchen and sets herself on fire.

A woman goes to the neighbourhood temple with her husband. On the way, some young men standing by the road pass lewd remarks. The woman, deeply offended, sets herself on fire as soon as she returns home.

Two slum-dwellers, one elderly and another young, have an argument, during which the young one abuses the senior. The old man, crushed by the insult, goes back to his hut and sets himself on fire.

A woman's son is involved in a few cases of theft, as a result of which policemen come looking for him often. The landlord, scandalised by the frequent police visits, asks her to vacate. She immolates herself.

A woman constable, who had been away at her parent's place to deliver her baby, returns home and suspects that her husband had been having an affair in her absence. One night, they have an argument over the suspected affair and the constable, in a fit of rage, walks to the kitchen and—well, you know the story.

Then there is my own story. About five years ago, I had hired a young man called Suresh as my driver. He was barely twenty-two, and of cheerful disposition. His lips always wore a smile and his eyes shone with loyalty. It was his first job, and it was my first car, fresh out of the showroom; it wasn't a good idea to let someone test his driving skills on a car bought with money that would be hard-earned in the next four years, but I trusted him instinctively. He turned out to be an efficient driver—he even gave me a surprise gift once by getting an ashtray fitted into the car—but he sought leave every now and then to visit some temple or the other, and that was his only drawback. He was too young to connect to—or to have even heard of—Periyar's movement.

Suresh lived with his parents in Royapuram, in north Chennai. He was their only child. His father, a labourer at the Chennai port, had just lost his job after he hurt his leg while loading cargo. Suresh's grandmother lived close to my house, in T Nagar, and on nights he got very late, he stayed over at her place instead of going all the way to Royapuram.

One such night, after he dropped me home and handed me the car key, he lingered at the door instead of saying good night and sprinting down the stairs, which he usually did. I asked him what the matter was.

'Sir, my salary. I want increase, sir.'

'But you have not even completed a year.'

'Sir, I know, sir, but these days driver's salary very high. My father not working now. He asking me, why so less money you getting? House rent very high, sir.' I could see he was very embarrassed to tell me all this.

I assured him I would hike his salary once he completed a year: it was just a matter of another month or two. But my assurance, far from pleasing him, made him sulk. He did not smile when he said good night.

The next morning, I was woken up by a call from an unknown number. The caller identified himself as Suresh's friend and told me that Suresh wouldn't be coming to work. I wanted to ask him if Suresh would be coming at all—a decision he might have taken the night before—or wouldn't be coming only that morning; but with my very limited knowledge of Tamil, I did not know how to phrase the question.

But before I could ask anything, the caller went on, 'Suresh father, Suresh mother, both dead.'

'Dead?' I sat up. 'How?'

'Suicide, suicide.'

The caller hung up, having fulfilled his duty of informing me about the tragedy.

What was I to do now? Call up Suresh and offer my condolences and ask him if he needed any help, or just let him be and wait for him to call in case he wanted to? Eventually I decided to call, but his phone was switched off. That evening, when I went to work, I got to know the details of the suicide. The crime reporter had already filed the story—the police version. An elderly couple living in Royapuram, the story went, had committed suicide by setting themselves on fire because they were unhappy that their son was not taking enough care of them.

The next morning, I looked for the suicide story in other papers. One English newspaper had invented a brother for Suresh, called Ramesh, and said the two sons had neglected their parents so much that the elderly couple was forced to take the extreme step. One Tamil paper, I found out, had gone a step further: it invented a wife for Suresh and held the young 'couple' responsible for the double-suicide. All this was amusing as well as sad. I alone knew the truth, but who was I? It is the version of the police clerk—who gives crime reporters a roundup of the day's murders, suicides, thefts and accidents—that is considered most authentic. It does not matter if a crime story, during its journey from the mortuary to the notebook of the reporter, gets embellished along the way, even to the extent of fact morphing into fiction.

About a month later, Suresh showed up at my door. His head was shaven. The sparkle in his eyes had gone. I asked him what had happened that night. That night, he told me, he had just reached his grandmother's house after dropping me (and asking for the salary hike) when he got the call. His father, who had taken to alcohol in a big way ever since losing his job, had got drunk and had a quarrel with the mother, and in a fit of rage, they bathed themselves in kerosene and set themselves on fire. They had charred their son's youth.

Death by fire, when it comes to suicide, seems to be the norm in Tamil culture—particularly in the case of poor people, especially women. They seem to be perpetually standing on the threshold of emotional turbulence and even a minor and an unrelated trigger can make them reach for the can of kerosene.

Those who have a better understanding of the culture argue that self-immolation among the poor is not unique to Tamil Nadu but is common across the country for the simple reason that kerosene is always handy in low-income or poverty-stricken households. But they vehemently agree that poor people immolating themselves for the sake of a political leader or a political cause is very typical of Tamil culture. No one has been able to put a finger on the exact cause of such behaviour, there are only theories; but the fact remains that each time a revered public figure dies or comes to any sort of harm, there are anguished followers who set themselves alight.

When Indira Gandhi was assassinated in 1984, as many as fifteen people committed suicide in the country, and fourteen of them belonged to Tamil Nadu and Pondicherry! That very year, when M.G. Ramachandran or MGR, the highly charismatic actor turned chief minister, was rushed to the US for treatment, over a hundred people attempted self-immolation across Tamil Nadu. When he died in 1987, at least thirty people committed suicide in grief. Many years before that, when Annadurai, the founder of DMK, died, many people had immolated themselves. A couple of MGR fans killed themselves when Karunanidhi took over the reins of the DMK and expelled MGR.

Karunanidhi, too, had many people dying for him: in 1986, when he was arrested by MGR's government for reigniting the anti-Hindi agitation, as many as twenty-one people reportedly committed suicide, mostly by self-immolation.

In Dravidian politics, such deaths are counted as feathers in the cap of a political party. Leaders never warn their followers against contemplating suicide. Instead, they hail such followers as martyrs and provide monetary compensation—called 'solatium' in Tamil Nadu—to the bereaved families. All that the father of Suresh, my driver, needed to do that night, before he and his wife decided to burn to death, was to leave a suicide note saying they were dying for the sake of a particular political cause or a political party. That would have made Suresh, my driver, richer by a couple of lakhs of rupees and perhaps earned him a better-paying job.

'In Tamil Nadu, politics revolves around personalities, cult figures,' Gnani, the well-known Tamil writer and columnist, tells me when I call upon him one afternoon. 'Here, when we talk about a political party, do we talk about its ideology? No. We always talk about a Karunanidhi or a Jayalalithaa. We are always concerned with the leader, the cult figure. So whenever a leader dies or is arrested, the fans go crazy. For poor people, who have only known suffering, the leader is the only hope. Once the hope dies, they are left with no choice [but to commit suicide].'

Even though other south Indian states, with the notable exception of Kerala, have from time to time found themselves in the grip of hysteria generated by politicians and film stars, Tamil Nadu remains streets ahead of them. Kerala, in contrast, places ideology way above personalities. Not a single Malayali committed suicide when E.M.S. Namboodiripad, Kerala's tallest Communist leader, passed away: the leader may have died, but communism was to live on.

'If you look at ancient Tamil history,' Gnani tells me, 'we have had a long tradition of worshipping personalities. We have worshipped the dead. Many of the gods and goddesses in village temples are real people, who lost their lives in some struggle or the other. Many such deities are actually victimised women, who went on to become cult figures in their village as well as neighbouring villages. Women who were not in a position to fight for themselves derived inner strength by worshipping the ones who died in a struggle.

'Over the centuries, when Brahminisation of religion took place in the south, all such village gods got absorbed in the Sanskrit tradition and the existing myths got interwoven into the discourse. Thus Murugan became Subramanya, the son of Shiva. In fact, Murugan, the typical Tamil god, was a village chieftain who fought and died for his tribe. Originally, he had just one wife, Valli, but after he got Sanskritised he acquired two. The second wife, Devyani, is the daughter of Lord Indra, but Indra does not exist in the Tamil tradition.'

Gnani is one of the few Tamil writers—he is fifty-six now—who does not hesitate to call a spade a bloody shovel. His outspokenness may have made him immensely popular among his readers, but the magazines publishing his column have not been always amused by the boldness with which he takes on the rulers of Tamil Nadu. There have been occasions when, facing a gag, he has deliberately devoted his political column to writing about mundane things such as the virtues of the potato—just to let the discerning reader know that his voice was being muzzled.

But the luxury of being allowed to sulk has been rare in Gnani's career as a columnist. Most of the time, his column, once it became too candid for the rulers' comfort, got the boot—only to be resumed, under the same title, in a rival publication.

The cycle continues for Gnani. He must have realised by now that it is easier to question the existence of Sanskrit gods than questioning the living gods of Tamil Nadu.

Chapter 4

A SACRED SUNDAY

*T*riplicane and Mylapore, were they to be nations, would probably be like Britain and France. The people look the same but have sharply distinct identities they are proud of—and a history of rivalry that may no longer cause wars but can still result in trading of taunts.

Triplicane, whose capital is the Parthasarathy temple, is the traditional home of the Iyengars. Mylapore, with its nucleus at the Kapaleeswara temple, is the traditional home of the Iyers. Separating them, like the English Channel, is the predominantly-Muslim neighbourhood of Royapettah.

The history of Triplicane and Mylapore long predates that of Madras: they were already thriving villages, existing since ancient times, long before the East India Company arrived. Unlike George Town, which is cut off socially from the rest of the city in spite of being the birthplace of Madras, these erstwhile ancient villages are vitally part of the psyche of modern Chennai. Even if you don't live in any of these places, there are bound to be a few occasions in a year when you will find yourself heading to or passing through Triplicane and Mylapore.

I too have made occasional visits to Triplicane and Mylapore in the ten years that I've lived in Chennai. At times to have idlis at Ratna Cafe in Triplicane, at others to visit the Kapaleeswara temple in Mylapore. I was not much into deities, leave alone rituals; but there is something about Shiva. To me he is not just a god, but more the footloose and fancy-free rock star of the heavens.

Lately, though, at the age of forty, I find myself bowing to the images that confront me in places of worship. Why take a chance? When you are young, you are complacent about your future; but as you grow older, fears of dreadful possibilities and inevitabilities begin to eat into the arrogance of youth. You pray to God in the hope that he will keep you out of trouble, even though God never ever gives you any guarantees.

But each time I visited Triplicane and Mylapore, I never found myself engaging with the sanctity that surrounds their names. To me, they were just like any other places in the city. Maybe because I always went there with a specific purpose, and was totally blind to things other than those related to the purpose. Had I walked around aimlessly, perhaps the sights and sounds and smells would have registered. But why would I walk around aimlessly, no matter how much I may love doing it, in neighbourhoods of my own city?

It was only my yen to write this book that necessitated a walk through these places. Also, because a friend from Mumbai, when she learnt that I'd started work on it, told me, 'I hope you are writing about Mylapore too.'

'How do you know about Mylapore?' I asked in surprise. She is barely twenty-five, Mumbai-bred and, as far as I know, has never set foot in Chennai.

'I just know. I have read about it,' she said.

'What do you know about Mylapore?'

'Temples, traditional people, flower-sellers, ethnic sarees, what else, well, that's about it.'

'Any other place you know of in Chennai?'

'No, only Mylapore,' she laughed. 'Do you by any chance live somewhere close to it?'

'As a matter of fact I do.'

'Oh my god, what are you waiting for!' She was ecstatic.

I knew the time had come.

■ ■ ■

Sunday morning: I have magically woken up with the chirping of the birds. I can't remember the last time I had watched the glow of dawn from my bed; I usually go to sleep when the sun is about to rise. Then I hear the slap of the newspapers outside my doorstep—the official announcement that a new day has begun. I feel impossibly good this morning. No hangover. No wife; she is out of town. I have the whole Sunday to myself. If the pilgrimage has to be made, today is the day.

My first port of call is going to be Triplicane because I badly need breakfast. I had not eaten the night before because as soon as my wife left town, the cook decided to fall ill. I hadn't been up to cooking for myself and went to bed early. That is why I have woken up feeling incredibly fresh. I could climb a mountain.

But all I want right now is four pieces of Ratna Cafe idlis, bathed in its inimitable sambar—that extra dash of coriander powder and asafoetida! Unlike in many other eateries where the sambar and chutneys are served in small bowls—and the waiters don't look exactly happy when you ask for a refill—here the man who serves you pours a generous mug of sambar over the idlis and hovers around to pour some more when your plate begins to look dry. That's the tradition of Ratna Cafe, since 1948, when it opened in Triplicane.

It is run, however, not by a Tamilian, but by a Gupta who has his roots in Mathura in the Hindi heartland. I had spoken to Rajendra Gupta a couple of times over the phone, regarding stories for the paper, but have never met him. I would love to interview him someday and learn more about the man and the secret behind his trademark sambar. All I know is that he runs the Hotel Picnic near the Central station; and that in 2002 he purchased Ratna Cafe, which was almost dying, from a distant elderly relative called Trilok Chand Gupta, who was also dying. The younger Gupta not only revived it but opened several branches of Ratna Cafe across the city. The sambar, however, is supplied in cans only from the Triplicane kitchen.

It being a Sunday, I find more people inside Ratna Cafe than on the road, even though it is ten in the morning. Sharing a table with a traffic constable who is morosely drinking his coffee, I have six of the soft, grainy-textured idlis that don't stick to each other—my first decent meal since wife left town. On the next table, a waiter is placing dosas in front of a family that seems to have spent the morning at the beach because the children have sand sticking to their feet. Overcome by temptation, I order a dosa too. Food served at the next table is always more interesting than what you are waiting for or have just eaten.

On my way out, I enquire at the cash counter if, by any chance, Rajendra Gupta is around. He is. Sunday has been very nice to me so far. I go behind the cash counter and walk into his office—a tiny wood-panelled room—and introduce myself. Gupta is about to leave—he is building a factory on the Old Mahabalipuram Road and he has to visit the site—but he kindly agrees to spare me a few minutes. It turns out that he is building a sambar factory—a state-of-the-art centralised kitchen that will supply food to all the Ratna Cafe outlets in the city.

'The kitchen will be almost fully-automated. There will be minimal human contact with the food. The cooking appliances alone have cost me some two crore rupees. All sophisticated and imported. In all, I am spending ten to twelve crore. When there is technology, we must make use of it. Don't you think so? It is a matter of ambition, a matter of vision!' The tiny beads of tulsi tied close to his neck stretch as Gupta, a short balding man with a dot of sandalwood paste on his forehead, makes his point.

Although Gupta is settled in Chennai and, like every prosperous Chennaiite, is an ally of technology, he religiously maintains his spiritual ties with Mathura, going there at least once in a month 'at the call of Thakurji'. Thakurji is Lord Krishna.

'I am not running this business. A lone man can't run such a business,' he declares. 'It is Thakurji who is doing it.' He points to the garlanded portrait of Krishna that hangs on the wall behind him along with many others. 'At times I go to Mathura with the intention of spending ten days there, but some work or the other makes me return to Chennai in two days. And there are times when I go there on a two-day trip but end up spending ten days. Why so? Because it is Thakurji who decides when I should go to him and how long I should stay there. I am just a puppet in his hands.'

However, Gupta does not leave the famous taste of his cafe's sambar to the divine machinations of Thakurji. Even as we are talking, a kitchen hand walks in with a tiny bowl of sambar for his employer to taste. Gupta puts a spoonful into his mouth and rolls his eyes upwards and meditates, as if making a mathematical calculation in his head. He takes another spoonful and meditates some more. He repeats the process three times until the tiny bowl has been scraped clean by the spoon. He personally tastes the sambar every day and if he finds something amiss or in excess, he orders for amends to be made during the preparation of the next lot. Today, he finds the measure of coriander powder excessive, and instructs the kitchen boy to tell the cook to go easy on it during the next time.

It is the distinct smell of coriander powder that sets the Ratna Cafe sambar apart from others, and Gupta perhaps calculates the exact amount to be used by meditating with his taste buds. He has of late started ordering coriander seeds from Gujarat instead of procuring them locally, because he believes that traders in Chennai mix in an inferior quality of seeds during bulk purchases.

'I *cannot* compromise on the quality of the sambar. The idli and sambar is our USP. If one kilo of tomato needs to be put in the preparation, we put one kilo, even when the price of tomatoes touches the sky. I cannot afford to cut corners. This sambar is my bread and butter,' Gupta, who is fifty-six, tells me.

Ironically, in spite of being born and raised in Chennai, Gupta never got to eat at Ratna Cafe until he bought it in 2002. 'I had my own restaurant. There was no need for me to come and eat here. Only when I came to pay the advance did I step in here for the first time and eat. I bought this place because of the brand name. It has a loyal clientele. If I had not bought it, Ratna Cafe would have shut down by now. There were employees who had been in service for thirty or forty years—they had become too secure in their jobs and complacent to work.

'I spent twenty lakh to pay off and get rid of them. I also revamped the kitchen. They were still using firewood to make sambar—the cook had to stand on his toes to peep into the huge vessel to check if it was ready. I bought modern boilers, which use steam for cooking. The steam heats the vessels evenly from all sides, so the consistency of the sambar turns out to be far better. In fact, the use of boilers enhanced the taste of the sambar by a hundred, by a thousand times. Even the water I buy for cooking is purified water. We need 36,000 litres every day, and it comes to us in tankers. If I were to use borewell water, which is hard, my boilers wouldn't last beyond three months,' he tells me.

I ask for the recipe of his sambar.

'That's our secret,' he smiles. 'But I will give you a rough idea. We boil the tur daal and the tamarind water separately. In the tamarind water, we put small onions and tomatoes. Then, in a little oil we fry coriander seeds, fenugreek seeds, asafoetida, dried red chillies and pieces of coconut—all of which are ground into powder. Finally, we mix everything together and add the seasoning.'

This is how even I make my sambar, so why doesn't it taste like his? The difference, I'm sure, lies in his secret.

Soon, Ratna Cafe's trademark sambar will become a product of technology rather than tradition. The upcoming centralised kitchen on Old Mahabalipuram Road has already been installed with sophisticated cookers imported from Switzerland, Italy and Germany. This morning, a team of technicians from Switzerland is on the site, and Gupta has to go there and meet them.

'The kitchen will have the capacity to produce food for 45,000 people every day. That should be more than sufficient for all my outlets, as well as for the cafeteria of IT companies where I supply food. I supply to HCL, Wipro, Tata Consultancy Services, and now to Foxconn. I think I have enough on my plate,' says Gupta.

As I shake his hand before leaving, he tells me, 'You know, people in Mathura often ask me, "Why don't you open a Ratna Cafe here too?"'

'Really, why don't you?' I ask him.

'*Arrey nahin saahab, hum to wahaan sirf ras aur anand ke liye jaate hain!*'—No way, sir. I go there only to seek divine nectar and happiness!

■ ■ ■

I step out into the gentle sunshine and walk down Triplicane High Road to find my way to the Parthasarathy temple.

Many of Chennai's prominent thoroughfares have the words 'high road' suffixed to them, but Triplicane's biggest road would at best qualify as a street in any other city. In existence even before Madras came into being, it is spacious enough for bullock-carts; you wouldn't imagine two buses passing each other on this road—but they often do. Right now I can see a red bus approaching at considerable speed and two burqa-clad women walking ahead of me step aside with alacrity. I walk past more women clad in burqas and a number of bearded men wearing skull caps, going about their chores.

Triplicane has a sizeable Muslim population, whose history goes back to the time when the army of the Sultan of Golconda, in 1646, overran the crumbling Vijayanagar Empire. Under the new regime, the East India Company had to renew its lease for Fort St George, which it had built just six years before. Thirty years later, the company also obtained on rent the village of Triplicane from the sultan. Triplicane thus became the first village in the region to pass into British hands.

In 1687, the sultan was dethroned by the forces of Mughal emperor Aurangzeb, who subsequently installed a nawab to administer the Carnatic region—whose expanse would cover today's Tamil Nadu with parts of Andhra Pradesh and Karnataka thrown in. The East India Company once again renewed its lease for the Fort and also obtained more villages from the Mughal emperor.

Since the nawabs had their court at Arcot, near Vellore, they were also known as the Nawabs of Arcot. In 1855, when the incumbent nawab, Ghulam Muhammad Ghouse Khan, died issueless, the Company used the Doctrine of Lapse to gain full control of the Carnatic. When Ghouse's uncle Azim Jah demanded recognition, the British crown, in 1870, created a new title for him, the Prince of Arcot, which entitled him to a pension. The British, since they had taken over the Chepauk Palace, the home of the Arcot nawabs, also built a new palace for the Prince, which was called the Amir Mahal.

Amir Mahal continues to be the home of His Highness the Prince of Arcot—a title the Government of India recognises even today even though royalty was abolished in 1971. Since this title was conferred by Queen Victoria, the government continues to honour the Letters Patent issued by her and grant him a modest pension besides certain privileges such as exemption from paying motor vehicles tax.

Amir Mahal stands in Triplicane, very close to Ratna Cafe. Rather, I should say Ratna Cafe is a stone's throw from Amir Mahal—lest the current prince, Mohammed Abdul Ali, take offence. But Abdul Ali is known to be a highly affable man who likes to stay connected to society. He routinely faxes his thoughts on social and political events to media offices, and then calls up to courteously enquire if the fax has been received.

I have never had the opportunity to meet or speak to the prince but have seen him once, from a distance, during a concert of the singer Lucky Ali held at the Amir Mahal grounds. The prince, who organised the concert, had followed up his welcome speech with a near-perfect rendition of a rather difficult Mohammed Rafi song from the film *Baiju Bawra* opening with the line:

O duniya ke rakhwaale, sun dard bhare mere naale...

Protector of the universe, please listen to my lamentations...

■ ■ ■

Even as long ago as when the British and the French were fighting for control over Madras, the Iyengars living in the village of Triplicane were quarrelling among themselves over how to address the protector of the universe. The centre of the dispute was the Parthasarathy temple, and the cause was the manner in which prayers were to be conducted.

The Thengalais, the 'Y'-mark Iyengars who come from a more orthodox school, would not allow the Vadagalais, sporting the 'U' mark and originating from a relatively more tolerant tradition, to invoke the name of Lord Vishnu in their own way. The aggrieved Vadagalais engaged in petitioning Fort St George for justice, following which there would be counter-petitions from the Thengalais. This went on for a number of years until, in 1754, Governor Thomas Saunders ruled that the Thengalais stick to the shrine of Lord Parthasarathy, facing the main, eastern entrance of the temple, and the Vadagalais to the shrine of Lord Narasimha, facing the western entrance, and ordered both parties 'not to interfere or molest each other in the performance of their respective rites'.

But the dispute was far from settled. In 1776, the then Governor Lord Pigot had to reiterate Saunders' ruling, and to drive home the message this time to every Brahmin household, ordered that 'public notice be given thereof by beat of Tom Tom'. In 1795, the Vadagalais once again complained to the government, saying the Thengalais, in contravention of Lord Pigot's order, had occupied both the shrines. The government, this time, refused to interfere, saying it could not give a decision on grounds of which it was not certain, and cause dissension among the inhabitants of Triplicane.

Rivalry between the two sects has cropped up in recent times too. In the 1970s, a dispute arose within the biggest Vishnu temple in Kancheepuram, just an hour's drive from Chennai, as to which mark the temple elephant should wear on its forehead, the 'U' or the 'Y'? The matter went to court, which sagaciously decided that the two marks be alternated on the elephant's forehead every week. That caused another dispute: which mark should the elephant start with?

If only the elephant could speak.

■ ■ ■

Parthasarathy temple is where I am headed now, walking past the burqa-clad women on Triplicane High Road. I decide to take a detour and turn left into a narrow lane. Suddenly, I am in Brahmin country.

Brahmin Triplicane is defined by its houses. Sealed off from the outside world by the main road, they huddle together, as if on guard to fight the onslaught of change that is sweeping through the rest of the city. Nearly all houses that surround the Parthasarathy temple are old—only the degree of oldness varies.

A majority of them seem to be at least fifty years old, some others not less than a hundred. And the houses, whether modest or once-opulent, have one thing in common: a narrow enclosed verandah on which rests a cement bench. The bench, I learn subsequently, is a symbol of old-world hospitality: in bygone days, visitors to Triplicane, strangers though they were, could step into any of the houses for a brief respite from the Madras sun.

Then there are houses, much fewer in number, that are straight out of a *Chandamama* folk tale. They are part of the agraharam, the traditional Brahmin quarter. In the olden days, houses of Brahmins lined the street leading to a temple, thus, architecturally, forming a garland around the temple—therefore the name agraharam. Low-hanging, tiled roof; wide front door flanked by niches to hold oil lamps; windows with vertical rods as grilles; and in the shade of the slanting roofs, an open verandah where one can easily imagine people sitting in close circles engrossed in discussion or plain gossip—that's a typical agraharam house. You expect such houses to exist only in villages, but then, Triplicane was a village until a couple of centuries ago. In no other metropolis in the country will you find relics from an ancient tradition still standing in the heart of a city and continuing to be in use. I won't be surprised if some of these old houses are equipped with broadband connection.

Even today, if you were to remove all the cars and the cables and the motorbikes from its lanes, Triplicane would easily resemble an early twentieth-century hamlet—the very air is so charmingly another age. Traversing the lanes and byways, I eventually come upon what seems to be the main square of Triplicane, where you can buy everything your larder may possibly need—from vegetables to foodgrains to spices to utensils.

Few things can beat the sight of fresh vegetables being sold on the pavement—the blood-red of the tomato vying with the bright-green of the ladies' fingers. Then there are smug heaps of potatoes and onions—smug because they may not be as colourful but they know they are indispensable. There is something delightful about vegetables being sold in the open—you not only feast on the colours but also on the indefinable but delectable scent that raw vegetables give off. The delight may be completely lost on a man from a small town or village where such open markets are commonplace; but when you are used only to supermarkets, where the spectrum of colours is dulled by the plastic packaging and where the only scent hitting your nostrils is that of the disinfectant circulated by the air conditioner, the sights and smells of an open-air vegetable market tickle your taste-buds long before the meal is cooked.

Right now, what's working my salivary glands are the curving pieces of raw tamarind, laid out in tiny heaps on sacking, sold by an old woman. Tamarind is the staple ingredient in any Tamil kitchen, and every grocer or supermarket worth its rock salt stocks it. But when and where did you last spot pieces of raw tamarind carefully handpicked for sale? Didn't I just say there is something old-world about Triplicane?

I lose no time in walking over to the elderly vendor. Ten rupees for a bunch, she tells me. All I want is a couple of pieces, and I am more than willing to pay ten rupees for them, but that would not only appear rude but also disturb the evenness of the bunches. So I buy the whole bunch, shove it into my pocket and walk on. Unable to resist the temptation, I pull out a piece and bite into it, careful that no one is watching—what would people think of a forty-year-old man munching on raw tamarind with childlike delight? The Parthasarathy temple is only a step away now.

It is a very old temple—dating back to the eighth century. Right across the road once lived the nationalist journalist-poet Subramania Bharati, spending the fag-end of his life in a pretty two-storey house in front of which I am now standing. It has been turned into a memorial—I know because I'd read about it, otherwise the black plaque designed in front by the Tamil Nadu government gives no information to a visitor who does not read Tamil.

Bharati's poetry was resurrected briefly for the younger generation in the Tamil film *Kandukondain Kandukondain*, which was made about ten years ago. This was the film which I had watched in a Delhi theatre and which had inspired me to pack my bags and move down south. Most often, you don't need to understand the language for your ears to detect that a poet is saying something beautifully profound—words have their own rhythm that is independent of the script.

Bharati, even though only in his late thirties, was physically a broken man when he came to live in this house with his family. He had returned to *Swadesamitran*, the newspaper that had made him a fiery patriotic journalist before the British government ban forced him into exile and then into jail, and was drawing a handsome salary of seventy-five rupees—this was in 1920. But the fire had mellowed down. Being proscribed by the British, and addiction to opium, had taken their toll on his health.

Bharati then turned to God. He went to the Parthasarathy temple every morning and evening, and on the way out, fed the temple elephant. One morning, while making the offering to the elephant, he got knocked down by the force of its trunk as the animal turned towards him. Bharati survived the blow, but died two months later, of dysentery, in September 1921. He was only thirty-nine.

Bharati's life was not only short but also very sad. During his lifetime, even though the British found him provocative enough to ban him, recognition by his own compatriots eluded the poet. Only a few of his friends showed enthusiasm when he repeatedly—and desperately—sought monetary help from them to publish a forty-volume illustrated collection of his works, promising them that the books would sell faster than kerosene oil and matchboxes. When he died, barely fifteen people showed up for the funeral. His songs were sung after his death, but he died unsung.

There is another house I want to see, that of the mathematician Ramanujan, who also lived in Triplicane. I spot an elderly man, dressed in a white shirt and dhoti, emerging from one of the lanes. He is carrying a shopping bag and is obviously on his way to the vegetable market. In Bengal he would be called a bhadralok.

I intercept him and ask him for directions to Ramanujan's house. He kindly obliges but at the same time cautions me, 'I am not sure if you can find the exact house. Earlier, there was a tablet that indentified the house, but they have now removed it.'

I notice that the man, unlike many others I see passing by, is sporting the holy ash, smeared horizontally across his forehead, and not the 'U' or the 'Y' mark.

'You must be an Iyer, sir?' I ask him.

'Yes sir, I am an Iyer,' he smiles.

'And you live in Triplicane?'

'Why not, sir?' he asks even as he motions me to the sidewalk so that the traffic does not interrupt our chat that is taking place right in front of the Parthasarathy temple. He has realised that the conversation is going to last more than just a few minutes.

'You see, we Shaivites are pretty flexible people. We worship all gods, even Vishnu. But that's not the case with Iyengars. They worship no god other than Vishnu. As a result we Iyers don't get any respect in this temple,' he tells me.

'Forget Iyers,' he goes on, 'even the Vadagalai Iyengars don't get any respect here. The temple is run by the Thengalais. They don't let any other sect of Brahmins participate in the rituals or prayers.'

The elderly gentleman identifies himself as Sundararajan. He tells me he was born in Madras, and after a long stint in

Hyderabad as a pharmaceutical consultant, he returned to settle down in Triplicane. Sundararajan, now seventy-five, has been living in Triplicane for thirty years now. And what he just told me is something I have heard often during the ten years I have lived in Chennai.

When I first set foot in Chennai, I had absolutely no idea about the caste distinctions among Brahmins there. But over the years, I derived my own conclusions—that the Iyengar considers himself a notch above the Iyer in the social pecking order, and that the Iyer, instead of disputing the claims of superiority, resents the snootiness of the Iyengar.

I once knew a woman, an Iyengar, who would remind me now and then how fortunate I was to have met her. Iyengar women, she would tell me, are not only beautiful but also elusive. Unlike the Iyer women, she would add. She eventually married an Iyer, though.

Then I have a male friend, a devout Iyer, who does not tire of telling me the same story over and over again: how he and an Iyengar colleague once happened to visit a Brahminically-secular temple, which had both the Shiva lingam and an idol of Vishnu, and how the Iyengar colleague made sure to keep his back to the Shiva lingam. The Iyer friend, each time he narrates the story, stands up to imitate the Iyengar's cautious walk.

And now Sundararajan, the man of science who once guided pharmaceutical companies in setting up formulation units, is echoing the same thoughts. But he, like most others, has long made peace with the Iyengar-Iyer distinction; it is an internal matter of the Brahmins. What is bothering him more is the increasing number of inter-caste marriages, that is, Brahmins marrying Tamils from a different caste.

'You see, sir, our traditions have a scientific basis, and it is not for nothing that our ancestors kept them alive for thousands of years. It is true that certain people have misused the traditions, but it is also true that they are based on science. For example, why is one asked to fast on ekadasi? That's because when you fast once every fortnight and break the fast with certain types of greens, the amoebas get weeded out of your digestive system.

'Similarly, why do Brahmin scholars shave their heads? Because when a head is shaven, it is able to absorb certain rays from the sun which help the brain function better. But why do they leave a tuft of hair at the back of the head even when the rest of the head is shaved? That's because in the olden days, people bathed in tanks. If someone slipped and fell, the tuft of hair acted as a cushion. And if someone was drowning, he could be pulled out by that tuft.

'So you see, sir, how every custom has a scientific basis. Even with marriages. When you marry outside your caste, you are only laying the grounds for conflict, because it is difficult to adjust to cultural differences. Something as basic as food habits can lead to conflict, especially when one side is non-vegetarian and the other side considers meat-eating taboo. So these days, the man does his own thing and the woman her own, especially since the woman is also working. In the olden days, even though the woman rarely stepped out of the house, her opinion was always sought in important matters. She was placed on a pedestal. But these days, as I said, each one does their own thing. Where is the family? There is no consensus, there are only differences.'

I ask Sundararajan if he has seen Triplicane change much in the thirty years he has been here.

'Definitely, sir,' he is unequivocal. 'You see, earlier, weddings took place at homes. A wedding is the most sacred and prestigious ceremony to take place in a family, and what better place to conduct it in than your home? But these days they hold it in community halls. I don't like the idea.

'One more thing,' he tells me, 'earlier, there was great respect for Brahmins. Now there is none.'

I watch the frail figure of Sundararajan disappear into the road leading to the vegetable market. Nice man, I tell myself. I have always envied men like him, who have made careers out of science and yet know their traditions like the back of their hand. It is only in Chennai, or Madras, that you find such people in abundance, who can reel off a shloka and a scientific formula with equal ease. They will explain to you even the science behind a shloka.

■ ■ ■

I am standing in a queue that hasn't moved in twenty minutes. I am one of the few hundred people waiting for a darshan of Lord Parthasarathy. I ask the woman ahead of me what could possibly be causing the delay. Her guess is that some ritual might be on, and that once it is over, the queue will start moving. I consider abandoning the line to generally look around the temple, but I tell myself that if bad luck were to visit me the next day, I would have none to blame but my impatience. I stay put.

Suddenly, my eyes fall on a man seated at a table with bunches of pink coupons. I see some people buying them and heading straight towards the sanctum sanctorum. I figure that if you pay, you have a shorter wait for a glimpse of the god. I lose no time in buying a coupon and am now standing in a new, much shorter queue. I wonder what the people in the queue that I have just abandoned must be thinking of me.

Once I join the new queue, I learn that there are also coupons of higher denomination that would have taken me straight to the lord, but it is too late now. I have already spent twenty bucks.

As we wait, confined into single file by iron rails, I notice a temple palanquin in an enclosure. The palanquin has the 'Y'-mark painted on it. There is a boy standing ahead of me, who must be seven or eight, and I ask him, just to test his knowledge, whether the mark is Vadagalai or Thengalai.

'Thengalai,' he replies even before I can complete my question, delivering the word in a hoarse voice that belongs to a much older male.

At the sanctum sanctorum, all the queues—the privileged and free-of-cost—converge and transform into quite a jostling crowd. Finally, I am face to face with the black idol of Lord Parthasarathy, the charioteer of the Pandava prince Arjuna. I barely have a few moments in front of the lord when a guard pushes me into the queue of the outbound crowd.

The courtyard of the temple bears the look of a village classroom. Young girls, in corporation school uniform, are sitting cross-legged on the floor in rows. Each row faces a teacher, also sitting cross-legged. The students seem to be taking a recitation test. The teachers listen to the girls attentively and scribble the score ratings on sheets of paper.

To find out what's going on, I approach three women who are sitting in a circle on the floor and keeping an eye on the proceedings from a distance. I introduce myself and join the circle. Very rarely does someone say no to a journalist—most of the time you are actually welcome.

'We are having a contest, sir. The girls are reciting from the *Thirukkural*,' one of the women tells me. 'You know Thirukkural?'

Thirukkural I know. It is a collection of aphorisms, running into 1,330 couplets, attributed to the Tamil saint-poet Thiruvalluvar, who is believed to have lived in Mylapore around the time of Christ. Every student studying in the Tamil medium must know his Thirukkural, considered the Bible of Tamil culture and literature. Karunanidhi, whose fountain pen has written the script for many a successful film, and who happens to be a great devotee of Thiruvalluvar, often chides his followers for likening him to the ancient poet, though such public admonishments make one wonder whether he secretly relishes such praise.

'Children these days hardly know Thirukkural. Most of them go to English-medium schools. So it is a good idea to have this contest. They must not forget their culture, don't you agree?' the woman, who must be in her early forties, asks me.

'But these students are from corporation schools, who must be learning the Thirukkural anyway?' I ask her.

She pauses to think up an answer when another woman, who must not be more than thirty and who turns out to be as articulate as she is ravishing, explains to me:

'You see, every year we hold the *Thiruppavai* contest in the temple. You know Thiruppavai? It is a collection of songs written in praise of Lord Vishnu by Aandaal. You know Aandaal? She was a saint who lived more than a thousand years ago. So every January, when we celebrate the Triplicane festival, we hold the Thiruppavai contest here. But now the state government has asked us to host a Thirukkural contest as well. That is why you see these children here today.'

One would have understood if well-fed children, studying in expensive and exclusive English-medium schools, were being introduced to the practice of sitting in lotus position on bare floors, awaiting their turn to recite couplets from the Thirukkural. But all I can see are impoverished young girls from corporation schools sitting obediently in rows to which they are long-accustomed. The contest, clearly, is symbolic—perhaps the Dravidian government's way of needling the devout Iyengars by having the maxims of Thiruvalluvar, who is associated more with ancient Tamil tradition than Brahmin, read out in the hallowed courtyard of a temple where only praises of Vishnu have hereto been sung.

The three women, it turns out, live very close to the temple. But only one of them, the young and the articulate one, happens to be an Iyengar. Just the right time and the person, I think, to bounce off what Sundararajan, the Iyer man I met a short while ago, had told me about Iyengars.

'Do you think Iyengars are superior to Iyers?' I ask her. The other two exchange glances and suppress their smiles.

'I wouldn't say superior,' the young woman boldly takes up the challenge, keeping a straight face. 'But yes, we Iyengars are more exclusive.'

'Exclusive?'

'We have a certain identity, and we continue to maintain that identity. We don't dilute it.'

So, neither does she contradict the opinion of Sundararajan, the elderly Iyer; nor does she offend her two non-Iyengar companions. My admiration for her grows manifold.

'But it does not matter much these days,' she continues. 'We no longer live confined in Triplicane. We all go out to work. I do too. I don't like it when people call me mami. Why should I be branded a mami? I don't like to be stereotyped.'

Traditionally, in Brahmin society, as in most Indian societies, an older unrelated man is respectfully addressed as mama—or uncle—and a married woman as mami. But over the years, in the aftermath of the Dravidian movement, the term 'mami' has come to sarcastically denote a Brahmin woman in general—a woman who is supposed to be loyally wedded to tradition.

So the Iyengar woman I am speaking to now does not want to be seen as a prisoner of tradition. I ask her if at her home menstruating women are still confined to a corner of the house.

'Yes, they are, but no longer in a corner. We remain in our rooms,' she tells me.

'But why? You are a modern woman, you are working.'

'Why not? If such small gestures make the elders in the family happy, so be it. Once you are out of the home, you can do your own thing; you can have all the freedom you want. They are happy, you are also happy.'

I ask for her number. She hands me her card.

'But Triplicane,' she continues, 'is slowly becoming more orthodox'.

'Why so?'

'It happened because of the IT boom. When Iyengars from the smaller towns pass out as engineers and take up jobs in Chennai, they prefer to take up residence in Triplicane. Here, they strictly follow the traditions they have been practising back home. They are far more rigid and orthodox than people like us who have actually grown up in Triplicane and have adapted to the changing times,' she tells me.

Just then, she gets a call and excuses herself. 'Nice meeting you,' she smiles, and disappears into the Sunday crowd at the temple.

Left sitting with the two other women, I examine her card. 'That's her mother,' one of them tells me, pointing to the name on the card. 'And that's the name of the cultural organisation she (the mother) runs. You can call her anytime sir, in case you need more information,' she tells me.

So the ravishing Ms Iyengar not only turned out to be articulate but also elusive. All I am holding in my hands is her mother's name and number.

■ ■ ■

Coming out of the temple, I set out in search of the house of Ramanujan, the mathematician, following the directions given by Sundararajan. I walk along the length of the temple, and in the process pass many other traditional Iyengar houses—from the front door of most of them you can see several rooms in a row, as if they were one long corridor—and finally pass the temple tank and get into a lane.

The lane is deserted at the moment except for the presence of two women who seem to have run into each other after a long time and are now catching up, chatting. I decide to approach them. One of them is silver-haired; she must be over sixty. The other looks around forty.

They are startled as I walk up to them. 'Excuse me,' I interrupt their conversation, 'would you by any chance know where Ramanujan, the mathematician, lived?'

They breathe easy. The younger woman bids goodbye to the elderly one and asks me to follow her. She happens to live just a few steps away, in a building which has a deep narrow passage on one side that leads into a cluster of rooms.

'Ramanujan stayed in one of those rooms,' she tells me, pointing towards the deep end of the passage.

'Can I see the room?'

'No one is sure in which room he stayed. He lived here only for six months or so, as a tenant. While in Madras he lived in three houses, all in Triplicane only.'

'Have you lived in Triplicane all along?'

'Yes, sir, born and brought up here,' she smiles.

'Do you see any changes around you, from the time you were a child?'

Her answers, rather concerns, turn out to be the same as that of Sundararajan, the elderly Iyer man, even though she is much younger. 'The way people dress has changed. Then, a lot of inter-caste marriages are happening. And in the earlier days, there was a lot of respect for Brahmins in the city. These days nobody cares. But why are you asking all this? I thought you were writing a book on Ramanujan?' she enquires politely.

'No, ma'am, it's a book on Chennai.'

Since she is already in reflective mode, and since she herself brought up the subject of Brahmins, I decide to ask, for one last time, the same question:

'Why do Iyengars consider themselves superior to Iyers?'

She blushes at first. But when she speaks, minces no words. 'We believe in Lord Vishnu because he is the only god. Shiva and Brahma were appointed to their respective positions by Lord Vishnu only. That is the truth.'

■ ■ ■

Later in the day I land up in Mylapore.

The smell of Mylapore often precedes its sights. The moment your nostrils are hit by a cocktail of scents—of fresh jasmine, of burning incense, of raw vegetables—you know you are entering the sacred quarter of Chennai's most famous neighbourhood.

Mylapore—or the land of peacocks—has existed forever, it seems. It was called Maillarpha by the astronomer-geographer Ptolemy (AD 90-168) who described it as a great port, and has also been known as Maila, Meliapor, Maliapur and so on. St Thomas, the apostle of Jesus, is believed to have spent the final years of his life here. He was speared to death, for proselytising, on a hillock some distance away, which came to be known as St Thomas Mount, close to which lies the Chennai airport. On the spot where he is said to have been killed, stands a Portuguese-built church dating back to the sixteenth century.

At four in the afternoon, Mylapore has begun preparing for the evening. I smell the flowers and the vegetables even before the autorickshaw driver has deposited me on the edge of one of the four streets that form a rectangle around the Kapaleeswara temple. The streets, which are the unofficial boundaries of Shiva's territory, are coloured with the merchandise on the pavement—flowers and garlands; heaps of vegetables, coconuts and bananas; posters of actors such as Vijay, Vikram and M.G. Ramachandran; masks of the poet Bharati.

Elderly Brahmin men and women move about casually, stopping to talk to a familiar face. Their conversations take place in a mix of Tamil and English. The streets are lined by eateries and shops that meet all the needs of a traditional family. Like Triplicane, Mylapore is a self-contained village within a large city, its devotion-laden air insulated from the Chennai of malls and supermarkets.

Completing the village-like setting is the greyish-green, serene water of the temple tank that lies right in the middle of the rectangle, with ducks floating in a corner. Also, the sprinkling of surviving houses from the agraharam, just the kind you get to see in Triplicane.

I find myself gravitating towards the Kapaleeswara temple. That is the edifice that matters most in Mylapore. The temple is said to have been by the sea once upon a time, before it was demolished by the Portuguese in 1566; the present temple is about 300 years old. New, perhaps taller, buildings have now come up in its vicinity, but they are eyesores next to the temple tank. The damage, however, is limited only to the skyline; on the ground, Mylapore remains as traditional as ever, the almanac still followed here to the last word.

Just as I am taking my sandals off to deposit them at the shoe counter before entering the temple, I hear the *Hanuman Chaalisa* playing in one of the nearby shops. Now, I've grown up in Kanpur listening to the Hanuman Chaalisa, live as well as in the recorded form, but never before had I heard a woman sing it, that too in a voice so powerful and persuasive that I slip my sandals back on and walk into the shop. I ask the shopkeeper to show me the CD he is playing. The singer turns out to be M.S. Subbulakshmi.

I buy the CD and once again remove my sandals to walk into the temple, gliding past devotees in the courtyard. A few of them are lying prostrate on the stone floor, praying earnestly; many others are sitting in small groups, as if out on a picnic; but a majority of them are walking in the same direction as I, to queue up for the darshan of Shiva.

The queue here is short, and soon I find myself pressed up against the iron barricade in front of the sanctum sanctorum, trying to look inside. The darkened chamber containing the Shiva lingam is always lit up by oil lamps and never by electricity, and that's the beauty of this temple. Oil lamps may be too weak to fully illuminate the black Shiva lingam or the aged walls of the hallowed chamber, but they beautifully light up the air between them, providing the Shiva lingam a large and natural halo.

I am still admiring the halo when a young priest, one of the several shuttling between the sanctum sanctorum and the barricade, comes out with a brass plate that holds a piece of burning camphor and sacred ash. You are expected to lightly hold your palms over the flame, rub the warmth on your head, smear your forehead with some of the ash, and place an offering on the plate—if you wish. Many regulars place a ten-rupee note on it but the majority still makes do with coins. I pull out my wallet and try to peer into it discreetly. The lowest denomination I am carrying this evening is only hundred-rupee notes. Since I have to part with one anyway, I pull out a note with a flourish and place it on the plate.

I am not quite prepared for what happens next. As soon as I make the offering, the priest opens the barricade, motions me inside and leads me right into the sanctum sanctorum. He makes me sit on the stone floor, at a little distance from the god, and performs a puja on my behalf.

Even before I can decide whether to have a proper look at the lingam and its surroundings—now that I have come this close—or to pray doubly hard since I am sitting almost at the feet of the god, the priest is standing in front of me and gesturing me to get up. He is holding a smaller brass plate, bearing some flowers and a pair of bananas— the blessings of Lord Kapaleeswara. He hands over the goodies to me and asks for dakshina, the Brahmin's fee for an audience with god. Gratefully, I pull out another hundred-rupee note. The young priest looks equally grateful as he closes his fist over the crisp note.

Outside the temple, on one of the roads, a kolam-drawing contest appears to have just taken place. On the tarred road, contestants have drawn designs that they draw outside their door every morning; only, these kolams are much larger and more intricate and bear the names of the women who have drawn them.

The judges seem to have already rated the kolams because pedestrians have now started walking over them, much to the horror of two European men who are standing in a corner and marvelling at the works of art spread out on the road, waiting to be wiped out slowly by footsteps and wheels.

One of them, a Frenchman on his way to Pondicherry, tells me, 'I just don't understand this! I saw the women spending hours drawing these beautiful designs, and they have left their art on the road to be destroyed! They are remarkable women, I must say, they are not at all possessive of their work.'

What the Frenchman does not know is that the art of drawing a kolam is a way of life for the Tamil woman—it is as integral to her existence as bathing and cooking. This is something a Frenchwoman called Chantal, whom I happen to meet at the spot, understands very well.

Dressed in a red kurta and an off-white churidar, Chantal is squatting on the road, poring over the kolams and taking pictures, when I walk up and introduce myself. Chantal, who is fifty-two, has spent as many as twenty-five years of her life in India, most of them in Kerala while learning Kathakali and Mohiniattam. There she stayed as a tenant in the home of a Tamil family, where she got interested in kolam—the deceptively simple design drawn outside thresholds. She went on to write a book on the art of kolam, published recently in France, and is collecting material to write another.

'The best part about kolam,' Chantal tells me, 'is that you don't have to be an artist to draw one. When I conduct workshops, people often ask me whether they need to know drawing or painting, and I tell them, "No, not at all. All you need is a sense of geometry."'

A fragile Brahmin woman, who has been standing around us for a while and is now keenly listening to my conversation with Chantal, interrupts to tell us that every Tamil woman, even the illiterate maid, knows how to draw kolam. I suddenly think of my mathematics teachers in school. They invariably happened to be Tamils—all women.

Chantal, who now lives in France, is staying in a hotel in Mylapore. Ever since she arrived a couple of days ago, she hasn't stepped out of Mylapore and has been wandering on its streets taking pictures, mostly of doorsteps.

'I have been out since ten this morning,' she tells me as I walk her to the hotel. 'I was wondering how to get into people's homes and see the kolams in their puja rooms, when I happened to stop at a fruit stall to take pictures of a colourful Ganesha idol. Just then, a young woman dressed in Western clothes walked up to me and asked if I was a professional photographer. When I told her that I was looking for indoor kolams, she got very excited and asked me home. We jumped into an autorickshaw and in a few minutes we were in her flat. There was no one else at home at the time. While I looked around, she changed into a lovely red salwar-kurta and showed me into the puja room. I was mesmerised by the two kolams I saw there. Seeing my excitement, she made fresh rice paste and redrew one of the kolams for my benefit. She drew another at the entrance of the flat. In between, she ordered lunch for us from Saravana Bhavan. Only in India can you see such kindness. Her gesture was totally spontaneous. She believed it was Ganesha that brought us together.'

The temple bell has started clanging. It's the call for the evening ritual. The streets are now crowded and noisier. Peak hour is beginning in Mylapore.

'What strikes me about the temple is the Dravidian-style gopuram with multi-coloured sculptures. They are an invitation to plunge into mythical India,' Chantal strikes a philosophical note. 'In Mylapore, it feels as if different periods of history overlap and condense. The streets transcend time. Just look at the fortune-tellers and their lovely green parrots. They must have been here since forever. Their birds gently hop out of their cages and pick out the card of your destiny. Next to them you find palm-readers who predict events and suggest remedies, which send you on a trip to many more temples!

'Another fascinating sight here is that of the women weaving jasmine buds into ornaments all day long. Oh, I can go on and on. The oleographs of gods and goddesses, the banana leaves in hotels, the colourful sarees... Mylapore is a whirlwind of colours. Two eyes are not enough to appreciate them.'

At the gate of the hotel, Chantal enthusiastically greets another European woman. They speak in French.

'Meet Sylvie,' Chantal tells me. 'She is a flautist. We became friends from the moment we met. She is also staying in the hotel.'

Sylvie puts an arm around Chantal and exclaims, 'We are like sisters. We must have been sisters in our previous birth.'

When Chantal introduces me, Sylvie withdraws the arm to greet me with a namaste. Like Chantal, she too is clad in salwar-kurta. They seem to be the same age.

'I think, in my previous birth, I lived in Mylapore,' Sylvie tells me.

I learn that she is not just a guest at the hotel, but almost a resident: for the past twelve years, a particular room on the second floor has been her second home, where she spends six months every year. On the eve of her arrival each year, the hotel makes sure the room is vacant and ready for her.

Sylvie would like to leave France and make Mylapore her permanent home, but she cannot do so because she is on a tourist visa—something that makes her very sad. I ask her why she is so fascinated by Mylapore, upon which she invites me to her room to talk. I say goodbye to Chantal and tell her how lovely and Indian she looks in a red kurta.

'Are you trying to flirt with me, monsieur?' Chantal asks me with a mischievous glint in her eyes.

■ ■ ■

A hand-drawn 'Please do not disturb' sign is pasted on Sylvie's door. She opens it and leads me into the room, which is sparsely furnished, like a monk's, and onto the balcony. 'Take a look,' she tells me.

I now know why she wants to live in Mylapore. The balcony gives a VIP-gallery view of Shiva's territory. Until moments ago, I was part of the crowd and the cacophony, and now I have risen some thirty feet above it. I can still see and hear the people below, but they can't see me; I can also see what they can't see—such as the tops of trees, the dome of the temple emerging majestically from among them, no longer looking as intimidating, the temple tank in its entirety. Sylvie's balcony directly overlooks the tank—the luxury of such a close and complete view most

Kapaleeswara devotees and Mylapore lovers would never have had.

'Here, only God can see me,' Sylvie tells me, pointing to the dome of the temple. True. No eyes, other than God's, break into her privacy in the hotel—which wasn't the case when she lived as a tenant in various houses in Mylapore. The families of the landlords would be curious about her and walk in and out of her room, even when she practised on her flute. So, twelve years ago, she moved into the hotel.

Sylvie was born in Paris, and grew up to train in Western classical music. Her mother was a violinist, but Sylvie learned to play the flute—she had a silver one. Her boyfriend, Don Cherry, was an accomplished jazz cornet-player. 'He always told me that we need two lives to learn and understand music,' she said.

In 1977, she happened to attend a concert given by N. Ramani, the Carnatic flautist, in Paris, and decided that Carnatic music was her true calling. 'Until then I had heard records of Ravi Shankar and Pannalal Ghosh, but Ramani's music was a revelation for me! I decided to give up Western classical music,' she tells me.

The very next year, she sold her silver flute to buy a one-way ticket to Madras. 'At the time, I believed that every Indian was a yogi, a Mahatma Gandhi,' she laughs.

The truth hit her as she landed in Bombay, but all was well once she reached Madras which, in 1978, was charmingly sleepy enough to match her mental image of India. She signed up as a disciple of Ramani, who gave Sylvie her first bamboo flute, and took up a pretty garden house in Mylapore on a monthly rent of ₹ 400, finding a strong and inexplicable connect with the neighbourhood—'as if I had lived here in my previous birth'.

The first visit lasted for a year, when she survived on the money that was left from the sale of the Japanese-made silver flute. 'All I had back then was just two sets of clothes, a clear mind, and a strong desire to learn Carnatic music,' she reminisces.

Three decades on, her possessions remain pretty much the same—she still learns from Ramani and practises for six hours daily. She now wants to buy a house in Mylapore and settle here to avoid shuttling between France and India. But she can't do that because she is on a tourist visa. Unless, of course, she marries an Indian—something she has contemplated for long (her boyfriend Don Cherry, the globetrotting musician, died in 1995).

'But the musicians I would have liked to marry are all married,' she tells me with a laugh. 'The problem with me is that I have set myself very high standards. If I marry a poet, he has to be the best poet. If I marry a painter, he should be the best painter. If I marry a musician, he should be the best musician.'

So Sylvie is waiting. There is something else she is still waiting for: a big break in the Carnatic music circuit. Meanwhile, she continues to persevere, the bamboo flute her steady and sole companion. Many years down the line, if you happen to walk down South Mada Street in Mylapore and hear the strains of a flute wafting down the balcony of a hotel called Karpagam, you will know that Sylvie is still there—still in love with Carnatic music and still to find an Indian husband.

Come to think of it, I wasn't even aware of the existence of this hotel until I came to Mylapore this Sunday. Two Frenchwomen showed me the way here.

■ ■ ■

I hail an autorickshaw to get home. Just when it is about to leave Shiva's boundaries I spot a hawker selling wood apples.

'Stop, stop!' I tell the driver.

He gets down too and helps me choose the ripe ones by bouncing them gently off the ground, much to the irritation of the woman hawker. If a wood apple tends to bounce, it means the pulp inside is still raw and hard. The driver buys one for himself too. 'Very good for stomach,' he tells me.

So I have finally found what I have been actually looking for all this while in Mylapore, even though I hadn't mentioned it to anyone—not even to myself.

Chapter 5

SEX AND THE CITY

'The thing is,' the elderly man tells his companion, 'I am here today, gone tomorrow.'

'Why do you say that, sir!' protests the companion, who looks equally old.

'Why not? I am eighty-one. Anything can happen to me anytime.'

'Nothing is going to happen to you for many more years, sir,' assures the companion. 'You are still healthy. Touch wood!'

The two men, as they contemplate mortality, are eating hot alu bondas off paper plates. I have missed the context of their conversation since I have just arrived. I am tempted to listen on, but the bondas look more tempting at the moment and I head for the stall to help myself to a couple of them. There are quite a few people flocking the stall and you never know when the bondas might run out. I fill my plate, take a seat and look around.

We have gathered this evening at the Freemasons Hall to listen to a talk—part of the numerous events being organised across the city to celebrate 371 years of Chennai—which is about to begin in a few minutes. Until then, we are meant to enjoy the hot bondas and coffee.

Most of the men who have come are elderly; a handful of them are accompanied by their wives. There is a lone woman, in a sky-blue saree, sitting alone and eating. She must be in her forties. On her lap is a shiny carry-bag from a famous saree shop; she might have been purchasing sarees before she decided to drop by. More people trickle in—among them a dark young man whose attire I shall never forget. He is wearing denim shorts that are hemmed with strips of patterned silk, a brown vest, over it a leather jacket, and suede shoes. I see him gravitating towards the woman.

The speaker arrives. He is the only familiar face so far—Dr Vijay Nagaswami, his thick silver hair stylishly set against a youthful face. He is a well-known psychiatrist in the city who has written bestselling books on how to preserve marriages. Journalists from the features departments reach out to him for quotes when writing about relationships.

The crowd follows him into the hall. Inside, it is chilly because of the efficient air conditioners. Yet, the young man in denim shorts takes his leather jacket off, exposing the sleeveless vest and a lot of dark skin. A vacant seat separates him from the woman in the sky-blue saree. They obviously wanted to sit together, and sitting a seat apart was as together as they could get without attracting the eyes of the others. My ears, though, are tuned in their direction: I have decided to sit in the row ahead of them.

'Do you go for a game?' the woman asks him.

'What game?' the young man asks.

'Do you play any game?'

'Not anymore. I used to.'

'Then why are you attired like this?'

'This is how I am usually.'

'But you said you are a software consultant.'

'Yes. My laptop is my office. Only when I meet my clients I am formally attired.'

'But are you not feeling cold?'

A third voice, belonging to a male, interrupts loudly, 'The topic of today's lecture will generate enough heat!' They all laugh.

The subject of this evening's talk is 'Sex and the City'. The fact that there is a highly popular television series and a film by that name has spared the organisers the trouble—and perhaps embarrassment—of having to think of a title.

A matronly woman climbs up the dais. She is the emcee for the evening. 'Good evening, ladies and gentlemen,' she says. 'Before we go any further, can we just take thirty seconds to switch off our phones or put them on silent or something? Thank you! On behalf of Chennai Heritage, it gives me great pleasure to welcome you all to one more beautiful evening of lectures brought to you by Chennai Heritage over the last few years. We started off with Madras Day, graduated to becoming Madras Week, this year it is Madras Fortnight, and hopefully one fine day, we will have Madras Year. This evening we have a well-known figure speaking on a very interesting subject which, I am sure, has brought most of you here.'

She then goes on to read out an introduction to Dr Nagaswami before welcoming him onto the stage. But not once does she mention the word 'sex'. All she tells the audience is that they are going to be treated to a lecture on an 'interesting subject', keeping herself miles away from spelling it out.

On the other hand, Dr Nagaswami, an extremely soft-spoken man, does not mince his words. He opens his lecture by calling Chennai a 'wild city' before going on to talk about its changing attitudes towards sex. Even though he draws from his long experience as a psychiatrist, what he says during the hour-long lecture could be true for any other city, not just Chennai.

What is, however, typical to Chennai is the woman abstaining from mentioning the word 'sex'. Here, you should not be seen openly associating with sex in an approving manner, even though Chennai, as a city, celebrates sex in a big way. Sex is always in the air—and on the airwaves.

The display of ample cleavage on the cover seems mandatory for many Tamil magazines; film songs can be vulgar and often border on pornography; television channels showcase the choicest of such songs late in the night when children are supposed to be asleep. Sex traders seem to be a prosperous lot too, slipping in advertisements in the classified columns of newspapers under the 'healthcare' category:

- DREAM GIRL massage services. Relax by high profile female masseurs. In call, out call selection available.
- MALE TO MALE inch by inch cool massage. Anytime hygienic smart guys.
- ESCORTS SERVICE High Profile Females. Special Package available. Door-step also.

- DEAR CUSTOMER We are doing Good Massage and Relaxation. Attached A/C and car park.
- SPECIAL ESCORTS Service. North Indian girls available.

At the same time, newspaper offices in the city routinely receive statements from the police regarding the busting of some prostitution racket or the other. While the pimps are promptly arrested and packed off to jail, the women caught in the act are always 'rescued' and sent to a government-run rehabilitation home in Mylapore. In the age of political correctness, police can no longer arrest the women but only 'rescue' them and confine them in the home.

Chennai may not have a designated red-light area, but prostitution is a flourishing business in the city, and its links with the film industry are uncovered from time to time. In October 2009, Chennai police arrested an actress called Bhuvaneswari on charges of running a prostitution racket. She had been arrested in 2002 too, for prostitution, but was let off for want of evidence. This time, in custody, she opened a can of worms. She reportedly told the police that she was only small fry in the trade, charging a meagre amount and that too to support her son's education, while there were high-flying actresses who charged up to one lakh rupees an hour and yet the police was turning a blind eye to them. She even named seven actresses and claimed she had evidence against them.

What she told the police was published by the Tamil newspaper *Dinamalar*, along with mug shots of the seven actresses, all of them well-known faces. The headline of the report screamed, *Top Actresses into Prostitution: Bhuvaneswari Reveals the List*. An enraged film industry came out in protest, holding a rally in which top actors including

Rajinikanth made angry speeches and took the media to task. The government was caught in a tricky situation: on one hand it faced the might of the all-important film industry, on the other it risked the wrath of the equally powerful media in case it proceeded against the newspaper.

Eventually, police went to the *Dinamalar* office and arrested not the publisher or the editor, but the news editor, who ranks much lower in the pecking order and legally cannot be held responsible for the contents published in a newspaper. Journalists, as expected, held a protest meeting. The news editor spent two nights in prison before he was released.

Bhuvaneswari too was released a few weeks later, and after coming out of jail she joined a little-known political party and was made the secretary of its women's wing. By then her arrest was long forgotten by Chennai. No one ever raised slogans against her; no one pelted stones at her house; no activist rushed to the court to file cases against her for outraging public decency.

In a shocking contrast, actress Khushboo, whose fans once built a temple to her, had twenty-two cases slapped against her in 2005 when she expressed her views on pre-marital sex to a magazine. All she had said was that in the present day and age, young men should not expect their brides to be virgins, and that women, if having sex before marriage, should take adequate precautions. Hell broke loose. Tamil activists, led by Pattali Makkal Katchi and the Dalit Panthers, accused her of insulting the Tamil woman and her chastity. Cases were filed against her in various courts. Activists would shout slogans against her whenever she appeared in courts, and in at least one place, in Mettur, they threw slippers, eggs and tomatoes at her car as she left the court. She was the same woman who once ruled their hearts, and now they were asking her to go back to Bombay, from where she had come to work in Tamil films.

The whole controversy was actually triggered by a Tamil tabloid. Seizing upon her statement that young men should not expect their brides to be virgins, it ran a story, complete with reactions from film stars and politicians, implying that Khushboo thought very poorly of the Tamil woman's chastity. The result: an actress, who had merely advised young women to take precautions in case they wanted to have sex before marriage, had to run from pillar to post, from one court to another, for the next five years.

It was finally in April 2010 that the Supreme Court dismissed all cases against her and set her free from the prolonged legal tangle. Ironically, the very day the Supreme Court gave its verdict, I happened to be sitting in Khushboo's house—only that she wasn't living there anymore. She had just sold the house to a friend of mine from Kolkata, who had absolutely no idea that his grihapravesh—house-consecrating ceremony—had coincided with the day of the judgment. In fact, until I told him, he wasn't even aware of the 'breaking news' flashing on TV channels—so busy he'd been looking after his guests who were being treated to a lavish Bengali lunch.

Like Bhuvaneswari, Khushboo too joined a political party once her travails were over. Given her stature, Khushboo joined the ruling party, the DMK. But the difference in the reaction each woman drew from society best illustrates Chennai's attitude towards sex.

A few weeks after she joined the DMK, Khushboo happened to be on the panel of a debate organised by *Outlook* magazine. The magazine was holding debates in big cities to celebrate its fifteenth anniversary, and for the Chennai debate it had chosen moral policing as the subject. The debate not only turned out to be entertaining but also enlightening, in the sense I could see for myself how the minds of even the highly educated worked here.

One of the panellists, Dr D. Viswanathan, a former vice-chancellor of the Anna University who, during his tenure in 2005, had banned jeans and T-shirts for female students, stoutly defended his decision, saying that tight-fitting clothes distracted male students as well as teachers. He even went on to say that America admitted six lakh students from abroad every year for higher education courses only because local students dropped out of colleges due to such distractions. Students may be complaining about the dress code, he said, but not a single parent had protested.

When Khushboo reminded him that in Indian culture, teachers were placed above god and that their minds were not expected to waver, Dr Viswanathan retorted, 'But they are also humans.' He, however, found support in a vocal woman panellist, Dr Tamilisai Soundararajan, a gynaecologist and also a local leader of the Bharatiya Janata Party.

Dr Tamilisai asserted that as a doctor, she could vouch for men being prone to getting aroused by provocatively-dressed women. I was quite tempted to ask her whether the same logic should be applied to prevent male doctors from examining female patients, and perhaps vice-versa; but it is more fun to be a fly on the wall on such occasions. Dr Tamilisai was also against the idea of women consuming alcohol—for medical reasons, of course. 'If you see your sister or daughter drinking in a pub, won't you feel like giving her a slap and dragging her home?' she asked shrilly.

Quite interestingly, even though their remarks drew jeers from the noisy youngsters in the audience, there was a sizeable section that seemed to silently agree with

Dr Viswanathan and Dr Tamilisai. When I thought about it, I realised that the two panellists could not be considered the villains of Chennai's society but only upholders of the traditional middle-class belief that watching films, wearing fashionable clothes and mingling with the opposite sex are the biggest enemies of education.

That such mentality still prevails is evident from the fact that the most sought-after engineering colleges in Chennai also happen to be ones that strictly prohibit mingling of male and female students. One such college has even ensured that no tree ever grows on its sprawling campus, out of fear that young couples might seek privacy under their shade; and bars male and female students from using the sole ATM on the campus at the same time—boys are supposed to use it only on Mondays, Wednesdays and Fridays, and the girls on Tuesdays, Thursdays and Saturdays. On Sundays, the ATM remains closed.

Chennai seems to be comfortable with such arrangements. As a society, it has always encouraged segregation of sexes—at least in public. Until a few decades ago, men and women attending concerts were separated by a rope. Even today, 'ladies seats' in public buses must remain vacant even if there are no women passengers travelling. Recently, the transport corporation changed the seating arrangement in buses plying on two busy routes by shifting the 'ladies seats' to the right side from the traditional left. This was done after women passengers complained of indecent behaviour by men travelling on the footboard. But it took a couple of days for the women to realise that they had to now squeeze their way through the men to get to the seats reserved for them—which, they thought, was worse. So the 'ladies seats' returned to the left.

In the past, too, the transport corporation had tried to segregate men and women passengers by partitioning buses—lengthwise as well as breadthwise—but such arrangements did not work out because they only succeeded in splitting families, which is a dangerous thing to happen when travelling in a crowded bus. All this had to happen in Chennai, where men are far better behaved than in other metros!

Segregation is the norm here; any deviation is at your own risk. In 2005, shortly after Khushboo got herself into that mess, *Dinamalar*, the Tamil daily, front-paged a picture shot in the newly-opened discotheque of Park Hotel, showing a handful of men and women dancing. The women in the picture were wearing sleeveless tops and one of them was drinking beer straight out of the bottle. The newspaper sought to know from the police commissioner 'how in a society where even married couples are reluctant to hold hands in public, women can sing and dance with men'.

The police commissioner, an officer with a prominent handlebar moustache whose edges nearly touched his sideburns—the trademark of a macho man in this part of the country, fell for the bait. Two managers of the hotel were promptly arrested and notices were sent to other hotels warning them against playing host to similar 'obscenity'.

I blame neither the newspaper nor the police commissioner. I happened to be in Kolkata during Durga Puja last year when one evening, I found my car trailing a truck that was carrying the idols for immersion. The truck was packed with cheerful men and women—from teenagers to the middle-aged—who behaved like college kids out on excursion for the first time. Even though

Goddess Durga and her four children, wearing dignified expressions, watched over them from a corner, it was noise that now acted as the presiding deity of the truck as the men and women indulged in laughter and banter and frequently broke into jigs to the beats of the dhaak.

Such uninhibited mingling of the two sexes struck me as odd—even mildly obscene. But I was quick enough to remind myself that, in the ten years I had lived in Chennai, my eyes had grown used to the segregation. Here, even when you see couples spending time together on the beaches or in parks, you can detect a sense of unease on their faces. A part of them tries to make the most of the hour or two they have in hand, while another part is always on the lookout for the cop—real or self-styled—who likens lovers to petty criminals. It is not uncommon to read reports about policemen harassing hapless couples in public places.

There is one aspect of sex, though, that Chennai has taken to celebrating publicly of late—alternate sexuality. The LGBT parade, which is an assertion of their identity by the lesbian, gay, bisexual and transgender community, has become an annual event in the city ever since the Delhi high court decriminalised homosexuality in 2009. But sex—as an idea, as a need—continues to remain in the closet in Chennai, finding an outlet in the form of cleavage on the cover of a magazine or a wet saree in a film song.

■ ■ ■

This evening I have an appointment with Susie. I am waiting for her on the terrace-lounge of Park Hotel, overlooking the Gemini flyover. I have arrived early because the friend who has set up this meeting has specifically asked me not to keep Susie waiting. I kill time by gazing at the moon. It is peeping from between the clouds like a curious child—a child that is too intimidated to walk into the drawing room where guests are being entertained but at the same time is eager to observe and eavesdrop from behind the curtains.

The first thing you notice about Susie is her breasts. She has a perfect pair, on the ampler side, which she flaunts at the top of a short black dress—and why not? She has, after all, earned them.

She was not born with them. Today Susie, who is twenty-eight, is one of the stars in Chennai's transgender circuit.

'I was born and brought up in north Chennai. When I was in the fourth standard, I found something was wrong with me. I wouldn't say wrong, I would say I found myself to be different from other boys. They would play cricket, but I would like to stay with the girls and play with dolls. Since I was too young then, nobody found anything unusual about my behaviour or tried to stop me.

'By the time I reached the tenth standard, boys had already started teasing me. I used to feel very sad. There was nobody I could talk to about why I was like that. I didn't know who to approach. Fortunately, my school was only five minutes' walk from home, and whenever the boys teased me, someone from my family would come and hit them. I come from a Chettiar family, and many of my relatives are into politics. So the boys began to be scared of bullying me, and I was able to complete my schooling.

'After that I joined a hotel management institute. You see, people like us are physically male, but mentally female. People can tell from our mannerisms, from the way we talk. But what to do, that is our nature. We can't hide it.

At the hotel management institute, we were a class of seventeen. Sixteen boys and one girl.'

'You mean you were the only girl in the class?' I interrupt, completely forgetting, due to her current appearance, that she did not always look like a woman.

'No, no,' Susie laughs. 'I was a boy then. I was one of the sixteen boys in the class, and there was only one girl. I was very close to that girl. I told her my problems. She would stop the other boys from teasing me. She also helped me in my assignments and in preparing for exams. The boys thought we were having an affair.

'After that I joined a four-star hotel (she names the hotel, a well-known one). That was the turning point. I joined as a trainee steward. In six months I became a steward, in another six months a senior steward, and in another six months a trainee captain. At that time they all thought I was gay. I let it be. You see, most people don't know the difference between a gay and a transsexual. A gay means a man who likes another man. You have another category, called the shemale, which means a female with a penis. If you go to Bangkok and Pattaya, you will find many of them. Then there are the transsexuals, people like me, who undergo surgery to become a female. But most people still don't know the distinction. So at the hotel, they all thought I was gay. The problems began when I became a trainee captain. Many managers did not like the idea of having a gay man as a captain. But the general manager was very supportive. He was a kind man. He would say that my sexuality was my personal matter, and that it wasn't an issue as long as I was good at my work, which I was. I could handle the guests really well. But the managers kept pointing fingers at me.

'Meanwhile, I had become friends with a senior captain. I really liked him. One day both of us decided to quit and

The fort at Chandragiri, 150 km north of Chennai, where its ruler signed the deed in 1639 granting land to the East India Company to build a settlement in the village of Madraspatnam. (Photograph by author)

Fort St George, where modern India originated. Its construction began even when building of the Taj Mahal was yet to be completed in Agra.

The author strikes a pose at the Royapuram station (in north Chennai), the oldest surviving railway station in India. (Photograph by Murali Krishnan)

Chennai wakes up to such posters each morning. A composite picture showing Jayalalithaa and her mentor MGR (top) and Karunanidhi and his son Stalin.

The Kapaleeswara temple in Mylapore. Mylapore has been in existence since ancient times and is Chennai's most famous and venerated neighbourhood.

Chennai without its flower-sellers would be like a sea without water. A young florist poses for the camera in Mylapore.

An enterprising palm-reader awaits customers on the sands of Marina beach, which draws visitors from all over the country

Usman Road in T Nagar, where you can buy almost everything under the sun. On the eve of festivals such as Diwali and Pongal, nearly ten lakh people descend on this road every day.

The Marina on a calm morning. The view from the beach helps soothe the nerves of many a troubled soul.

The caste-mark of the Thengalai sect of Iyengars painted on the wall of Parthasarathy temple in Triplicane. It is the oldest temple in the city, dating back to the eighth century.

Saroja Devi and Gemini Ganesan in the Tamil film *Kai Raasi*.
(Photograph sourced by author)

Dr Kamala Selvaraj and actress Rekha. Both are daughters of the actor Gemini Ganesan, but born of different mothers (Photograph sourced by author)

join another hotel (she names yet another well-known hotel). But even there, while they hired my friend as a senior captain straightaway, they asked to me to start all over again as a steward. I had no choice but to go back to the position in which I'd begun a year-and-a-half earlier. I felt very sad but what to do, I needed the job. To make things worse, one of the managers from the hotel I previously worked in also took up a job here. Things became difficult.'

One day, Susie was visited by a doctor—a shemale of Indian origin—who lived in the US and periodically visited Chennai. The two had got to know each other during Susie's stint in the hotel she worked earlier: the doctor had stayed in that hotel during one of her visits to Chennai. During a subsequent visit when she checked into the same hotel and enquired about Susie, she was told that Susie had taken up a job in another hotel. So she landed up at Susie's new workplace.

'I told her everything about myself, A to Z. I told her what I was going through,' Susie goes on. 'She told me that abroad, the gender of a person did not matter. You are accepted the way you are. If you are a transsexual, you went to work as a transsexual; you did not have to hide your gender because everybody is treated as an equal. When she told me all this, I wondered what I was doing in a job where I had no respect? I decided to quit. I went with her to Bangalore, where she introduced me to a very kind person who became my guru. In the transgender community, we have gurus. After I returned from Bangalore, I lived alone in Triplicane for three years. I was earning money by going out with people. I used to inject myself with Progynon Depot (a drug containing the female hormone) because of which I had even grown small breasts. I used to go out with all kinds of people, from the lower class to the VVIPs. You see, in India, people like us have only three ways of earning money. One, by singing and dancing during weddings, which is common only in north India; you don't see it happening in the south. Two, by begging, going shop to shop, which I could not have done because I was educated. The third option is sex work, which was the only option left for me. Why would I have wanted to lose out on that? At least I had money coming my way. When I was being discriminated against, nobody stood up for me. The people I was going out with were at least giving me money.'

After three years of going out with people as a shemale, she had earned enough money to be able to purchase a new identity. 'I found a doctor, a plastic surgeon, working in Apollo Hospitals. He was trained in the US. I met him and got proper surgery done. It's called SRS, or sex reassignment surgery. It costs about three lakh rupees. But the doctor was kind enough to give me a discount and I had to pay only two lakh. After six months, in Bangalore, I got my breast implantation done. It cost me about one lakh. Until then I wore specs, so I also got laser treatment done for my eyes, which cost me ₹ 35,000. Actually it costs around ₹ 50,000 but the eye-surgeon waived off his fee and asked me to pay only the hospital bill.'

But medical science is not miracle science, notwithstanding the wonders it can work. It may bring a dead man alive, but to transform a man completely into a woman—that can happen only in mythological stories and there too, gods are known to switch genders, when required, only for a short period of time. In real life, many subtle as well as vital signs are left behind in spite of the surgery—signs that are easily apparent to the discerning eye and that always keep the person who has undergone the surgery on the fence between the two genders. Even Susie, in spite of having rid herself of the burden of manhood, calls herself a transsexual and not a woman. But then, she is today as close to being a woman as science is capable of making her—that has not only set her free from the anguish of being born a man but also boosted her business like never before.

'Today wherever I go, they say, "Oh my god! A hot girl is coming!"' she giggles. 'I make a lot more money. And people are also satisfied. They feel they have slept with a woman.'

'Do you ever miss your penis?' I ask her.

'Not at all,' she laughs. 'I had always looked at it and thought, "I just want to cut this off!"'

'How did you feel after the surgery? What was the very first thought that came to your mind when you woke up to find your penis gone?'

'Before the surgery I went to a psychotherapist. But he began to ask me all sorts of silly questions—all kinds of rubbish. I told him very clearly that I would love to be a girl. Before the surgery I prayed to all the gods. I prayed for a second life. The moment I opened my eyes after the surgery, I was so, so, so happy. It was the happiest moment in my life. After that I spent forty days in the house of my guru in Bangalore. She put me up in a room where there was only a bed. For those forty days I was not supposed to look at the mirror or at a man's face or visit a temple. On the fortieth day there was a big celebration—it is the custom.'

After the celebration Susie returned to live in Triplicane. Occasionally, she would go home to meet her mother, unknown to other members of the family. She did not want her brother to be teased by his friends or colleagues.

As it was, her sister's engagement had been called off a few times when the prospective groom's side found out about Susie. After three years of living as a woman in Triplicane, her parents called her back. By then, the sister was married. They have made peace with the fact that their son is now their daughter.

'My mother tells me, "Now you are a girl. Wherever you go, whatever you do, you must come back home. We don't want any more trouble." They are fully supportive of me. Even people in the neighbourhood respect me.

'In one way I am happy. I have become what I wanted to. But in another way I am sad. I need a support, I need a partner, I need a guy to hold my hands. I want to work. I want to be an air hostess; I want to be a manager. Why doesn't anyone give me the job I want? What's wrong with me? I am educated. The work I am doing, I am doing it by force, because there is no choice.

'I want to have a career, I want to have a home. Whenever I see young couples, I feel very sad. Whenever I see a baby, I feel very sad.'

Just then, in a cruel coincidence, a toddler takes small steps past our table, holding on to an arm each of his young parents. The baby's tiny shoes make a squeaking sound. Tears start rolling down Susie's cheeks. I find one of the most awkward moments of my life staring me in the face.

■ ■ ■

I first met Dr Narayana Reddy about seven or eight years ago at the Gymkhana Club, where a writer friend of mine had invited me for drinks one evening.

'Do you see that man in specs?' my friend asked me.

'Yes, who is he?' I asked.

'Have you heard of Dr Prakash Kothari, the sexologist?'
'Of course, who hasn't? But that's not Prakash Kothari!'
'Prakash Kothari is the no. 1 sexologist in India. And the man in specs you see there, he is the no. 2 in the country. He is Dr Narayana Reddy,' my friend said softly.

'Of course I have heard of him too.' I remembered reading in a magazine, many years ago, about a survey he had conducted on changing sexual mores in India—one doesn't forget articles on sex easily. And at the time—I must have been barely fifteen then—I thought of Dr Reddy as one lucky man to be privy to such juicy statistics.

'Great,' my friend said, 'if he happens to pass by, I will introduce you to him.'

So that evening, I finally got to shake hands with Dr Reddy, the man I once envied and perhaps envy even now. After all, he knows the bedroom secrets of countless people, from the rich and the famous to the couple next-door—people who are eager to get their sex lives back on track. The voyeur in me would like to trade places with him for a day.

Dr Reddy turned out to be soft-spoken and charming—it was easier to imagine him as the CEO of a multinational company than a doctor who dealt with sex. We exchanged cards and promised to meet up for a drink. Dr Reddy and I have stayed in touch ever since, and this is largely due to my occasional visits to his clinic.

Every now and then, which is to say about once in six months, my hypochondria drives me to him. Dr Reddy's gentle persona inspires so much trust that when he puts the stethoscope on my chest and tells me the pain I've been experiencing has nothing to do with the functioning of my heart, I instantly feel assured and relieved. I always walk into his clinic with anxiety writ large on my face and walk out smiling, with an extra bounce in my step. So far, fortunately, nobody known to me has spotted me entering or going out of Dr Reddy's clinic. They just might attribute the extra bounce to the joy of having rediscovered an erection.

'You are not the only one. Nobody likes to be seen at my clinic,' Dr Reddy laughs, as I settle for a chat with him one evening after he has seen his last patient. 'I see a lot of men who are unable to get married because they have a sexual problem. Once I cure them, they are so happy that they don't forget to invite me for their wedding. They come to the clinic personally to hand me the card, but when I ask them about the date and the venue, they say, "No doctor, please bless us from your clinic." They know if I show up at the wedding, tongues might start wagging. After all, people know me as a sexologist,' says Dr Reddy.

Being a sexologist has not been easy for him.

'When I started my clinic in 1982, everybody discouraged me. My family and friends were worried that sexology was not a respectable specialty, unlike cardiology or ophthalmology, which would have given me a better status. My medical colleagues and seniors, too, felt there was no need for this specialty and I wouldn't be able to earn anything.

'Probably it was the desire to be different. At the time I was thirty-two and had the guts to do something new. One of the very first patients I had was a sixty-plus man. I had presented a paper at a conference in Madras and *India Today* had published a report. The man had read the report and he came to see me. And the first question he asked was, "But how old are you?" When I told him, he said, "My marriage is older than you. I am sorry, I don't think you can help me." He walked off.

'Then came another patient I can never forget. You see, my doctor-friends had advised me that if I had a stand-alone clinic to treat sexual problems, people may hesitate to visit, so I should simultaneously join a multi-specialty hospital to have an income. So I joined a hospital. But the owners, who were known to my family, said I could not call myself a sexologist. I asked them what I should call myself. After much deliberation, they said I could call myself a reproductive biologist. I didn't even know what that meant, but beggars can't be choosers.

'I was allotted a room in the maternity section. I was sharing it with a senior gynaecologist, who was my teacher in college and who had delivered my two children. For six months I hardly had any patient. Every doctor used to make fun of me. When passing by they would peep in and wink, "If you have any interesting case, do let us know. We will come and watch." I would read magazines, drink tea and then go back to my clinic.

'One day a man knocked and walked in. I was so happy I could have garlanded him. But he said, "I don't have a problem, it is my wife who is admitted here for surgery. I was just walking around when I happened to notice your board. I am curious to know what 'reproductive biologist' means." I was crushed. But this man became the turning point of my career.

'He was a Muslim, orthodox, well-to-do man who had been married for a number of years but did not have any children. He had taken his wife for treatment to Bombay, to Singapore, but nothing happened. Finally, he came to this hospital because he had heard that the gynaecologist, my teacher, had a good hand. The surgery was to be done to see if internal organs were fine. He was hoping that his wife would become pregnant after the surgery.

'I asked him about the reports. He said the reports were all fine, both his and his wife's. Then I asked him if he was regularly having sex. He said he was. I found it strange that the wife should not be conceiving. Something was amiss. I wanted to speak to the wife, but she was a purdah-clad woman who would not speak to me. So I got hold of a staff nurse and made her sit with the woman in a room while I spoke to them over intercom. The nurse conveyed my questions to her. I asked her if they were having proper intercourse, to which she said yes. But my hunch was that vaginal intercourse was not taking place.

'I realised this was a make-or-break case for me. I hadn't had a single patient in six months. I requested the gynaecologist to ask certain questions of that man's wife. But she refused, saying, "At my age how can I ask such questions?" I did not know what to do. Those days there was no internet or ISD. So I booked a call to America to speak to my teacher. My teacher said a vaginal swab test would establish whether vaginal intercourse had taken place and maybe the couple should be asked to have sex in the hospital.

'I pleaded with the gynaecologist to postpone the surgery. She said she could postpone it only by forty-five minutes because after that it would be rahu kaalam. So I asked the couple to have sex in the hospital and straightaway went to the chief pathologist, who was a highly respected doctor, and begged him to personally conduct the vaginal swab test. His word carried a lot of weight.

'True to my hunch, there were no sperms found in the vagina, which meant vaginal intercourse had not taken place at all. The surgery was cancelled once the pathologist wrote his report. The gynaecologist could not overrule him. I found out that the man did not even know where the vaginal opening was. He would simply lie on top of his wife and ejaculate between her thighs. They believed that was intercourse and were hoping to get a child. I had to tell him how to have sex.

'Three months later he barged into my room. He was ecstatic. He said his wife was finally pregnant. I got ecstatic too and went to the next cubicle to break the news to the gynaecologist, my teacher. And guess who I found there? The man's wife, the purdah-clad woman, who was presenting the gynaecologist a basket of fruit and a silk saree. Whereas I was the one who done all the work! From then on, the gynaecologist began to refer such cases to me. My life changed.

'I stayed working in the hospital for about eight years. Of all the cases referred to me, I found twenty-five to thirty per cent of the couples did not even know how to have sex. Meanwhile, in my clinic, I was seeing only about thirty patients—thirty in a year, mind you. It can be very discouraging for a doctor not to get patients, and also detrimental financially. Today I see thirty-five to forty patients in a day. I can't cope with the load.

'Things started changing gradually since 1985, when Prakash Kothari and I conducted the World Congress of Sexology at the Taj Palace in Delhi. The media coverage was tremendous. That made the Indian public realise that sexual problems didn't have to be hush-hush and that they could be dealt with scientifically. But, as I said, the change was gradual; it was not an overnight process.

'The flood, for me, came in 1997. You see, I had been knocking at the doors of the print media for a very long time, but while they would give me coffee and be nice to me, they would shy away from the idea of my writing a column for them. In 1997, the Tamil magazine *Nakkeeran* asked me to write a column. They were the only magazine who had the guts to publish such a thing.

'So I started a column, in which I would take up a real-life case history—of course, by changing names—and suggest various solutions to the problem. Neither I nor the magazine was confident that the column would be a success. We presumed that women would not even read such things. But our eyes opened once the column started. There was a flood of letters from women in small towns, asking for their cases to be highlighted.

'Soon after, I started writing a column for *Vanitha*, the women's magazine of the Malayala Manorama group. Even today, the best questions come from the readers of *Vanitha*. I don't know if this has anything to do with the high literacy level in Kerala, but to answer their questions I often have to refer to my books.

'Now I am also writing for the women's magazine *Kumudam*, a popular Tamil publication. In between, I had a column in the *Deccan Chronicle* for a few years. I can tell you that my columns are mainly read by women. Among the men, only elderly people and youngsters read them. The other day I was at a party and a man came up to me and said, "You look familiar." I told him he might have seen me at some Rotary meeting. Immediately his wife said, "He writes a column in *Deccan Chronicle*."

'Very often, when I the see the list of patients who have made appointments, I find a number of women among them. But when the patient arrives, he turns out be to a man. Then I realise it is the wife who has made the appointment on his behalf. When I started my practice, men would come alone. Today, they are either accompanied by their wives or are sent by their wives.

'Women are far more open about sex today. Only two days ago, I had a patient, seventy-seven years old, who was walking with the help of a stick because he had a fractured femur. He was accompanied by his wife, who was seventy-one. They were a traditional Brahmin couple. The man had been unable to have an erection for the past two years, so the wife had brought him to my clinic.

'When couples come to see me, I also speak to the man and the woman separately. When I spoke to this woman, she didn't bat an eyelid while explaining her husband's problem. Mind you, she was a very traditional woman. People are lot more forthcoming today than they were when I started my practice. Which I think is a good thing.

'Since 1995, when I began consulting for Apollo Hospitals, the number of patients coming from north and east India has also steadily increased. First they would come because of the Apollo connection, but now they come directly to me. I get patients from West Bengal, Bihar, Assam, Arunachal Pradesh.

'The women coming from the east, especially Bengal, are not only more vocal but also direct. Some time ago, a Bengali couple came to see me. I asked the man in Hindi, "*Bataiyye aapki kya samasya hai* (What problem do you have)?" Immediately, his wife replied, "Doctor *saab, mere* husband *ko* sex *nahin aata* (Doctor, my husband is unable to perform)." The man sat quietly all through. Here, in the south, women may not be so forceful, but they are vocal.

'Recently, a newly-married woman from Chennai came to me with her husband. Her complaint was that the husband's penis was too small. I examined the fellow and found him to be fine. I asked the woman what made her think his penis was small. She said she knew it because she was a zoologist. I told her she must have seen only a donkey's penis so far and that is why the human penis looked small to her.

'Many patients, even the educated ones, since they are not taught the right vocabulary in school or college, use all sorts of colloquial, or wrong words, or slang to explain their problem. One woman, who was the head of the department of economics in a college, came to me because she had pain in the vagina during intercourse. She kept on referring to the vagina as "urinals". For a long time I did not understand what she was saying.

'At times, the words they use to describe a condition happen to be related to their profession. For example, one patient who was suffering from premature ejaculation kept on saying "Dispatch, dispatch." When I asked him about his job, I found out that he was a postal dispatch clerk in small railway station in Andhra Pradesh.

'All kinds of people come to see me—you could say—from the manual labourer to the nuclear scientist. Also industrialists. And of course, politicians. You see, in 1950, the average life expectancy of a man was forty and of a woman thirty-eight. In 2001, the figures went up to sixty-five and sixty-three respectively. In 2011, these figures will go up even higher. Any living adult will have sexual desires. So there is nothing unusual about an elderly patient coming to me. To say that you become asexual after a certain age is not true; it cannot happen.

'Age is no bar for sex. Several elderly men come to me after they have been dismissed by other doctors. One sixty-plus man who came to me for erectile dysfunction had already visited a senior doctor, who was my professor in medical college. I asked the man, "Why did you come to me? This doctor would have treated you better, he was my professor." The man replied, "Sir, he shouted at me. He said at this age you should be taking care of your heart and prostrate and not thinking about sex." So the medical fraternity is also responsible for making people believe that sex is taboo after a certain age.

'While on the one hand, it is heartening to see older people wanting to lead a full life, on the other, I feel sad for the younger generation. Many couples are drifting apart because there is no sex in their marriage. They may not be legally separated, but there is no intimacy. The reason being, people don't have the time for anything, leave alone time for sex.

'We may talk of globalisation and liberalisation, but I think we are going backward. A young professional today draws one lakh a month and his family is very happy. But he works thirty kilometres away from the city, which means he has to be up by five or six, and by the time he is back it is about nine in the evening. Where does he have the time?

'Nowhere in the Western world do airports function between eleven in the night and five in the morning. Nowhere in the West do they work beyond five in the evening or during Christmas holidays, come what may. That is because they respect the body clock, they understand the value of quality in life. But our boys are working according to their timings, working even on holidays like Diwali and Pongal, because they want to earn those dollars. At what cost?

'A husband and wife hardly spend time together these days. They spend more time with their colleagues. Whatever little time they get at home, they catch up on sleep. Their sex life is bound to be affected. Just the other day, I was visited by a high-profile couple. The man was a vice-president in a multinational company and the wife was the head of HR in another multinational. They had not had sex for almost a year. When I asked them why, they said they rarely met. When one of them was at home, the other would be travelling. In fact, they had met each other only once in the past six months, that too at the Changi Airport in Singapore.

'Now, do you call this marriage? Are we going forward or backward?'

■ ■ ■

The amorous septuagenarian couple who visited Dr Reddy's clinic must be among the very fortunate few who, even in advanced age, not only retain mutual attraction and an appetite for sex but are also bold enough to see a doctor to fix the glitches in their conjugal life. They are an exception and perhaps, in society's eyes, even an aberration, for wanting to have sex at a stage of life when they should be out on a pilgrimage. The fact remains that an overwhelming number of senior citizens living in Chennai make do with loneliness for company.

Each time you blink, yet another young man or woman is flying out of the city to study or work abroad, perhaps never to return, certainly not for good. The inclination to pursue a career abroad is particularly common among the academics-obsessed Tamil Brahmins—a contributing factor being the indifference they suffer at the hands of the Dravidian government at home.

But each time an international flight takes off, a certain number of houses in Chennai turn into old-age homes. You can't blame the visa-holding young person: they are only fulfilling the dreams of their parents, who would have invested a chunk of their own youth in their education so that they would get absorbed by the West someday.

For the parents, the pride in having a child settled in America seems to far outweigh the pain of them resigning themselves to a soundless and lonely life. Occasionally, they get invited to America, mostly to babysit a newly-born grandchild, and once they return, they show off their knowledge of America to fellow morning-walkers. Fellow walkers too would have similar stories to share. Through such stories they live vicariously the lives of their children—it's their way of escaping the dreariness back home. But for how long? Once their spouses pass away, many of the elderly in the city find themselves prisoners in their own homes—and quite often, in old-age homes.

Once, when I was lamenting this trend to a Tamil Brahmin friend, herself a young engineer, she told me: 'You know, the other day, my mother and I were talking just about this. We were thinking about starting an old-age home for all our relatives whose children are now living abroad. And our conversation was not sombre: it was matter-of-fact.' Irony of ironies, the friend now lives in Canada.

Until I visited an old-age home, I thought hospitals were the most depressing places on this planet. But in a hospital, there is hope; in an old-age home there is none. The inmates are like passengers of a bus that is taking them to sunset point. In the fading sunlight, they can only observe the world from the window of the slow-moving bus; they are not permitted to alight until the bus has reached its final destination.

Quite symbolically, the sun has begun to set by the time I can locate the old-age home I have chosen to visit. And quite ironically, the home happens to be situated right next to a park where elderly men are out in their walking shoes—some of them will go home to have their quota of two small drinks before dinner, some others would play with their grandchildren or help them with homework. But in the old-age home, the inmates have no home to go back to—this is their home.

A stony silence greets me when I step into the compound. Not a soul in sight. I remove my shoes and tiptoe into the corridor—still no sign of life. I listen for footsteps or the sound of coughing, but all I can hear, in the silence, is the chirping of birds coming from the adjacent park. I pass by a room where an emaciated woman, her cropped hair all grey, is sitting motionless on a cane chair. She stares at me blankly. I walk on. I feel as if I've entered a never-ending maze of silent corridors from where there is no way out to the bustle of life.

Before I begin to feel nervous, I am spotted by an attendant who has been informed about my visit. She shows me into a hall and goes about rounding up the inmates, who soon troop in and take their seats. I am now being regarded by about half-a-dozen eager pair of eyes. They are all curious to know who I am and what I am there for. I don't have the heart to tell them that they are subjects of my story because they have aged, a process they've had no control over, and are now living in an old-age home.

I start with Mr Ramanan, who happens to be sitting right next to me. He is seventy-two, a retired bank employee and has been living in this home for five years now. He is the only one in the hall who is of cheerful disposition and does not seem to mind living in the home.

'My wife is long dead. I have two children, one daughter and one son. My daughter married a Mudaliar while my son got married to a girl from the Gounder community. I did not have any objection to them marrying out of caste, but, you see, I am a Brahmin and a strict vegetarian. Once my children got married, they began to prepare non-vegetarian food at home. I could not take that. So I left the house and came here. Not that I have any other problem with them. They come to visit me once in a while,' he says. 'That's it,' he smiles.

He has nothing more to say. Perhaps he doesn't want to say anything more. Since he speaks fluent English, I urge him to stay on to be my interpreter. He agrees.

But Mr Viswanathan, the only other man among the inmates gathered in the hall, happens to speak English even more fluently. Once upon a time, he worked with Tata Steel in Jamshedpur. 'Let me make it very clear before you ask me anything,' he tells me in a firm voice, 'I am here out of choice. Nobody has forced me to live here. And you will also have to tell me who you are and which organisation you represent.'

Once he learns that I am a Bengali, he softens a bit. He actually smiles. He had a number of Bengali colleagues while working in Jamshedpur. 'Now I've lost touch with the language. I was there long ago, in the 1950s and '60s,' says Mr Viswanathan, who is now eighty-four. 'I was a foreman, and I was getting a salary of ₹ 800. Today a person doing the same job gets ₹ 40,000. Those days a steel plant worker used to earn only ₹ 4 a day, now he earns ₹ 35 an hour. Those days rice used to cost...' He goes on to compare life between then and now.

On one hand, I don't feel inclined to stop him because then-and-now stories always fascinate me—just how the span of a few decades can turn the impossible into possible, and the possible into impossible. But on the other, I am also curious to know how he came to live in an old-age home—something that might have seemed impossible to him during his Tata Steel days in Jamshedpur. Finally, during a longish pause, I steer the conversation in the desired direction.

In 1967, when he was forty, Mr Viswanathan returned with his family to Chennai, where his parents lived. Unfortunately, within three years, his wife passed away. Mr Viswanathan was left to take care of his three young children—two sons and a daughter. Fortunately for him, his parents were around to look after the children while he reinvented his career in the steel industry as a consultant—his long stint with the Tata group holding him in good stead.

In 1985, when Mr Viswanathan was fifty-eight, his mother passed away. In 1987, his father passed away too. By then both his sons had become engineers while the daughter had finished her BA. Also by then, Mr Viswanathan had made sufficient money to build a three-storey house in south Madras. He built three storeys in order to give one floor each to the three children.

But by 1990, all the three children had migrated to the United States. The sons took up jobs there; while the daughter, who is now working with the US government, was married to an engineer settled there. Mr Viswanathan had played a good father. Only that he himself, in a span of just five years, was left all alone in his hometown.

He tried watching movies in the theatres to kill time, but realised it was no fun sitting in the cinema hall all by oneself. 'The last time I went to a cinema hall was in 1991. After that I never went to a theatre. For the first few years after they left, I would visit the US once in a while, but you see, they don't give a visa for more than five or six months. Moreover, life in the US is more boring than in Chennai. What do you do there? So I have stopped going there now.

It is so much better here. I watch cricket, browse the internet, listen to songs that are stored in my laptop. Once every year, my children come to see me,' he says.

But why did they have to leave in the first place? As soon as I put this question to Mr Viswanathan, the firmness in his voice returns. 'Did they have a choice?' he asks. 'What do people like us get here? Do you give us proper jobs? Do you give us good pay? Do you give us respect? If we get all these things here, why should we go abroad?' When he says 'people like us', does he mean people from his community—Tamil Brahmins—or bright young graduates in general? I somehow run out of courage to probe that. He could have meant either—or perhaps a bit of both.

But I do ask him why he has chosen to move in here when he could have stayed on in his own home—the three-storey house that is now vacant?

'Who will look after me there?' he asks me, looking into my eyes. 'I am eighty-four now.'

'You could have hired a servant,' I suggest.

'Sir, you are a journalist. You should know what's happening to elderly people living alone in the city. You know how difficult it is to get a good servant? Only one in hundred turns out to be good. The rest can't be trusted,' says Mr Viswanathan.

He leans back and regards me with grandfatherly eyes. 'You Bengalis are very emotional, isn't it?' he smiles.

I don't know what to say. I smile back. He gets up. 'I have to go now. But before you publish this article, please show me the draft. I want to see if you have got the facts right.' I watch his tall frame disappear into the corridor. He would easily be six-foot—the owner of a three-storey house located barely a couple of kilometres away, now retiring to an eight-by-eight room which has been his home for seven years now.

I now turn to the women. There are five of them, waiting eagerly. The eagerness, I sense, is not so much to tell their stories as about having a chat with a stranger who seemed to be interested in listening. Mr Ramanan acts as the interpreter.

It is the same story repeated over and over again: once upon a time they were a happy family until the sons landed dream jobs in America and the daughters got married to respectable professionals settled abroad. The elderly parents suddenly found themselves stranded in their own city. When one of them died, the surviving parent was persuaded by the children, all leading prosperous lives abroad, to move into an old-age home.

But none of the women—or for that matter, not even the two men—blame their children; all of them claim they moved into the old-age home of their own choice.

One woman, however, strikes a discordant note.

Ratnamma, who is seventy-four, turns out to be bitterly critical of her daughter. 'My husband died two years ago. He worked in the railways. Within ten days of the funeral, my daughter, instead of taking me along with her, brought me here. Imagine, my only child doing this to me!' she seethes.

Even though Ratnamma can only speak Tamil, she has sufficient understanding of English to sense that Mr Ramanan is presenting me with toned-down versions of her outbursts. Even I have enough understanding of Tamil to realise that Mr Ramanan is censoring her emotions: it is quite obvious that he doesn't want to bring a bad name to the 'children'. Ratnamma rebukes him: 'Let him know what I have been through.' After which Mr Ramanan begins translating her sentences verbatim.

'I would have liked to stay with my daughter after my husband's death, but no, she did not allow me to!' Ratnamma goes on. 'She just dumped me here!'

'What does your daughter do?' I ask Ratnamma. 'How old is she?'

'She is forty-two now. She is an engineer. She is earning quite well. She has a son who goes to school.'

'Why doesn't she want you to stay with her?'

'She says, "Amma, who will look after you when I go to work and the child goes to school?" Am I bedridden that I need to be looked after, tell me? I get my husband's pension. I was not going to be a burden on her.'

The other inmates look away in an uninterested manner. They do not want to be seen in the same boat as hers.

'What does her husband do?' I ask.

'She is divorced. She and her child are living alone. Still, she wants to keep me here!' she says.

Suddenly, there is silence in the hall. The anger on Ratnamma's face begins to melt into embarrassment. 'But I must say that my daughter's character is good,' she seeks to clarify.

'Good? Ha!' Mr Ramanan mocks at her, seeking his revenge. 'And all this while you were saying how bad she is.'

'She may be bad,' the mother in Ratnamma fights back, 'but her character is good.'

Chapter 6

THE RICH GIRL AND THE KING OF ROMANCE

Sometimes, coming a long way in life can just be about crossing the street.

For nearly five years since I came to Chennai in 2001, my evening haunt was a dingy bar on Commander-in-Chief Road, or Ethiraj Salai, off Mount Road—a bottle's throw from the offices of the *New Indian Express* group where I worked. The bar was actually the garret of a liquor shop. That dimly-lit space, the air always thick with cigarette smoke, the smell of fried food and the cacophony produced by its occupants, was the back office of my life where new dreams would be hired and frustrations fired.

Cockroaches and laughter flew across the grimy tables with equal abandon. Nowhere else in the world would you see people from such disparate backgrounds socialising under one roof: emaciated drunks who could collapse any moment; labourers who needed their daily fix; dangerous-looking rowdies; decently-paid professionals and businessmen who were not permitted to drink at home and who found bars such as this most convenient to wind up a long day.

Then, there were vagabonds like me, living from paycheque to paycheque, who had no one waiting at home or to take out.

Though that bar has been shut down, there are a few hundred others that continue to flourish: they are the backbone of popular drinking culture in Chennai. A chunk of the heat-of-the-moment murders that take place in the city result from drinking sessions in these hellholes. I no longer go to such places. I now drink at the Presidency Club, which is right across the road from my old haunt. When I sit on the terrace of the club, where I love to be, I oversee the same stretch of Commander-in-Chief Road that would be visible from the attic of the liquor shop. Looking at the passing traffic, at times I feel like the same vagabond I was, except that I now sit on the other side of the road.

■ ■ ■

Nine-thirty at night. Wife and I are sitting on the terrace of the club. She is, as usual, sulkily sipping on a cocktail. She hates spending the evenings on the terrace. It can be hot in the open; moreover, the mosquitoes from the potted plants are always on the loose, like a murderous mob. Above all, the tables on the terrace are invariably empty because most people like to drink in the air-conditioned comfort of the refurbished bar. My wife believes that if you don't see people and people don't see you, you're not really spending an evening out. It is as good as drinking on the balcony of your home. But I like to park myself on the terrace because I can smoke here. Also, there is something about drinking under a starlit sky. I find it a luxury.

I've just begun my second drink when I spot a female silhouette that I cannot mistake because of the long hair that reaches down to her calves. It is Priya Selvaraj, who, like her mother Kamala Selvaraj, is a well-known fertility specialist in Chennai. Priya is also the granddaughter of the actor Gemini Ganesan who, along with M.G. Ramachandran and Sivaji Ganesan, once formed the triumvirate of Tamil cinema.

Even as a small boy in Kanpur, I had, thanks to my mother's Madras connection, heard of Sivaji Ganesan and Gemini Ganesan. I had always thought they were brothers because of the common second name. Like Raj Kapoor and Shammi Kapoor. It was some decades later that I was to be introduced to the south Indian system of nomenclature where, especially in showbiz, the landmarks of your life—be it a place or a memorable role or a quirky thought—often decide your first name.

Sivaji Ganesan was born Chinnaiahpillai Ganesan, but he happened to portray the Maratha warrior Shivaji in a popular play and was rechristened as Sivaji Ganesan. Gemini Ganesan earned his first name because of his association with the Gemini Studios, where he made his entry into filmdom as a casting manager.

In the present day, there is a theatre actor by the name of Crazy Mohan. In the music circles, there is Bombay Jayashri, a respected Carnatic vocalist, and Malgudi

Shubha, a popular singer. Malgudi, as far as I know, is a fictitious town invented by the writer R.K. Narayan; I hope to meet Shubha someday to ask her how she came to be named after a non-existent place. Though there is indeed a place called Lalgudi near Tiruchirapalli. The famous Carnatic violinist Lalgudi Jayaraman hails from there.

Priya Selvaraj, the granddaughter of Gemini Ganesan, is in the club this evening because she has come to see actress Saroja Devi, who happens to be passing through Chennai and is spending the night at the club. For the uninitiated, Saroja Devi, in her heyday in the 1960s, was as popular in the south as Hema Malini and Rekha, put together, were in the north during the subsequent decades. She paired with the reigning idols of the time, including M.G. Ramachandran, the hysteria-generating superstar who first noticed her in a Madras studio in 1957 and instantly stamped her passport to immortality. She had then barely stepped into her teens.

Priya, who has come with a friend, gushes about her meeting with the yesteryear heartthrob. For her it was an emotional reunion with the 'aunty' she had known since childhood. Her grandfather paired with Saroja Devi in many landmark films. I ask Priya if she could take us to her. It is 10.30 at night now—not exactly the time an elderly actress would like to entertain a fresh set of guests. But Priya makes a call.

Though a part of me is eager to meet the actress, there is another part that secretly hopes the actress refuses to meet us because I am not even carrying a pen, leave alone a notebook. Moreover, I have just begun to enjoy my drink. Unfortunately, we are summoned to her room right away. Fortunately, my wife fishes out a small notebook and a pen from her bag.

Saroja Devi is at first startled to find a male among the visitors trooping into her room at that hour, but graciously motions me to take a seat. She is already in bed, in a nightie, the bedcover pulled up to her chin. A pair of brown Bata chappals sits under the bed. Priya's friend, in order to help me begin the interview, asks her, 'Aunty, which are the Hindi films that you have done?'

Saroja Devi, instead of answering, starts singing, very softly:

Teri pyaari pyaari surat ko, kisi ki nazar na lage, chashme baddoor;
  Mukhde ko chhupa lo aanchal mein, kahin meri nazar na lage, chashme baddoor...

I am taken aback. This is a landmark Mohammed Rafi song from a movie called *Sasural*, filmed on Rajendra Kumar, one of the most saleable stars of the 1960s. I suddenly remember watching an interview of the celebrated lyricist Hasrat Jaipuri many years ago, when he explained how he got the first line of the song after grappling with words for several days, or perhaps weeks. Hasrat's wife had just delivered a baby, and she would always put a black *tika*—or a smudge—on its forehead to ward off *nazar*, the evil eye. One day, when Hasrat Jaipuri was admiring the child, its forehead bearing the protective marking, the lines occurred to him:

Teri pyaari pyaari surat ko, kisi ki nazar na lage, chashme baddoor—May evil glances not fall on your lovely face, may God ward them off.

So all along, I had known everything about the song—the film, the hero, the lyricist, the composer, and how it came to be written. But what I did not know, until only now, is that the 'lovely face' celebrated in the song belonged to the woman who is now ensconced in bed right in front of me. Today she is lovely and graceful in a grandmotherly way—Saroja Devi is close to seventy now—but her face retains a youthful charm that belies her age.

Saroja Devi was only twelve, still studying in a school in Bangalore, when she made her debut in Kannada films after being spotted by a filmmaker at a function where she happened to sing. The film became a hit, and more offers came in. But she did not want to be an actress.

'I did not want to come into the film industry. I wanted to study. I wanted to become a teacher. But my mother told me, "So many girls are waiting to become film stars, but you didn't even have to try." But I was not interested at all. I told her, "Amma, I don't want to work".'

But the mother had her way.

Saroja Devi would come to Madras to shoot the films and return to Bangalore. After every visit to Madras, where not only all south Indian but also many of the Hindi films of that era were shot, she would tell her mother that she had had enough and that she would like to continue her studies and become a teacher. The mother would have none of it.

In 1957, Saroja Devi was in a Madras studio to shoot for yet another Kannada film when M.G. Ramachandran happened to walk into the sets. He had been shooting on another floor of the studio. 'He kept looking at me and then asked me if I wanted to have coffee. I said no. After he left, I asked people, "Who is this man?" They told me, "You don't know? He is MGR." I said, "Oh, *he* is MGR!"

'He then went and told others, the producers, "There is one girl, very cute, why don't you take her?" But those days everybody was scared of signing a new face, that too as heroine. At the same time they could not say no to MGR. He understood their predicament. So he himself produced and directed a movie. Bhanumathi *amma* (a top star of the time) was there in it, and he took me as the second heroine. The film was called *Nadodi Mannan*. Part of it is in black and white, and part of it in colour. When my character enters, the film becomes colour. I play the queen of an island, Queen Rathna. MGR plays a double role. Today you can do so many trick shots, but those days a double role was not a joke. MGR was a great, great, great man. Really a great man. I was so nervous during the shooting. But he put me at ease. In the film I am smiling most of the time, smiling like a child.'

Nadodi Mannan became a huge hit, making Saroja Devi a star. In 2006, fifty years after it was made, the film was re-released in a couple of several theatres in Chennai and ran for fifty days, drawing mostly young crowds. But back then, Saroja Devi was not even aware that she had become a star. She never got the chance to mingle with the public to discover her new-found status. She was always in the shadow of her mother like a young, obedient south Indian girl of those days. In fact, once the film was completed, she had asked her mother to take her back to Bangalore so that she could pursue her ambition of becoming a teacher.

'My mother asked me, "Why do you want to become a teacher?" I told her that was my idea of doing something for society. She told me, "When you have fame and money, you can do a lot more for society." Then I thought I should become a big star,' says Saroja Devi.

She was soon cast opposite Gemini Ganesan, and Sivaji Ganesan as well, and overnight she became the top heroine in the Tamil film industry. Most of MGR's films that met with dizzying success, such as *Anbe Vaa* and *Enga Veetu Pillai*, have her playing the female lead.

Enga Veetu Pillai was a remake of *Ramadu Bheemadu*, a Telugu film starring yet another south Indian idol, N.T. Rama Rao. *Ramadu Bheemadu*, in turn, was inspired by *The Corsican Brothers*, the 1941 film based on Alexander Dumas's story of that name. We are all too familiar with the Indianised version of the story. At least half-a-dozen remakes have been made in Hindi alone over the decades: twins separated at birth and growing up in different circumstances; one living amid the riches that legitimately belong to him but who has been terrorised by the villain into being timid and slave-like, the other a good-natured ruffian who has been brought up on the streets. By a twist of fate they happen to swap places, and the swashbuckling brother lands up in the palatial house where he sorts out, in style, the very people who had been ill-treating his twin brother. Eventually, the twins are united and live happily ever after.

Ramadu Bheemadu came in 1964, *Enga Veetu Pillai* in 1965, and the first Hindi version, Dilip Kumar's *Ram Aur Shyam*, in 1967. All three were huge hits, all three produced by the legendary B. Nagi Reddi, and all three directed by a former army telegraphist, Tapi Chanakya, who delivered quite a few hits in the 1960s but was so grossly overshadowed by the stars he directed that not many are familiar with his name today.

Of the three, it was the Tamil version of the film that had the maximum impact on the audience targeted. *Enga Veetu Pillai* went on to alter Tamil Nadu's destiny. The native audience, already in awe of the swashbuckling, fair-skinned MGR, now saw him as the messiah who could deliver them from their woes just like he had done for the oppressed in the film. His image as the future leader was bolstered by similar saviour roles he played subsequently, and by the time he became chief minister in 1977, he seemed so infallible that he was never voted out of power until he died in 1987.

The high point of the film is the high-pitched, racy song, *Naan aanai ittal*, in which MGR cracks the whip—literally—on the evil characters and embraces the ones who had been oppressed. The image of a whip-cracking MGR still stirs emotions. Recently, when a contestant chose to sing the song during a karaoke contest at the same club where I am sitting now, a middle-aged man from the audience pulled out his belt and, brandishing it like a whip, took to the dance floor. For the next few minutes he danced and lashed around in a frenzy, as others watched him from a prudent distance. 'That's what they call belting out a song,' the DJ remarked, once the song had ended.

It is past eleven now, but the walk down memory lane has made Saroja Devi come alive. She drops no hint that we should leave now because it is late, though I am expecting it any moment, considering she had already changed and was in bed when we showed up. She is childlike now, bubbling with memories. The TV in her room is on, the volume muted, and what a coincidence: a channel is showing *Padagotti*, another of her hugely popular films with MGR.

'If you go to a temple and pray to God,' says Saroja Devi, 'it will take a while before God answers your prayers. But if you went to MGR and asked for something, he would get it for you in one minute. Not even one minute, but in one second. Such a great man he was. Whatever promises he made to the people through his films, he kept them when he became the chief minister.' Saroja Devi played the rich girl in most of MGR's films. The costumes she wore in them became a fashion statement in that era. 'Those days we were very dignified when it came to clothes. We wore dresses that covered the full body. There was no vulgarity,' she tells us.

I ask her to compare the three giants she worked with—MGR, Sivaji Ganesan and Gemini Ganesan. How different was each from the other?

'Gemini was a jolly person. I had never seen him get angry, not even for a second. He would always teach me, teach me, teach me. But as soon as the director said, "Action!" he would forget his own lines. I would laugh, and he would tell me, "Amma, what to do! Because of you I keep forgetting my lines." Sivaji used to breathe acting. For him, life was only about cinema, about acting, about the script. MGR was an all-rounder. He wanted to know about every aspect of filmmaking, from direction to camera to editing to music. Those days as many as twenty-eight departments were involved in the making of a film, and MGR wanted to know about them all.'

I ask Saroja Devi about Jayalalithaa, MGR's latter-day heroine and political successor. 'Jayalalithaa was a very talented actress,' she says. 'If the director said two steps she would only take two steps. She scrupulously followed whatever the director said. With me she was friendly. I have got great respect for her. She became the chief minister in a man's world, that too succeeding a man like MGR. So many problems came her way, but she faced them in a very dignified manner.'

Saroja Devi was interested in neither politics nor the men she worked with. She was, in fact, one of the very few in the industry who was not romantically linked to any of the heroes she was paired with. 'Nobody saw me as a bad woman,' she tells me. 'They all wanted to marry me. That was a great thing. I was so lucky.'

'Great thing', 'lucky': not because they wanted to marry her, but because they considered her marriage-worthy and not mistress material. She, of course, said no to them because the men worth marrying were already married. Moreover, there was her mother, watchful as ever.

'My mother had told me very clearly that I should not fall in love with anybody. I belong to the Gounder community, and my mother had told me, "You can only marry someone from the Gounder community." So they found a boy for me. He was working as an engineer with Siemens in Germany.

'My mother used to decide everything, you see. Even after I became a star, I had to take permission from my mother for everything. Suppose if I wanted to go to Priya's house (she points at Priya Selvaraj), I had to ask my mother and she would also come along. Those days, even though we were stars, we did not tell producers we want this food or that food. Sivaji and MGR would get food from their homes in big tiffin boxes. We would all eat together. My food mostly came from Sivaji's home. Gemini, I remember, would go home for lunch and return by two o' clock. Those days there was hardly any traffic, it would hardly take him ten minutes to reach home.'

Saroja Devi: the 'rich girl', the big star, the style icon who fans wanted to touch to see if she was for real. But in reality she was an obedient daughter, an obedient actor and, eventually, an obedient wife. She got married in 1967, and with her husband's permission, continued to work in films for a while, mostly wrapping up the projects she had been signed up for. In 1972, she finally returned to Bangalore, the city she had badly wanted to return to way back in 1957. In those fifteen years, she must have been a reluctant resident of Madras.

'If you want to know about the Madras of those days, you should watch our films. Madras was exactly the way it looks in the films of that time. The LIC building was the tallest in the whole city. The roads were all empty, only one or two cars going past you. It was so wonderful. We used to shoot on the beach, which was also empty.

'Today, Madras has become so crowded. We drove down from Bangalore last evening in a BMW. The BMW, I am sure you know, is a very comfortable car. But I got a headache as soon as we entered Madras. The traffic is so bad. Today, everything has changed. Those days, even in films, there was no vulgarity, no fighting. But can you imagine the same thing happening today? Life has changed. Today if you came to my home as a lone man, I would not allow you in because I wouldn't know who you were. I wouldn't trust you. If you send your child to school, you cannot be sure if the child will come back home safely. Back then, there were no terrorists, no bombs, no fear. During our time, our parents could hit us, even our teachers could hit us. We did not mind. For us, teachers were God. Even parents were God. Today, if the teacher hits a child, the parents will go to the school and hit the teacher.'

After she returned to Bangalore, in 1972, Saroja Devi did a few films every year, most of them in Kannada, her mother tongue. Most of them were mythological films, revolving around gods and goddesses. And the men she had been frequently cast with had become living gods.

Those men are no longer alive. Neither is her husband. In 2009, she returned to Tamil cinema after a gap of twelve years, making an appearance in a film called

Aadhavan, which had current heartthrobs Surya and Nayantara in the lead roles. I ask her what she thinks of the present generation of actresses. 'You see, today the girls are well-educated. They know exactly what they are looking for. During my time, things were different. Before I got married, I had never seen a hundred-rupee note even though I was a star. My mother took care of the money. My job was to act.'

It's not always easy to be the progeny of a highly popular, good-looking actor. Life maybe a bed of roses; but the person who should be sitting on the bed and telling bedtime stories is rarely there. Ask the daughters of Gemini Ganesan, who was hailed by his fans as Kadhal Mannan, or 'king of romance'. He lived up to the image in real life too, siring eight children, including the actress Rekha, with three different women.

The four daughters by his first wife, Alamelu, fondly known as Bobji, grew up under the belief that a father is someone who does not return home at nights. When they were old enough to understand why he went missing at nights, they were caught between the love for a father and the jealousy of having to share him with other sets of children. Love prevailed, but the pangs remained. Today, six years after his death, only fond memories remain.

Rekha, however, always remained bitter. She was the first child of Gemini Ganesan to be born of an extra-marital affair, and he did not acknowledge her for a very long time. Perhaps he was too guilt-ridden since it had been the first time he had strayed from his wife. He had met Rekha's mother, Pushpavalli, during the shooting of his second film. She was the heroine's sister. They fell for each other, but guilt kept tugging at him.

'I even contemplated taking my life,' he writes in his autobiography *Vaazhkai Padagu*, or 'The Boat of Life'. 'When I looked at myself, my body, I imagined it was stained with some indelible ink. Could I wash away my sins if I showered repeatedly? I just couldn't look Bobji in the eye. I resolved never to meet Pushpavalli again.'

But, according to him, Pushpavalli insisted on continuing to meet him and was remarkably unfazed when she became pregnant. He goes on to write, 'She was sure that this was what she wanted. She said she considered herself fortunate to bear our child. I explained to her that I could never be, in practical terms, a father to this child. She was adamant. Pushpavalli's adamant decision to have the child turned out to be Bollywood's gain.'

An emotionally fragile woman might have even considered taking her life after reading these lines, just the way her father had when she was about to be conceived. But the weak-hearted don't rise up the ladder in the Hindi film industry on their own steam and manage to stay there. Moreover, the autobiography came out in 2002, when a lot of water had flowed under the bridges of the lives of the people concerned. It didn't matter anymore. But in spite of his guilt, and reluctance to accept Rekha as his daughter, Gemini Ganesan went on to father another child with Pushpavalli just a year after Rekha was born.

Rekha, who also contributed a piece for the autobiography along with the seven other children of Gemini Ganesan, does not hide her bitterness about his absence from her life. 'I have lived with my father all my life, in awe of him, appreciating his achievements—but only mentally,' she writes. 'I have never known Appa as a father in the conventional sense. So we never had a father-daughter relationship—seeing each other every day, chatting, sharing ideas. My encounters with him have been fleeting. I have never sat with him for a long time and had a normal conversation.'

The autobiography contains many touching scenes that describe the torment his innocent daughters, borne by different mothers, went through while at school. They all studied in Church Park on Mount Road.

One afternoon, Narayani, Gemini Ganesan's third daughter from his first wife, was waiting for the car to pick her up as usual when a girl walked up to her and asked, 'Why don't you and your sister go home in the same car?' Narayani, who was in sixth standard then, was taken aback. Her two elder sisters had long passed out of school and her younger sister was still a baby. How could she have another sister?

'You must be mistaken,' Narayani told the girl.

'No way,' the girl argued. 'Come, I will take you to your sister.'

To quote Narayani from the autobiography:

'She led me to the playground where I met Rekha—who is a year younger than I am—for the first time in my life. "Hello," I began, in a faltering voice, "what is your name?"

"Bhanurekha Ganesan," she replied.

'I stared at her confident, huge, mascara-lined eyes. "What is your father's name?" I enquired politely.

'"Gemini Ganesan," she declared.

'"Huh? But that can't be, he is *my* father," I protested, my eyes filling up with tears.

'"Go ask your grandma," she said, moving away.'

Rekha's own account of her childhood is equally touching. During an Independence Day celebration at the school, Gemini Ganesan, a big star by then, was invited to be the chief guest. Rekha and her younger sister Radha were dolled up by their mother and taken to school so that they could see their father distributing sweets. They watched him only from a distance. The father would not have liked to recognise them, or be recognised by them, in public.

Distance: the word was to define Rekha's relationship with her father till the very end. Although, once she had become a star, Gemini Ganesan would taunt his other daughters, asking them if they could ever be as famous as her. In 1979, Rekha was in Madras to shoot for a Tamil film with Kamal Hassan. She eventually quit the project because she was said to be unhappy about Sridevi, the upcoming sensation, getting a bigger role. Had Rekha stayed on, it would have gone down in history as the only Tamil film she acted in. It was during that visit to Madras that she went to see her father. The meeting was arranged at the initiative of Kamal Hassan, and this was the first time that the father and the daughter ever sat face to face.

But distances, once they are established at a very tender age, are difficult to demolish. After all, in spite of having her biological—and famous—father living in the same city, she grew up in a fatherless home. Of what use now the acknowledgement of paternity when the tables had turned? He was now an ageing star, while her ascent to superstardom had just begun. Rekha saw her father for the last time barely a month before he died. It was a chance meeting. She had come down to Apollo Hospitals to inaugurate a wellness clinic, and Gemini Ganesan happened to be admitted in the hospital at the time. She did not return for the funeral.

However, Gemini Ganesan's relationship with the two children from the third woman in his life—the legendary, national award-winning Telugu actress Savithri—was cordial. That was because he married Savithri and set up a nest with her, unlike in the case of Rekha's mother Pushpavalli.

Savithri was in a different league: she was as successful as he, if not more, and the Tamil films they did together became huge hits. From reel-life they became a real-life couple and moved into a rented house in Abhiramapuram. The year was 1956, the rent ₹ 400. Savithri soon bought two plots of land in T. Nagar and Gemini Ganesan personally supervised the construction of their new nest. During the same time, he also built a sprawling house in Nungambakkam where he would live with his first wife and her daughters. He effortlessly shuttled between the legitimate home and the other.

Under the Hindu Marriage Act, a man can't be legally married to more than one woman at the same time. The illegality of their marriage troubled Savithri. She realised she would always be the other woman. Cracks began to appear in their relationship, even though Gemini Ganesan was a doting father to their children. Savithri eventually shut the door on him and took to the bottle in an excessive way, dying a horrible death at the age of forty-four, a skeleton when taken for cremation. Their son, who was still young, was brought by Gemini to his legitimate house. He was looked after by his first wife Bobji, who emerges through the Gemini saga as a saintlike woman who had been born with inexhaustible reserves of tolerance and magnanimity.

Or maybe she didn't have a choice. She was a simple dusky-complected girl whom Gemini Ganesan had married only because her father had promised to fund his dream of becoming a doctor.

Gemini Ganesan was only twenty and still studying in Madras Christian College when he got married. But destiny had other plans: Bobji's father, sister and sister's husband died within months of their marriage. His dreams of becoming a doctor were crushed. Burdened with looking after a family and armed with a science degree, the young graduate set out looking for a job, eventually landing up at Gemini Studios (the Park Hotel stands in its place). The studio was to give him a new name—he was Ramaswamy Ganesan until then—and fame. Tamil cinema's King of Romance was born.

Gemini Ganesan was good-looking, spoke and wrote near-impeccable English—an evidence of education—was a sportsman, had a philosophical bent of mind, and, above all, was a celebrated actor who kept his hands clean of politics. All the ingredients that draw women. While MGR was the hero you worshipped and Sivaji Ganesan the actor you were in awe of, Gemini Ganesan was the man you wanted by your side if you were a woman.

Rumours abound about more affairs other than the publicised ones. Then, at seventy-eight, he had a whimsical marriage to a woman from Bangalore who was half his age. The two moved to a rented house—a case of history repeating itself. But now he was too old and too much of an alcoholic to start a nest all over again. Also, his daughters were no longer the children who thought a father was a man who did not come home at nights. They were in dignified professions, in respectable positions: they were not going to allow him to cause them embarrassment.

Before long, he found himself admitted to G.G. Hospital, which he had built for his gynaecologist daughter Kamala. That was the end of his relationship with the Bangalore woman. Gemini Ganesan eventually died at home, at the age of eighty-five. His first wife and their children were by his side—just the way it would have been for an ordinary family man.

■ ■ ■

The most famous of Gemini Ganesan's daughters in Chennai is Kamala Selvaraj, who put together the autobiography by goading him and all his children to write. She is a pioneer in the field of fertility. In 1990, she commissioned south India's first test-tube baby, and since then has been the most sought-after gynaecologist in the city. Besides her daughter, her husband and son are doctors too.

At the G.G. Hospital, the number of abbreviations that accompany their names on the brass plates is as dizzying as the crowd that arrives every morning. Women with protruding bellies, women with not-so-protruding bellies and, above all, women who desperately want protruding bellies. They are mostly accompanied by their husbands: some look hassled, some proud. I am the free bird here, flitting around the hospital as I wait for Kamala Selvaraj to arrive. I look at the various notices taped to the walls: most of them warn attendants of summary dismissal if they are found demanding or accepting tips from women who have just delivered. One notice announces a vacancy for the post of 'cleaning lady'—a term easily understood in Chennai where they hesitate to use the word 'sweeper'—to take care of the Ganesha temple on the hospital premises.

It suddenly occurs to me that the hospital is so aptly named, G.G., after India's most fertile film star. I can't think of any other popular actor who has fathered eight children. A member of the staff, who spots me loitering and knows why I am there, shows me into a room. 'Dr Kamala Selvaraj will see you soon,' she says and shuts the door.

Five minutes later, Kamala Selvaraj walks in. Her face is resplendent with good health. She is wearing a traditional south Indian saree and looks every bit a kind mother rather than a hotshot doctor who helps women become mothers. But as she settles down to talk, she transforms into a daughter and I can see her eyes travelling back to the time when she wore skirts. Our chat gets briefly interrupted on four occasions: twice when an attendant walks in to get papers signed, and twice when she breaks down while recalling certain memories of her father.

'My daddy was born in Pudukottai. He was a very energetic man, terrifically handsome, and very literate. In Pudukottai he used to read under street lamps, and he had read everything. Just about everything. He could lecture you about the *Ramayana* and *Mahabharata* the whole day. If you asked him to talk about nothing, he could talk about nothing the whole day. I was born in Trichy, and in 1948 or '49 we came to Madras—me, my elder sister and my mother. I was about five years old. My daddy had already become an actor.

'We lived in a house in Thirumoorthy Nagar [in Numgambakkam. She lives on the same location now but in a new house]. There were three houses in a row on one side of the road, and three houses on the other. That's it. Maybe one house here, one there. Nothing else. It was all paddy fields. Nungambakkam High Road used to be deserted. It had only Gemini Studios and the Income Tax office. Only one car would pass every two or three hours. If you were murdered, you wouldn't be discovered for hours, or not be discovered at all. We would walk to the school.

'My sister and I studied in Vidyodaya School near Valluvar Kottam. Today there is a park near the school, but in those days it was a lake. It was a Tamil-medium school at that time. When I was in the sixth standard, they were planning to make it English-medium from the next year. But my daddy was at the height of his fame and wanted us to study in Church Park Presentation Convent instead. The principal of the Tamil-medium school pleaded with my daddy not to take us away, but he insisted.

'We would walk to Church Park, or take a cycle-rickshaw. On the road hawkers sold fresh vegetables. The air was fresh, there was no noise. There were no phone calls at home, no TV. We grew up in innocent times.

'Even in Church Park, we had no airs about being Mr Gemini Ganesan's daughters. We used to mix with everybody. That's because my parents also had no airs. They never spoke ill of anybody, there was no gossip at home. If my father had so many marriages, we never knew about it. My mother kept it all to herself and my daddy made sure we never saw the newspapers. When we saw his movies as children, we would think he had gone inside the screen. We would start crying and ask him to come out. He would pat us, saying, "I'm here, I'm here." It took us quite a while to know what cinema is.

'We had a nun in Church Park, a plump woman with rosy cheeks. She would always carry chocolates for us. She would ask me, "So how is your daddy? Is he behaving himself? Tell him to come and see me if he does any mischief." She was so sweet. It was very nice to study in Church Park. It was a different experience.

'Today, I feel children are missing out on the joy of growing up. We used to only play. Rarely, when he was not busy, my daddy gave tuitions in maths. Otherwise, none of us were asked to study, none of us took tuitions. We had a very pleasant, very happy, very healthy childhood. We knew to respect elders. My mother would always say, always respect anyone elder to you. Even today, when a patient is accompanied by a person who is older than me, I stand up. We did not learn to say no to our parents. Whatever dress my mother gave us, we wore it. We were so innocent, life was so uncomplicated. Today, the children revolt, they retort, they talk back. It is shocking. We were not brought up like that.

'Gemini Studios was full of gardens. We had gone there only a few times. My daddy was determined to keep us away from cinema. S.S. Vasan (the owner of Gemini Studios) was related to us and he did not want my daddy to enter movies because he was an educated man. That is why he offered him the job of casting officer. My daddy spotted so many talents. He was the one who discovered Kamal Hassan and the singer S.P. Balasubrahmanyan. Then my daddy left Gemini Studios and joined Narayanan and Company, which signed him on as an actor.

'In 1955 the company gave him a used Ford car, which I recently got restored. In that car we would go to the beach. We played in the sand while he talked to a producer or a director. The beach would be almost empty. Only one or two people. And the sand absolutely pure. On the drive back home we would stop at the Woodlands Drive-in and have ice cream and Chicklets.

'And once, daddy took all of us to Kashmir. He was shooting for a film with Vyjayanthimala. The entire family, the entire crew went. We went in a Dakota, and as soon as we saw the snow-capped mountains we ran to the windows to have a good look. We stayed there for one whole month.

'One day, when we were in Church Park, he came to the school and told us, "Amma, if somebody asks you anything about me, just say you don't know." I think it had come out in the papers that he had married Savithri. We were twelve or thirteen years old, and we really did not know anything. We didn't even know that daddies slept at home at nights. Once, Narayani was playing with our neighbour, a boy called Ravi, who said, "Aiyyo, it's late, I have to go now or else my daddy will scold me." Narayani was surprised. She asked him, "Oh, your daddy sleeps in your house?" My daddy was not sleeping at home. He would be with Savithri. But we were too innocent to know all this. Also, it did not make any difference in our lives.

'He was a very kind father. We never knew anything for so many years. My mother brought us up so well, character-wise, behaviour-wise. Everything seemed normal, nothing was known in the house. Pushpavalli, Rekha's mother, was very nice. We liked her more than my mother. She would stitch silk skirts and send them to us; she would send us jasmine every day. Savithri was also very nice to us. We liked these women more than our own mother. They gave us love and affection which our mother could not give because she was going through her own problems. She had her frustrations which she could not show to anybody. She would vent her anger on us. But we did not understand it then. But she was extremely fond of my daddy, because she was fifteen and my daddy was twenty when they got married, and they lived together till she was eighty and he was eighty-five.

'She was very protective of him, and could not bear it if the children said anything against their father. She lived for him and for us. She was magnanimous to Pushpavalli and Savithri. People worshipped her. She is a model for an

Indian woman. I must write a book on her someday. But I don't blame my daddy. He was very handsome. Everybody wanted to marry him. At least, he was open about it. He did not hide anything. And he was the best father one could have ever had.

'My daddy would say the only dignified professions for women were teaching and medicine. When my elder sister and I finished school, he asked us whether we wanted to get married or study. Both of us said we would like to study medicine. We did not want to be teachers.

'But we are Brahmins, and in those days, forward communities were not getting seats in government medical colleges. They were giving admissions only to backward classes. My daddy happened to meet one Mr Shetty from Manipal medical college. It was sheer destiny that he happened to meet him. Mr Shetty asked him to bring us to Manipal. The capitation fee was ₹ 11,000 per seat. My daddy had a Herald car and it was driven down to Manipal for our use. One night, some engineering students stole the car and then met with an accident and abandoned the car on the site. The principal of their college wanted to expel them but my daddy said no. He was a very magnanimous person. When my elder sister and I got back from the medical college with MBBS degrees, my daddy was proud but he teased us, "Do you know Rekha has earned a name in her profession and is making lakhs of rupees? What are you two going to do?"

'I resolved that I would do so well in my chosen field that one day my daddy would say with pride, "This is my daughter, Kamala." It did happen when I held south India's first test-tube baby in my arms.

'When we came to know about daddy's relationships, I don't think it made any difference to us. As I told you, he was the best father one could ever have. But we did have some hostile feelings towards Vijaya and Sathish (Savithri's children), because no one likes to share their father. As for Rekha and her sister Radha, we had no contact with them. Rekha must have had her own grievances. Look at her situation: her father does not own her, then she becomes famous and the father owns her. If she had not become famous we would have never known who she was.

'As I matured, I realised, they are all innocent. It is not their fault for being born. So when my son got married about ten years ago, I invited them all to the wedding. Now, we talk on the phone frequently, meet frequently. There are no hard feelings. They don't have parents, I don't have parents. Only we are there for each other. During my son's wedding, my daddy saw everybody together and happy. He died peacefully.'

Chapter

7

CHANDAMAMA AND MADRAS MISCELLANY

I must have been eight, maybe nine, when I wrote my first job application. It was a five-paisa postcard addressed to the editor of the children's magazine *Chandamama*, enquiring if it needed artists.

I could sketch well. That was one talent I was born with, which invariably got me the first prize in drawing competitions but which was never honed professionally. My parents, like most parents, wanted me to follow the time-honoured route: study hard, get into an engineering college, land a decent job, get married, produce kids, and finally take care of them—the parents.

It was the standard middle-class trajectory: the suggestion of any deviation was met with scorn or cynicism. So drawing, unless it was related to academics, was considered a waste of time—at best, a good pastime.

But it was my ambition, at the time, to be an artist for *Chandamama*. I could not comprehend the stories entirely on my own: they had to be explained either by my mother or father. But to admire the illustrations I required no help. That was my area. I would spend hours looking at the pictures, studying the lines and trying to copy them. The first thing I would instinctively look out for was the name of the artist—signed legibly enough to be deciphered by an eight-year-old. I had my biases: I admired some artists more than the others. My favourite was Sankar. Most of the illustrations I liked in *Chandamama* bore his signature. I found his works very real-life. I wanted to draw like him. I wanted to be him. The editor, of course, never replied to my letter.

It was Sankar who drew the pictures for the popular 'Tales of King Vikram and Vetala' series. It was also he who created the signature image for the series, showing the sword-wielding King Vikram walking through a cremation ground in the dead of the night with a corpse on his shoulder. Even as he walks, the king looks behind for a moment, as if someone has called out to him—that's the pose in which Sankar had captured the king. For me, as a child, this image was the ultimate symbol of bravery. I would look at it every now and then—at times at the fearless expression of the king, at times at the skulls strewn in the cremation ground, at times at the bats and the dangerous snake, and at times at the name of the artist, 'Sankar', which was signed over a grey rock for easy visibility.

So: yet another childhood connection with Madras. This one was direct—my first ever official correspondence was addressed to Chandamama Buildings, Vadapalani, Madras. Then the years rolled on and *Chandamama* got archived along with my childhood.

Then, about a quarter-century later, in 2007, I set out looking for its offices. I had come to know that the magazine was completing sixty years—the occasion merited a story because, for generations of people, *Chandamama* and childhood had gone hand in hand.

The offices were no longer in Vadapalani, but in a quiet neighbourhood in Guindy. A few minutes into the conversation with the editor and I mentioned to him what a great fan of Sankar I used to be. I wanted to enquire about the artist but feared that the reply would be heartbreaking. But a surprise awaited me.

'Sankar is still there,' the editor smiled. 'He must be over eighty now. You see, at *Chandamama* we don't retire people.'

The editor—an extremely soft-spoken man called Viswanatha Reddi, whose name appeared in the printline as Viswam—was himself sixty-three then, technically past retirement age. But owners don't need to retire. It was Viswam's father, the legendary film producer B. Nagi Reddi, who started *Chandamama*, and Viswam has been in the editor's seat since 1975. So I was now face to face with the man I had written to as a nine-year-old, asking for the job of an artist.

Chandamama is a month older than Independent India. The first editions came out in July 1947—in Telugu and Tamil. The founding editor was a writer called Chakrapani, who had earned a literary reputation of sorts for translating Sarat Chandra Chatterjee's stories from Bengali into Telugu.

Chakrapani had taught himself Bengali while recovering from tuberculosis at the Madanapalle sanatorium, where the patient in the next bed happened to be a Bengali.

Nagi Reddi ran a printing press in George Town, and in 1945 had started a Telugu monthly, *Andhra Jyothi*. In the glow of the freedom movement, he also started a youth magazine called *Yuva*. It was for *Yuva* that he first teamed up with Chakrapani, and they took forward their association to start *Chandamama*.

Chandamama was an instant success. The first edition, priced at six annas, sold six thousand copies, and for a very long time the circulation stood at that figure. Apart from editing *Chandamama*, Chakrapani also wrote stories and dialogues for many of the Telugu and Tamil films produced by Nagi Reddi who, by 1949, had acquired the Vahini Studios in Madras after its owner ran into tax problems. 'The idea behind starting *Chandamama* was to introduce the post-Independence child to Indian culture and tradition. Even today, we stick to the Indian ethos,' said Viswam, who became the editor when Chakrapani died in 1975.

By then, the magazine had become a household name across the country, being published in as many as twelve languages. The English edition had begun in 1955. The magazine's popularity peaked in the early 1980s when its combined circulation touched nine lakh. This was also the period when Nagi Reddi's reputation in Bombay as a producer of movies that promised clean, wholesome entertainment was at its pinnacle. He had given Hindi cinema memorable films such as *Ram Aur Shyam*, *Ghar Ghar Ki Kahani*, *Julie*, *Swarg Narak* and *Swayamvar*.

But in 1980, Nagi Reddi's eldest son Prasad, who helped him in the film business, died. Nagi Reddi went into depression. Sanjeev Kumar, who had acted in *Swarg Narak* and *Swayamvar*, sought to bring him back to his element by successfully persuading him to make another film, *Shriman Shrimati*. I distinctly remember seeing advertisements for this film in the pages of *Chandamama*: they were a welcome distraction from the illustrations of numerous kings and queens, gods and sages.

'Sanjeev Kumar was a great support to my father. We were planning to ask him to take over our movie business, but he died suddenly,' Viswam told me.

The movie-making business was now part of family lore, just like a story from *Chandamama*: once upon a time there was a producer called Nagi Reddi. *Chandamama*, too, had almost become history. In the mid-1990s, labour problems began to brew in the press at Vadapalani, where the magazine was headquartered for decades. A scuffle between workers and a supervisor spun so much out of control that publication had to be suspended in May 1998.

'It was the most painful decision of my life. I could have done much better in life had I not taken up *Chandamama*, but it was a passion for me,' said Viswam. Adding to the labour trouble was a dispute within the family, which Viswam gently put as a 'conflict between ideologies of the second and the third generation'. The patriarch, Nagi Reddi, meanwhile lay immobile in his Vadapalani home, having suffered a stroke. Publication remained suspended for more than a year until two investment bankers, who had an emotional attachment to the magazine, came to its rescue.

So from a new, modest office in Guindy, Viswam started all over again. 'Once you shut down a publication, it is not easy to come back. But by November 1999 we managed to print in all the twelve languages and I presented the first set to my father on his birthday on 1st December. That was the happiest day of my life.'

The magazine's circulation was six lakh when it shut down, but when it was revived, it could sell barely two lakh copies.

'For sixty years we survived on sheer goodwill. We never promoted ourselves. And we will continue to survive on goodwill,' Viswam said with a sad smile that was accompanied by a nod indicating the interview was over.

I asked him if I could meet Sankar. Viswam picked up the intercom and made enquiries. 'I am sorry, he hasn't come in today. These days he comes in only thrice a week. After all, he is over eighty now. You will have to come some other day,' Viswam told me. As a parting gift, he handed me some recent issues of *Chandamama*.

On the way back home, I browsed through them. The 'Tales of King Vikram and Vetala' series was still alive—the trademark image of the king carrying the corpse on his back intact. I regretted not having been able to meet Sankar.

Soon, *Chandamama* and Sankar were once again forgotten.

■ ■ ■

Three years later, in early 2010, I got the news that *Chandamama* had been taken over by Geodesic, a Mumbai-based firm that made telecom software. So Viswam had given in to the conflict between the second and the third generations of his family and finally sold the magazine. The patriarch, Nagi Reddi, had died in 2004, never recovering from the debilitating stroke.

The offices shifted once again, this time to Neelankarai on the East Coast Road, where the rich of Chennai own beach houses. I called up the new office asking to meet the new editor. I was asked to contact the head office in Mumbai. I enquired if Sankar was still around. Yes, he was. Could I come and see him at least? No sir—I was politely told—you will have to get permission from the Mumbai office.

When I called up the Mumbai office, a young female voice at first regarded my call with some suspicion and then asked me to email the questions I would like to ask the editor. I did as told. She called back, this time sounding warm, and said the editor would be glad to meet me and answer my questions the next time he travelled to Chennai—which was to be in a few days' time. And yes, I could meet Sankar too.

One rainy afternoon, I travelled to Neelankarai to keep my appointment with the new editor, Prashant Mulekar. I showed up a few minutes early and was asked to wait in the conference room. A member of the editorial staff stopped by to ask if I wanted tea or coffee. I asked her if I could meet Sankar instead.

'I am so sorry, sir,' she said. My heart stopped for a moment. 'This morning we were coming here together in the office van. Sankar sir was very excited that you were coming to see him. He had read your previous article on *Chandamama*. But he suddenly fainted in the van and we had to take him to the hospital. The doctor said there is nothing to worry but he needs to take complete rest.'

'Can I see him at home sometime? Can I have his number?' I asked.

'Yes sir, but not now. He needs to take rest.'

'But can I have his number?'

An office boy came to say that Prashant Mulekar was ready to see me. As I climbed up the stairs, I decided I was not going to like him. Only three years ago I had such a cordial meeting with Viswam, and now I had to go through several phone calls and emails to get an audience with the editor. How can the warmth and the charm of the world peopled by kings and queens and sages be corporatised? At the same time, it occurred to me that this man had saved *Chandamama* from folding up and thus rescued a pillar of my childhood from crumbling. Shouldn't I instead be grateful to him?

The first thing I noticed about Mulekar was the pair of Mont Blanc pens sticking out of his shirt pocket. I liked him instantly. Men who are particular about their pens are usually meticulous about their jobs. Mulekar, forty-five, is not a professional editor. He is a techie-cum-MBA—the ultimate cocktail of qualifications an Indian student aspires to acquire—who can fit into any industry. He is the executive director of Geodesic, the software company he set up with friends; the editorship of *Chandamama* is an additional hat he is wearing, with seeming ease.

'The magazine is not only a strong brand but also has a strong brand recall,' Mulekar told me. 'That's what makes us determined to take it back to its glory days. We cannot compete with television and internet, but we can always complement them.'

Today *Chandamama* comes out in thirteen languages, including Santhali, the tribal language; and has a combined circulation short of two-and-a-half lakh—a pathetic figure compared to what it was twenty-five years ago. But just look at it another way: the fact that the magazine sells so many copies—in the age of television and internet—shows how deeply rooted its reputation is. And having been in the story-telling business for nearly sixty-five years now, *Chandamama* has built a volume of archives that no channel or magazine can match. It is this rich library that the new management is banking on.

'But we don't want to restrict it to print media alone. We are also on internet now. *Chandamama* is now available online in as many as six languages. The number of hits may not be very high at the moment, but we are getting there slowly. Since we can't stop change, why not be a part of it?' he said.

Change is not something you can easily associate with *Chandamama*. Insulation from change has been its forte: all along it has been an island peopled by temperamental gods and goddesses, duty-bound kings and brooding queens, valiant princes and pretty princesses, benign sages and benevolent hermits, friendly ghosts and moustachioed demons, simple-hearted villagers who lived in huts and travelled in bullock-carts. Innocence was the name of the island. But in the wake of satellite television and internet striking at the very roots of the two hallmarks of *Chandamama*—insulation and innocence—the magazine is adapting to change by becoming more informative and interactive.

But there is one employee of *Chandamama* who has remained immune to change. His life remains just the way it was in 1952, when he joined the magazine as an artist. Today, Sankar is eighty-seven but he continues to draw pictures depicting the timeless era of the gods and the goddesses, the kings and the queens. He now works out of home, though, ever since, a few months ago, he fell into a faint one morning in the staff van while on the way to office—the very day I was supposed to meet him at the *Chandamama* office.

'I suddenly saw a wall of light in front of me,' Sankar describes what happened that morning when I—finally—

succeed in meeting him at his home in Virugambakkam. 'I remember telling myself, "Oh Muruga! What is this! There are no clouds, then why this lightning?" The next thing I remember is the women (his colleagues in the van) sprinkling water on my face. They told me I had passed out.'

They took him to a hospital where the doctor, after keeping him under observation for a day, pronounced that he was in good health—except that he now had to take it easy and also eat more frequently but in small quantities rather than two heavy meals a day. In fact, the first thing you will notice about Sankar is that he is as portly as a priest: well-fed, fair-complexioned and healthy enough to look several years younger.

Arthritis, however, has taken its toll. He finds it difficult to walk, and his fingers, which have been drawing incessantly for more than half a century, are now gnarled. But the deformity has not interfered with his art.

For some inexplicable reason, I had always imagined Sankar to be tall, dark, lean, shy and withdrawn. But the Sankar I am meeting now turns out to be good-natured and garrulous in a very childlike way—he is very much the brand ambassador of the innocent era he portrays in his sketches.

Sankar and his wife today live alone on a quiet street in Virugambakkam. Two of his sons and a daughter also live in the city, while two other sons live abroad—one in Canada and another in Malaysia.

'Do you like the juice?' he enquires about the mango-flavoured drink which his wife has just brought me.

'Yes, sir.'

'Oh, very good, very good. Is it too chilled?'

'No, perfectly fine.'

'Oh, very good, very good.'
'Are you comfortable where you are sitting?'
'Absolutely.'
'Oh, very good, very good.'
And so the interview begins.

Sankar, or K.C. Sivasankaran, was born in 1924 in a village called Karatholuvu near Coimbatore. His father was a teacher in the local school. In 1934, when his aunt's husband living in Madras died, Sankar along with his mother and siblings moved to the city to live with the bereaved lady.

'My elder brother was already in Madras, studying in Pachaiyappa's College. My father told my mother that he would join us in Madras in a few months and asked her to put us in a corporation school in the meantime so that we would not be idle. Corporation schools did not charge any fees. So she took me and my younger brother to the corporation school in Broadway. There, as a test, we were asked to write the sentence, *George V is our king.* I immediately wrote it,' he tells me with great delight, his hand depicting the swift movement of pen on paper.

'I had beautiful handwriting. I was admitted to the fifth standard and my brother to the third. Because of my handwriting, the teachers always made me write the daily proverb on the notice board—this went on till high school. And because of my conduct, I was made the class monitor within ten days of joining school.

'I had a tough time managing the class. I was only ten years old, while there were some boys in my class who were fourteen or fifteen. They were from the fisherfolk community who had joined the school mainly for the free mid-day meals.

'Every day at eleven o' clock a van would come, and as soon as it entered the school the smell of sambhar would spread. Beautiful smell! The rice was also wonderful. Hot rice, sambhar and a vegetable dish: that's what we would have. I tell you, sir, those were wonderful days.'

Since it was a primary school, only up to the fifth standard, he could spend just a year there. 'My teacher, a Christian woman, wept when I left school,' he tells me.

After that he went to Mangadu Yellappa Chetty School on Linghi Chetty Street, and in 1939 joined the nearby Muthialpet Higher Secondary School on Thambu Chetty Street. All these schools were in George Town, where most of middle-class Madras lived back then.

It was at the Muthialpet High Secondary School, where Nagi Reddi had also studied some years before him, that the drawing teacher, a man called Veeraraghavachari, discovered Sankar's potential as an artist. The teacher would often make Sankar come by on Sundays, and together they would correct the sketches made by the other boys.

'The teacher would be waiting for me with a pile of drawing books. He would say, "See this! I asked them to draw a cat but it looks like a rat. What if the inspector of schools comes tomorrow? We will get a black mark." In return he would give me drawing books, pencils and erasers, which he got from the school. "Train yourself," he would tell me. Then one day he told me, "Son, do not go for BA or MA. I know your worth. You must join the arts college."'

Sankar took his advice and after finishing SSLC in 1942, went to seek admission in the government arts college in Egmore—the oldest art institution in the country, set up in 1850. When he met the clerk and showed him some of his drawings, the clerk was far from impressed.

'The clerk said, "Dozens of people like you come every day. Do you think they all get admission? You will have to take an exam." The exam was a three-week assignment: first week for drawing human figures, second week for table-top drawing—they would place objects on a table and ask us to copy, and the third week for outdoor sketches. They took the best from each week's work and assessed you on the basis of that.'

Sankar's elder brother, who had accompanied him to the arts college, had meanwhile got hold of an advertisement by Rajkamal, the studio started by the legendary filmmaker V. Shantaram in Bombay, which was inviting applications from young candidates for courses in the fields of art direction, cinematography and sound recording. The selected candidates were to be absorbed by Rajkamal after completion of their course.

'But I told my brother that I first wanted to try for admission in the arts college. If it didn't work out, I could consider going to Bombay. I told my brother that no way was I going to be demoralised by the remarks of a clerk. So I decided to take the exam. I was confident,' says Sankar.

For the outdoor sketch, the young Sankar chose to capture a sight that particularly struck him in Guindy where a hillock had just been flattened and labourers were carrying away the debris. There he saw, under a tree, a labourer rocking his child on a makeshift hammock and the wife squatting on the ground and preparing a meal. Using the silhouette of the labourers at work as the background, Sankar depicted the young couple and their child. As he worked on this picture, the paint-brush refused to cooperate with Sankar: it was not giving him the strokes he desired. But the effect that obstinate brush produced on paper surprised the principal, the legendary Bengali sculptor Debi Prasad Roy Chowdhury.

'He asked me, "Where did you learn the pen and knife treatment?" I just kept quiet. Silence, as they say, is golden. In my mind I asked: "What pen? What knife? What treatment?" He gave me ninety marks for that drawing and I was straightaway admitted to the second year,' Sankar gives out a joyous laugh.

All this while, Sankar had been living with his family in George Town on Thambu Chetty Street; his father had joined them as well, having taken retirement from the village school and making a living by giving tuitions. In 1942, however, when Sankar was in his final year at school, George Town nearly emptied out because of the fear of bombing by the Japanese. In fact, it was the government that had advised the citizens to evacuate, causing widespread panic in the city. Patients ran away from hospitals; animals in the zoo were killed as a precautionary measure just in case a bomb attack freed them from their cages; businesses shut down; residents either abandoned their houses or sold them at throwaway prices and hurried to their native towns and villages. The Japanese planes never came, but the few weeks of panic had altered countless lives.

Sankar's family too moved to a relative's house in Tiruchirapalli. Sankar, who was about to complete his SSLC, stayed back along with an uncle, who was a foreman at the Egmore railway station, and his elder brother, who was now the manager of the Bata showroom in Triplicane. The three of them moved to a rented accommodation in the nearby Linghi Chetty Street.

'There was hardly anybody in George Town during that period; the servants were enjoying the houses like anything,' recalls Sankar.

By the time he joined the arts college that very year, the family returned from Tiruchirapalli and this time took up a house in Mylapore.

'From Mylapore I would take the tram to college. Those days there were hardly any buses, only trams and rickshaws. I would take the tram from Luz in Mylapore and get down at Central station and from there take another tram to Egmore. A monthly pass cost only two rupees.

'The monthly college fee was also two rupees. Those days we had three scholarships: the Chettiar Scholarship, only for Chettiar students; Dr Rangachari Scholarship, which was only for Brahmin students; and Victoria Scholarship, which was open to all. The Victoria Scholarship was most coveted, because it carried a stipend of fifteen rupees a month. Rangachari Scholarship carried twelve rupees, and the Chettiar one I can't remember how much.

'You see, the Rangachari Scholarship, even though it was for Brahmins' —Sankar suddenly lowers his voice for a moment even though no one is listening—'first preference was given to Iyengars. In the fourth year of the course, one fellow called C. Ramaswamy and I, both stood first. Since he was an Iyengar, and me an Iyer, he was automatically entitled to the Rangachari Scholarship, whereas I should have got the Victoria Scholarship. But he wanted the Victoria Scholarship because it carried fifteen rupees. He complained to the teacher that since he had spent more number of years in the college—I had directly joined second year—he was entitled to the fifteen-rupee scholarship. The teacher somehow convinced him to settle for the Rangachari Scholarship.

'Eventually, Ramaswamy and I became best friends— *best* friends! He was appointed as art master in King George's School in Bangalore. Once, while visiting

Bangalore, I went to see him. He took me to his classroom and proudly introduced me to his students, "Do you know who this is? He is Sankar, who draws for your *Chandamama*." Such a great man, such a great man.'

But *Chandamama* was not Sankar's first job.

At the arts college, it was common for students to have their lunch at a nearby park. They would carry their works as well to the park for display. During his final year at college, in 1946, Sankar had painted a young Krishna surrounded by dancing gopikas. The work was on display in the park when it happened to be noticed by the chief artist of the Tamil magazine *Kalaimagal*—a man called Kumaraswamy. Since Sankar was not on the spot at the time, Kumaraswamy left a note with a fellow student asking Sankar to come and see him.

And so Sankar got his first job, on a monthly salary of ₹ 85. 'I can only be grateful to God. Right from the moment I left college until this day, I have never been unemployed—even for a day,' he says. 'Do you want biscuits?'

'No, I'm fine.'

'Oh, very good, very good.'

By 1952, Sankar was earning ₹ 150 a month, but that wasn't sufficient to support a large family. He had begun moonlighting for smaller Tamil magazines—such contributions were called 'piecework'. That year, one afternoon, the advertisement manager of *Chandamama*, a man called Venkataraghavachari, happened to drop by at the *Kalaimagal* office. He told Kumaraswamy, the chief artist, that Nagi Reddi was looking for good artists for *Chandamama*.

'Kumaraswamy looked at me and said, "Why don't you go and meet Nagi Reddi? You can do some piecework for them." So, soon after, I went to the *Chandamama* office in Vadapalani, where Venkataraghavachari took me to Nagi Reddi's room. Chakrapani was there too. I had carried my specimens from *Kalaimagal*. Nagi Reddi was very much impressed. He asked me to join his magazine. I told him, "Sir, I thought I was going to do only piecework for you." He said, "No, join us full-time." I said, "Sir, I can't do that without my chief artist's permission." He said, "Okay, go ask him. Once you have made up your mind, get back to me."

'I came back to Kumaraswamy and told him about Nagi Reddi's offer. He asked me, "How much are you getting here?" I said, "₹ 150." He asked me, "And how much are you making on the side, "Another ₹ 150, sir." Kumaraswamy said, "That makes it ₹ 300. Alright, ask Nagi Reddi to give you ₹ 350. If he agrees, you join them." Kumaraswamy said this because he wanted to retain me; he was sure Nagi Reddi would not pay so much to a young artist.'

But miracle of miracles, Nagi Reddi hired Sankar at ₹ 350 a month. On paper, though, his salary was shown as ₹ 300 because Chithra, the chief artist of *Chandamama*, was drawing ₹ 350. The editor of *Kalaimagal*, after overcoming his initial anger, ordered a warm send-off ceremony for Sankar. Money was collected. The farewell took place at the nearby Sanskrit College in Mylapore. Sankar was presented with a silver lamp and a vermillion container; the remaining money was spent on treating the staff to dinner.

This was December 1952. Since then—it is nearly sixty years now—Sankar has stayed with *Chandamama*.

Chithra and Sankar began as rivals but went on to become—in Sankar's words again—*best* friends. Nagi

Reddi, the wise proprietor, would often seek to defuse the rivalry by saying, 'Chithra and Sankar are the two bulls of *Chandamama*. Unless there is coordination between the two, the bullock-cart won't reach the village in one piece.'

Today Sankar has nothing but admiration for Chithra. 'He was a self-taught artist. No arts college, no training, nothing. He was a salesman with Oxford University Press but used to do piecework for Tamil publications. What maturity in his lines—just like a draftsman's! Nagi Reddi and Chakrapani went to his home in Triplicane and hired him. He joined *Chandamama* in 1946, the same time I joined *Kalaimagal*.'

Chithra, twelve years elder to Sankar, died of a peptic ulcer in 1979. His two other contemporaries, Razi and Vapa, are also no more. Today, since the magazine has become larger in format, Sankar is often called upon to expand on the illustrations in the archives that may have been drawn by him or one of his late colleagues thirty or forty years ago. For example, if a particular king or sage had been shown only down to the waist, Sankar is asked to add the legs and feet to the old image to suit the new requirement. This is something that cannot be done graphically on a computer—the lines drawn by the computer are far too impersonal to evoke devotion in the reader. Imagine the pictures of the various gods and goddess hanging in your home being computer-generated—would they still be worship-worthy? Not quite. It is the devotion of an artist—to his art and to God—that makes you hang a garland around the framed portrait of Shiva or Krishna.

The devotion he inspired through his art remains Sankar's greatest treasure. He has heard many stories about the effect his lines have had on readers—stories that keep him warm at eighty-seven. A woman in Kerala would walk five miles every month to the nearest library just to get hold of the latest issue of *Chandamama*. An elderly woman in Andhra Pradesh enrolled for adult education classes so that she could read the stories accompanying Sankar's drawings. A man from Karnataka, an ardent devotee of Lord Krishna, happened to be travelling by train on the day of Janmashtami, so he got down at a station, bought a copy of *Chandamama* and offered bananas to Sankar's Krishna. A shepherd boy from Orissa was so possessive of his copy of *Chandamama* that he would roll and insert it in a piece of bamboo he carried: his sole dream in life was to be able to draw like Sankar and Chithra. Then there is me, who wanted a job in *Chandamama* at the age of eight. At least I have now got to meet my childhood hero.

Sankar himself considers it a miracle that he is still around and drawing. 'My life is a series of miracles, sir. Getting the Victoria Scholarship was a miracle. Getting an appointment letter even before I could leave college was a miracle. Meeting Nagi Reddi was a miracle. That I continue to draw even today is also a miracle. God has been guiding me all along, or else how could an ordinary person like me have managed to stay around this long?'

■ ■ ■

'Did you speak to S. Muthiah?'

I've lost count of the number of times this question was put to me by well-wishers once they learned I was doing this book.

In Chennai, you don't ask back, 'S. Muthiah who?' Its English-speaking population knows him as the historian who has been educating them about the city's heritage for the past eleven years through his weekly column in *The Hindu* called 'Madras Miscellany'.

Then there is *Madras Musings*, a paper reaching out to readers who request it, which he started two decades ago. Even though small in size and circulation, it showed, to those who cared to see, the path leading to the rich past. Till then, the path had remained hidden by shrubs and bushes of ignorance and indifference. Muthiah's modest journal managed to nudge the local newspapers out of their obsession with politics into looking at the goldmine of stories that lay in their own backyard. Not to mention the definitive *Madras Rediscovered*, first published in 1981 and which keeps expanding with every reprint—it counts among the thirty-plus books that he has either authored, co-authored, ghosted or edited so far.

If it is Madras, it has to be Muthiah. So I rang the bell at his house in Teynampet one Sunday morning even before a word of my manuscript was written—it was like smashing a coconut or visiting a temple for the blessings of the goddess before beginning a venture.

I found Subbiah Muthiah sitting at the head of his dining table, under the glow of a reading lamp whose peeling paint was testimony to its long years of loyal service. The table was laden with books, files, bunches of papers—they seemed to have been sitting there untouched for months. Right in front of him, where his lunch was soon to be served, lay a small heap of manuscripts. They were all articles on Chennai, written by various people in various fonts and type sizes, meant for publication in *Madras Musings*.

One of the first things Muthiah, a recipient of the MBE from the Queen of England, told me was that he doesn't like the tag of historian: 'I *never* call myself a historian. I am a chronicler.' The man who carefully weighs every word he writes—he still types his *Hindu* column on a portable Olivetti—knows best. Nevertheless, the title sticks. Newspapers, when quoting him, always call him a historian and perhaps they always will. He is, after all, linked eternally with the chronicles of Madras.

But how many in Madras—as he likes to still call the city—know the history of Muthiah? Who is this man, after all, who has taken it upon himself to illuminate the bridge that connects the past and present of Madras? How many in Madras will know that Colombo is the city he loves the most and remains emotionally connected to, and that in 1968 he nearly became a citizen of Sri Lanka? Wouldn't it be only fair for someone to chronicle the life of the chronicler?

And so I go back again, this time on a Sunday evening. He has just returned from his walk in the grounds of the Madras Club. As usual, he is sitting at the head of the dining table that continues to groan under the weight of the written word.

'Would you like to have a drink?' he asks me. I decline at first—more out of the Indian instinct to not drink in the presence of an elderly person whom you know. 'Are you sure?' he asks, 'because I am going to have one'. Muthiah gets up and from a cabinet pulls out two glasses and a bottle whose label I am unable to read. He pours the drinks and returns to his seat. I take a sip: it is brandy.

The 'historian' begins to tell his history.

Muthiah comes from Kanadukathan, one of the seventy-five villages in southern Tamil Nadu that constitute the region known as Chettinad, home to the Nattukottai Chettiars. Like all Chettiar families, his was a traditional business family with interests in Ceylon, Burma, Vietnam,

Sumatra and Singapore. Traditionally, among Chettiars, education was largely confined to the hands-on training in finance that one received while working in family concerns. But in the early twentieth century, several Chettiars began to look toward Western education. Many of them sent their children to Ceylon, because the standard of English education there was streets ahead of that in India.

'My father, M. Subbiah, went there to study when he was nine. He was educated there, made friends there, and decided that he was going to settle there as well. He started with stockbroking and then took over a large German engineering and agency house which handled all German goods before the Second World War. The businesses overseas were financing, agriculture and land-lordship.

'In the mid-1930s he got involved in politics; he was three times deputy mayor of Colombo and acted as mayor several times during this period. He founded the Ceylon Indian Congress—which is now the Democratic Workers Congress—representing Indian workers' interests, especially on the plantations. He was very active on the political scene; he knew everybody in the Sri Lankan political setup.

'After he got married, he brought my mother to Ceylon. This must have been around 1928. We have this tradition of women coming back to their parents' homes for childbirth, so I was born in Chettinad, in 1930.

'I was taken to Colombo when I was three months old. I grew up there and went to St Thomas's Preparatory School. You see, in Colombo, there were a dozen leading schools, but the two best-known ones were Royal College and St Thomas's College. These were like Eton and Harrow, and the rivalries were also like that, especially in sports.

'St Thomas's College effectively started from the First Form—that is Sixth Standard—onwards. There was an

Englishman, W.T. Keble, who taught at the college and who started St Thomas's Preparatory School in 1938 as a feeder to it. I was one of the first forty pupils to join Prep. I joined in the Third Standard, I think. I was eight years old at the time.

'Keble was the single biggest influence in my life. He was an amazing man, and all of us who went through that school went on to become well-rounded persons—who spoke and wrote English well, were widely read, well-informed on a whole range of subjects, and passionate about sport. All this because of one man: Keble.

'The first thing he did was to start a library, and fill it with popular fiction for boys. He had a very simple theory which to this day I advocate: get a child interested in reading *anything*—comic books, popular fiction, adventure stories, you name it. Once a child gets interested in reading it will carry on reading, even the serious stuff.

'The other thing he did was to start a magazine which he wanted us to bring out every month. He did that within three months of the school starting and insisted that everybody write for it. And the prize was that the two or three stories that he thought were the best would appear in—he would ensure that—in the children's pages of Colombo's newspapers. In those days, there used to be a regular children's page in every newspaper. I was eight years old when I started writing and getting published in a newspaper.

'During my last year in Prep, in 1941, he wrote a book called *Ceylon: Beaten Track*, in which he told Ceylon's history through places in Ceylon and the stories connected with them. So you learnt about Anuradhapura through stories connected to Anuradhapura, you learnt about Kandy through stories connected to Kandy. It is a fascinating book, still a classic, still being reprinted. When I look at my *Madras Rediscovered*, I begin to realise how much that book has enabled my writing style and the kind of things I do in terms of writing. If someone reads *Ceylon: Beaten Track* and *Madras Rediscovered*, they would think both authors had some connection.

'Those three years in the preparatory school made a considerable impact on my life—and it lasts to this day. Normally, I should have got into St Thomas's College given the connection and toppers' scholarship, but the college was way out of town. More importantly, it insisted that you learn swimming, and I hated the water. So I went to Royal, which did not insist on swimming.

'Royal College had excellent teachers, but only one person made a difference in my life, a person called Basil Mendis. He was a young man just out of university and had been looking for a job, when he came to his old college to teach. He taught me English for a year. He was an inspiring English teacher, and again played a major role in my writing. He went on to become a priest. The interesting aspect was that his father was the biggest branded arrack manufacturer in Ceylon—the family is still in the business.

'In 1944, the educational policy in Ceylon changed. C.W.W. Kannangara, the education minister, made education free—from kindergarten through university and started up educationally elite schools in every district. The only flaw in his plan was, you had to do your education in your mother tongue. And English became a second language.'

Since Muthiah didn't want to go into Sinhala or Tamil streams, he left Ceylon in 1944. His parents remained there. He went to a school called Montfort in Yercaud, where he did Senior Cambridge and the Anglo-Indian School Certificate. In Ceylon, together with the language policy, they had also stopped the Senior Cambridge exam, which he took in Montfort because his father was determined that he go abroad to study.

'I passed out in early 1945. Montfort was an interesting experience. This was the first time I was in boarding school, that, too, one which was almost entirely Anglo-Indian. The first thing I did was to take up smoking. I wound up smoking sixty cigarettes a day before I gave it up in the early 1960s.

'Father was determined that I become an engineer. And those days, when parents told you something, you didn't say no. He wanted me to go to America. He and a friend were the first Chettiars to go round the world. During a trip in the 1930s, as representatives of the Indian Chambers of Commerce overseas to the International Chambers of Commerce Convention, he was greatly impressed with America, even though those were the Depression years. I hated the idea of going there because I did not want to do engineering. Fortunately, I couldn't get a passport because I was under sixteen.

'So I joined Lawrence College in Murree, near Rawalpindi, to do my Intermediate. The college, again almost wholly Anglo-Indian, came under Punjab University; it was the only university at the time that allowed you to do your Intermediate in one year if you got through your Senior Cambridge in first class.

'Murree was a typical hill station. I had my first drink there. It had a famous brewery, run by a Parsi family. With three girls' schools around, there were lots of dances. Lots of lovely Anglo-Indian girls. Lot of cafes were there, too. We went out on weekends and had bacon and eggs, sausages and stringy steak, or wonderful seekh kabab and lassi on the road into Kashmir.

'I would come from Colombo to Madras by train—one had to take the ferry in-between. From Madras I took the Bombay Mail to get to Bombay. And from Bombay I would take the Northwest Frontier Express to Rawalpindi. Then by road to Murree. I would spend six days on the train.

Muthiah's father's close friend, Oliver Goonetilleke, who went on to become the first Ceylonese governor-general of Ceylon, was very keen that the young Muthiah get into Oxford or Cambridge. That was the Ceylonese tradition: people there never looked at America. Goonetilleke was in London when Muthiah finished his Intermediate, and he asked Muthiah to come over. But both Cambridge and Oxford said they were full with people coming back from the war. As he marked time in England, Muthiah applied to American universities. One of them was the Massachusetts Institute of Technology, which wrote back saying they were full but they could get him a seat in Worcester Polytechnic Institute. So he wound up in Worcester, forty miles from Boston. This was in 1946.

'Until then, I would come to Madras on annual holidays. My father was into racing, and he would bring his horses here during the racing season, in winter. He wouldn't take me to the races, but there was a cousin of his of whom I was very fond, and he would take me all around Madras. We would watch the Pongal Test matches at the Chepauk, something I never missed at one time; we would go to the English cinemas; have ice cream at Jaffars; eat junk food on the Marina.

'My childhood experience of the Marina was a fearful one. We had a family friend living at San Thome, whose back gate opened onto the beach. They had three children about my age. We had gone out through the back gate and were playing on the beach and since I was the smallest of the lot, they decided to dig a hole in the sand and put me in, burying me up to my neck. Then they ran back to the house. It soon got dark and I began screaming my head off, but there was nobody around. They had completely forgotten that they had left me behind. Everybody was frantically looking for me. Finally I was found by a fisherman. But yes, Madras was a lovely city then, wide open. Half of it was paddy fields.

'At Worcester Polytechnic, I scraped through. But it was a great experience, because after the War, America passed the GI Bill of Education, under which every soldier would get free university education. The development of America today is due to this scheme. Till that time, education was a privilege. Because of this bill, people who came from the boondocks had the opportunity for education. There were only a few of us straight out of high school; the war veterans were much older than us. They had fought for two or three years. Many of them were married and had children. So if you formed friendships, you grew up very rapidly, looking after their babies and changing nappies. All that became a part of your life even while you were just sixteen.'

At Worcester, Muthiah wrote for the campus newspaper—eventually becoming its editor—and was also into athletics, running spring and winter track and cross-country for the college—he ran in Madison Square Garden and Boston Garden. In 1948, when he came to Colombo during the summer break, he wrote six articles on American life for the *Times of Ceylon*, then edited by Frank Moraes. That was his formal beginning in journalism.

Muthiah then went on to study international affairs at the Clark University in Worcester, after which he did his masters in international relations from Columbia University. He was working on his doctorate in international relations when, in 1951, he had to go back for his sister's wedding. That's when a citizenship issue cropped up.

'I had gone abroad as a British subject and had been living right through this period in America as a British-Ceylonese passport-holder. But when I came back, Britain and Ceylon had become two separate countries. The first thing Ceylon did was to confiscate my passport at the airport.

'I was entitled to Indian citizenship because I was born in Chettinad. But since I was brought up in Ceylon and had all my friends there, I was not interested in coming to India. Now, going back to America was also out of the question without a passport. I was stranded and stateless.

'Ceylon had, by then, enacted very strict citizenship laws, particularly aimed against people of Indian descent. My father, meanwhile, had applied for an Indian passport, even though he held a permanent resident permit for Ceylon. I did not apply for one—I had no interest in going to India. And with no possibility of going back to America to finish my doctorate, I joined the *Times of Ceylon*, which got me a permanent resident permit.

'When I joined *Times of Ceylon* in 1951, Tori de Souza was the editor. He was from a very old Goan family settled in Ceylon. His father had been a famous journalist who had gone to jail for advocating freedom. I was the only one with a degree in the whole editorial department. Tori had only done his Intermediate. His assistant editor, Francis Ashborn, who was my boss in the features department, was a Senior Cambridge pass. Yet they were so well-read. The Ceylon education system had been so good then that they were better than any graduate today.

'My learning in America was nothing compared to what they knew about the world. This is why I always say a degree means nothing, because the people who taught me at *The Times* were far superior in their knowledge and abilities than I was. Even today, I never ask anybody: Do you have a degree?

'Since I was desperate for a job, I joined as a features sub-editor for a hundred rupees a month. The normal starting salary was about three hundred at that time. Within six months they remembered the fact that I had a degree in international affairs and made me foreign news editor. My salary jumped up to ₹ 350. I was able to buy a car. I was foreign news editor from 1952 till '54. That was the time I, beyond being foreign news editor, got involved in writing and stringing for the London papers—first the *News Chronicle*, and then, when it folded up, the *Daily Mail*.

'In 1956 Solomon Bandaranaike came to power and the first communal riots broke out. The paper was mostly staffed by Burghers. A Burgher is the Ceylonese equivalent of the Anglo-Indian. A large number of Burghers left at this time. A lot of them left due to the new language policy because they realised that jobs later were going to depend on their knowledge of Sinhalese or Tamil.'

By then, Muthiah had already been placed in charge of features, all the supplements and also the *Sunday Times*. And after Ashborn emigrated in 1956, he also took over *The Times of Ceylon* Annual, a glossy publication that featured stories from the sahibs and the planters, and Christmas stories, and ghost stories. It was always meant as a Christmas gift to send home to Britain.

'When I got hold of it, I changed it completely and turned it into an ambassador for Ceylon overseas—in terms of our culture, tourism, heritage, nostalgia. From 1954 to '68, I also wrote a sports column every Sunday, 3,000 words. I never missed a week, unless there was a holiday for the paper. The column was very strong on comment, and if you see people like Sanath Jayasuriya in the Sri Lankan cricket team today, it has much to do with the campaigning I did to get cricket, rugby and other sports to the schools in the rural areas and get them the opportunity to compete with the snobbish elite schools.

'In 1968 I realised I could not become the editor unless I was a Ceylonese citizen. Mrs Bandaranaike was in power then. Her foreign secretary was a man called N.Q. Dias. The Bandaranaikes were friends of the family. Dias was a classmate of my father in school. And the only way to become a Ceylonese citizen at that time was to get distinguished citizenship. Every year twenty-five people were given citizenship at the will and pleasure of the government.

'In the early years the distinguished citizenship was really distinguished citizenship. Later, it became one of these things where all sorts of brokers became distinguished citizens by filling the party's coffers. But they still had one or two genuine candidates every year, like a nun who had put in thirty years of service or an old school teacher who had taught the prime minister. My name came up in 1968; by then I was fairly well known as a journalist. My papers were lying on Dias' table. I was fairly certain of getting a citizenship.

'Unfortunately, the government fell. When Dudley Senanayake came to power the first thing he did was to abolish distinguished citizenship, saying it was a corrupt practice.

'When you are young, you are ambitious. You want to run a newspaper. But now I was left with no alternative. I had to either stay No. 2 in the paper forever, or look for a job outside the island.

'So I came to India, went to the *Statesman* in Calcutta and *Times of India* in Bombay. I got offers from both. But my parents said both places were farther than Colombo. *The Hindu* had its own policies of recruitment, even though we were friends with *The Hindu* family. Ramnath Goenka's *Indian Express*, on the other hand, offered a pittance. The TTK group, at the time, had just begun a plant to produce maps, atlases and tourist literature. They had set up a large printing press in Pallavaram with German collaboration. (TTK was an agency house started in 1928 by T.T. Krishnamachari, who went on to hold several major portfolios—including industry, commerce and finance—in Jawaharlal Nehru's Cabinet. The group is now known for manufacturing Woodward's gripe water, Prestige pressure cookers and Kohinoor condoms). My father knew the TTK family well. They made me an offer to head the editorial section of TT Maps, a collaboration with a leading German publishing house.'

And so began Muthiah's Madras story.

'Within three months of my joining, the German who was the cartography specialist, and headed the company, decided to leave. T.T. Narasimhan and T.T. Vasu asked me to run the new firm. There I was, never having run a business in my life, with no knowledge of cartography which was the main line of business, no knowledge of Madras to get business. I learnt all about cartography, all about business, all about Madras.

'Once we were settled in 1971, we decided to bring out a map of Madras, and that's when I began reading up about the city to write some text to go with the map. Three or four people had written slim, sketchy books about Madras and they were my source.

'It was while reading these books that I came across four names which made a big difference: Robert Clive, Arthur Wellesley, Warren Hastings and Elihu Yale. They were all passing references, but people who had started their careers in Madras and went on to fame, fortune or notoriety. These were people we learned about as part of Indian history, but to discover that all these characters started their careers in Madras—that got me hooked.

'So I began reading, not so much about Madras but about people connected with Madras. In those days, access to archives was easy, not like today. Libraries were better organised. I discovered a whole lot of things. So many people who started their careers in Madras made such a big difference to modern India!

'Sometime in the early '70s, Abraham Eraly, a lecturer at Madras Christian College, was doing the house journal for MRF to make some extra money. Since he was living in Tambaram and the closest good press to him was ours, he came to us for printing. In the course of time we became good friends. I told Eraly that there was nothing about Madras in the local newspapers, which were obsessed with national politics, so why not start a magazine on the city itself. I told him I would help him with editorial material.

'So there started *Aside*, the first city magazine in India. An excellent magazine even if I say so myself. We had a fine crop of writers; most of them had been my students at the Bharatiya Vidya Bhavan. In 1971 I had started teaching journalism at the Bhavan, which had just started the first journalism course in Madras. I found that by adopting a conversational manner of teaching I got on well with the class. Since I had grown up in a journalism school which was an office where informality reigned and you could sit on the editor's desk and smoke a cigarette and call him by his first name, interacting with students was not difficult. I began to love teaching. In some ways I was catalytic in getting students to look at journalism differently, the way I had learnt it—focussing on the arts, entertainment, human interest stories, which are all now part of your dailies.

'In *Aside* I started writing a column called *Once Upon a City*, in which I put in all this stuff I was reading about Madras—stories about Clive, about Hastings, about buildings. That was really how people began to recognise me as somebody interested in Madras. *Aside* went on for several years. Then Eraly made the mistake everybody makes. Here he had a very good magazine, liked by all his readers and therefore supported by well-wishers in terms of advertising. But he wanted a larger audience and began featuring stories from all over south India. It became more and more a political magazine. It no longer got the advertising support it was getting earlier. He finally sold it to Sivanthi Adityan of the *Dina Thanthi*. Eventually, the magazine closed down. During the first ten years or so, it was a great magazine.'

The *Once Upon a City* column earned Muthiah a place on the panel of EPOCH or the Society for Environmental Protection and Conservation of the Historical, a heritage NGO set up way back in 1978. Much later, in the mid-1980s, he was also invited to be on the panel of INTACH—the Indian National Trust for Art and Cultural Heritage.

But the turning point, as far as Muthiah securing his reputation as the Madras Man is concerned, came in 1981.

By then, he had gathered plenty of material about the colonial history of Madras. Also by then, he happened to become friends with K.S. Padmanabhan, a partner in the Delhi-based publishing house Affiliated East West Press, which brought out scientific and technical textbooks.

Affiliated East West Press was set up in 1961 as an Indian arm of D Van Nostrand, the American publishing house. In 1974, Padmanabhan, who had lived in all other metros except Madras, happened to pay a visit to the city and he liked it so much that he decided to set up a branch of the company in Madras. His friendship with Muthiah, whom he first met in Delhi, went on to grow. When Affiliated East West Press decided to diversify into general books, Muthiah's *Madras Discovered* became one of the first to be published by it, in 1981—a slim volume, priced at ten rupees.

Much later, in the mid-1990s, Padmanabhan amicably separated from the parent company and started his own publishing house, East West Books (Madras), the predecessor of Westland Ltd., which owns the Tranquebar, Westland and EastWest Books imprints. In July 2011, Padmanabhan, aged seventy-five, formally retired from the business of publishing to play with his grandson.

On the other hand there is Muthiah, the Colombo-hardened journalist now known as the Madras Man, who shows no signs of slowing down even at eighty-one. *Madras Discovered*, rechristened *Madras Rediscovered* after the 1981 edition, is today not only larger in format but 450 pages thick. It is expected to get heavier when the seventh edition comes out in 2012.

Madras Discovered not only changed Muthiah's life but also changed the way the city looked at its history—a rich one at that. 'Sometime in the late '80s, I was asked to write the history of Parry and Co. for its 200th anniversary. From that time I've been writing one or two books every year—corporate histories, biographies, books on Madras. There have also been books on the Chettiars and on Ceylon.

"Madras Miscellany', the column I write for *The Hindu*, started in 1999. I have never missed one column except when the paper's been on holiday. I belong to an era when we didn't even get a byline. Till I started writing for *Aside*, I never used a byline. It was always a staff reporter or a special correspondent or correspondent or The Corner Flag or something like that. Today you join a paper and tomorrow you get a byline. The first time my picture appeared in a newspaper was with the *Hindu* column.'

'Madras Miscellany' firmly established Muthiah's reputation as the Madras Man. The column made him a household name. If it is Madras, it has to be Muthiah.

'The discoveries I write about in the column or in my books are not original—they cannot be original. There is *always* somebody who already knows, it's just that he does not know the value. For example, when I went looking for the Jewish cemetery after reading about it in the records, I found that it is being looked after by a family in Madras. Obviously, the family did not think this was something that should be publicised or known. And right next to the Jewish cemetery I found a Chinese cemetery, whose existence wasn't even known to most people.

'Today I find Madras overbuilt, congested and dirty and would any day prefer to live in Colombo. But the big question is: would I like to live in the Colombo of today? Most of the friends I grew up with or worked with have passed on or emigrated.'

Muthiah continues to maintain an eight-hour working day. 'Work keeps me going,' he tells me, 'so does the good life'. His two daughters, both Ivy League graduates, live abroad: one lives in California, another in Singapore. He visits them often along with his wife, Valli.

'Fortunately, I have a young and energetic wife. She is a company secretary, who manages the home as well as the finances. She makes sure I don't have to worry about anything other than my work.

'I go for a walk to the Madras Club daily at five. After the walk I sit with a group of men who are over seventy and gossip. Then I return home and have my two drinks. It's a habit I got from my father. He always had two drinks before dinner and lived up to ninety-seven. The only difference is that while he drank only Scotch, I drink only Indian whisky. The best thing about Indian whisky is that no matter what brand you drink, it tastes the same.'

Muthiah is so right about the taste of Indian whisky. All this while I thought I was drinking brandy.

Chapter 8

A SEASIDE STORY

It's three in the afternoon, and Sunanda and I are sitting on the sands of the Marina and gazing at the sea. She is a former colleague, who now lives with her husband in Florida and has travelled to some of the world's best beaches, but she refuses to let go of her Marina-fixation. The sands here, after all, bear the footprints of her growing years. Each time she returns to Chennai, which is once a year, she sets out to retrace those tracks in the sand. Today, she has me for company.

The Marina has often been said to be the second longest beach in the world, but dark clouds of uncertainty hang over the claim. What is certain, however, is that there are no bikinis on the Marina. Try wearing one and you will have a thousand onlookers encircling you in a matter of seconds, and soon a cop would be marching you to the nearest police station. The Marina is not really a beach in the Western sense, where you can go easy with your clothing and let your hair down. It is strictly a place for the masses—a monument, a water park and a picnic spot rolled into one. But that's also true of most public beaches in India.

Three in the afternoon is a bad time to be on the Marina. The sun and the sand can be cruelly hot. But today the sky is overcast and is merging seamlessly with the grey sea. The sea, otherwise furious, looks mellow, as if tired of pushing out the waves, and wanting a day off because the weather is lovely. It's rained in the morning, so the sand is wet and red. We are sitting on the crimson carpet that stretches around us as far as the eye can see. Not too many people around, mostly lovers who are sitting like small self-contained islands in that sea of red. To them, we must also be appearing like one.

'Time pass? Time pass?'

It's the peanut seller, a boy barely fifteen. But the authority with which he parks his basket in front of us is as if he was a cop sticking his lathi into the sand and glowering down at us over his generous paunch.

I wave him away. But he has made up his mind.

'Take, take, time pass, time pass,' he says, handing me a few peanuts.

I say no, but he is insistent. 'No buy, only taste. Take, take. First like, then buy,' he shoves them into my palm.

Sunanda, who is amused, speaks to him in Tamil. I don't understand the language well, but I can gather she is telling him that he is only wasting his time. A brief exchange between them follows. The boy keeps repeating, 'Time pass, time pass.'

Exasperated, he fixes his gaze on me. For a moment I feel inclined to oblige him, just to have him go away. But I do not like the aggressive stance he has adopted: you can sit on the beach only if you buy my peanuts. I wave him away. But he digs in his heels.

We are now eyeball to eyeball. Several seconds pass. The boy stretches out his hand and asks me to return the sample peanuts.

'Give them to him, what are you waiting for?' Sunanda asks.

'But I've already eaten them,' I tell her.

'When did you eat them?'

'While you were talking to him.'

'Why did you eat them?'

'He asked me to!'

'Okay, so what were we talking about? If we start talking, he might just go away.'

Her idea works. The boy eventually leaves, but not before giving me a long hard stare, as if to say he is going to sort me out some other time.

An old woman—a palmist—appears. Unlike the peanut-seller, she halts at a respectable distance and smiles at us genially. She begs us to get our palms read. I decide to indulge her. Normally, I avoid making eye contact with such people for the fear of being fleeced, even though I might be curious about what they have to say. But today I have by my side a Tamil-speaking woman who will not only translate the palmist's predictions but also, hopefully, intervene should a dispute about payment arise.

As I call her over, she breaks into a benign grin and squats in front of us. Her sun-baked face full of wrinkles, her nose blunt and pierced on both sides, her eyes pale and her hair grey—to describe her I would have to pick an antonym for the word 'beauty' and yet, I can't take my eyes off her. There is something very graceful about her as she prays to the small wand she is carrying—perhaps a mobile palmist's accessory—and touches it to our palms. Fifty rupees for each pair of palms—that's the fee we settle for.

'Your bad days are behind you,' she tells me rather confidently as she examines my lines. 'But be wary of your so-called well-wishers. They are casting an evil eye on you all the time.' I straighten my spine and thrust my palms closer to her.

I am quite taken aback by what she has just said, because this is exactly what an astrologer in Delhi had told me very recently. This is not to suggest that I keep running from one palmist or astrologer to another; but in a country like ours, you keep running into them all the time—they don't always have to be a professional astrologer but could be a friend's friend or a colleague's father who reads palms or horoscopes as a hobby. And since in a country like ours life is a constant struggle and is shrouded in uncertainties, it is soothing to the ears when someone predicts with confidence a bright future for you. Even though you may like to take such predictions with a pinch of salt, you feel good, for a moment or two, that life may not be unfair to you after all.

'You are married, correct?' the woman asks me. I nod. 'Your wife is your lady luck. If the worst is behind you, it is because of the luck your wife has brought. Always pamper her with gifts. Buy her gold, buy her a house... you won't lose anything, you will only prosper.' Sunanda is giggling. The woman looks at her and grins.

'But I don't even have that kind of money,' I protest.

'Not to worry, you will have it soon. You will lead a good life,' the woman declares. 'Any specific question you want to ask?'

'Will he be famous?' Sunanda asks on my behalf.

The woman straightens out my palm with her coarse fingers and says thoughtfully, 'Whatever he is doing, he must keep at it. Then he will be famous like a star. But as I said, there are people who are always casting an evil eye on him. He must watch out.'

I am elated, but at the same time, once again, astonished: even the Delhi astrologer had said that my wife was my lady luck. 'She is your Lakshmi,' the astrologer, who appears on a couple of TV channels, had told me. 'If you ever buy any property, buy it in her name. If you buy it in your name, the property will get sold off in no time.'

Two people foretelling the same things—yet look at the disparity in their lives. While one lives luxuriously in a south Delhi bungalow and is a highly sought-after man, charging a thousand rupees for every thirty minutes of audience he grants you, the other trudges the hot sands of the Marina like a beggar woman, seeking to make eye contact with vulnerable souls thronging the beach. Life can be unfair.

The woman then proceeds to read Sunanda's palms. The conversation happens in Tamil, but I can tell that a smooth future is being predicted.

'Hey, not bad!' Sunanda squeals once she is done showing her palms. 'She seems to know everything about me.'

The woman smiles. It's the I-told-you-so smile, but of the kindly, rather endearing, variety. Clutching the hundred-rupee note I hand her, she walks away and fades into the crowd. What surprises me is that not even once did she mistake Sunanda to be my wife or even lover—considering that Marina is teeming with couples who can't think of a better place to be together. She seemed to be acutely aware, without any obvious evidence, that we were two separate people leading separate lives with respective spouses and who just happened to be together on the Marina that afternoon.

Did she really have special powers to gauge that, or had she spent far too many afternoons on the beach watching the chemistry between visiting couples to mistake the nature of the relationship between them?

When we get up and begin our walk back to the road, with some of Chennai's best historical buildings waiting for us on the other end of the long stretch of sand, we discover that we are walking on a bed of used condoms. Maybe they are always there, the used condoms, but hide under the powdery sand. But this afternoon the sand is wet and its secrets now lie bare, to be trampled upon by us.

'What are the condoms doing here?' I wonder aloud.

'As if you don't know!' Sunanda punches my arm.

'But so many of them!'

'Have you ever heard of this saying, "*Kai-ku anju, vai-ku paththu*"?'

'No. What does it mean?'

'It means having five rupees in hand but spending ten rupees on the mouth. Basically, it's means living beyond your means. But in the context of the Marina, it means five rupees for a hand job and ten rupees for a blow job.'

'You seem to know a lot.'

'My husband told me about this. He also grew up in Chennai.'

I start counting the condoms but give up after I have counted one hundred and twenty-three of them. There are far too many of them—the Marina is a sea of used condoms.

'Really, I am wondering,' I think aloud, 'how was the woman so sure we are not married to each other?'

'Even I am wondering,' says Sunanda.

'Maybe because we are behaving ourselves?' I suggest.

'Are we?' she punches my arm again.

■ ■ ■

I first saw the sea at the age of eleven, at Puri. I was fascinated by the entire mechanics of this natural body of water: you just have to wait with joyful anticipation on the sands and a wave will come and drench you, every few seconds! Two black-and-white pictures, taken by a beach photographer stylishly clad in bell-bottoms, still exist as an evidence of that trip: one of me and my younger brother; and another of my father and mother. My mother looks shy as my father grabs her hand to steady her against the wave; she is clearly embarrassed at her hand being held in public and is trying to break away from his grip—that was the precise moment when the photographer took the picture.

That trip was just a trip, not a journey. Puri may be located in Orissa, but the lingua franca of the beach was—and perhaps still is—Bengali. The food we ate in the hotels of Puri was Bengali. The friendly rickshaw-pullers who took us around spoke fluent Bengali. Even though we had come all the way from Kanpur, the town of Puri, culturally, was merely an extension of home.

Twenty years later, as I walked on the Marina on the very day of my arrival in Chennai, I could tell the distinct flavour that permeated its sands. The sensation of the newness came like a splash of cool water on the face: large crowds surging towards the water to play with the waves or just to watch; vendors selling boiled peanuts and sliced raw mango; boys hawking cotton candies; bajjis and fish being fried in stalls; perambulating astrologers offering to tell your future. Above all, the language that was spoken around me: so far, in Delhi and in Kanpur, I had heard Malayalam being spoken, but rarely Tamil. And now it was only Tamil, and not Hindi, all around me. That made me finally realise I was in a new land, that I had travelled, that I had made a journey.

The journey continues even today, though Marina is rarely on the itinerary except when the occasional visiting friend demands to be shown the sea.

There was, however, one trip to Marina that I had planned solely for myself; the idea was to sit by the sea, all alone, and meditate upon life. The trip never materialised, thanks to a prolonged drinking session the night before; if it had, I might not have been alive to write this book. Or perhaps been alive to describe in detail one of the worst tragedies to ever strike mankind.

It was the Christmas of 2004, a Saturday. I had been invited to dinner by a Punjabi couple who had recently opened a restaurant in Nungambakkam. Their business had not picked up even though the restaurant was located in an upscale area, and they wanted me to eat there and write nice things about it. So, after putting the Sunday paper to bed that evening, I took my friend Saju along to the restaurant. On the way, we stopped at a roadside wine shop.

I cannot relish meat unless I've had a few drinks; the alcohol acts as an anaesthetic against the thought of eating flesh. That evening, though, I had some more reasons to drink. One, it was the last weekend of the year and we had managed to put together what we thought was a marvellous Sunday paper that celebrated the year-end mood. Two, in a matter of few hours, at the stroke of midnight, it was going to be my birthday: what better place to ring it in than in the dingy bar of a wine shop—a place where we felt at home and where alcohol nudged us to follow our ambitions. Three, my parents were arriving the next day and since they were going to stay with me for a month, I knew wouldn't be able to drink as often. They were very much aware that I drank, but they certainly didn't deserve to see me drink and smoke in front of them—the dutiful, caring, middle-class parents that they were.

My mother had planned to prepare an elaborate birthday lunch for me upon arrival—she was bringing along home-ground spices and coconut laddoos—but that seemed unlikely now because the train, which was to reach at seven in the morning, had been delayed by several hours due to the dense fog in north India.

So Saju and I drank on, from plastic glasses. And while we drank and talked about the stories that had gone into the paper, I entered into a silent conversation with myself.

'Tomorrow you turn thirty-four,' I heard my own voice telling me, 'and in another year you will be thirty-five. Considering that most men live only up to the age of seventy or so, you are touching the halfway mark, and what do you have to show for it? Not even a book? Why not make a fresh start tomorrow? Wake up early in the morning, have a bath, wear the brown Fab India shirt your boss has given you as birthday gift and go to the beach. Sit on the sands, maybe take a stroll, and give life a serious thought.'

Saju and I had three drinks each before we showed up at the restaurant. It was already past ten. The owner, who had been anxiously calling up to find out how long we would take, was extremely pleased to see us. But instead of showing us to a table, he motioned us into his car parked outside the restaurant. One of the boys brought whisky, chilled soda, roasted paapad and freshly-made chicken tikka into the car.

In Tamil Nadu, an eccentric rule forbids restaurants from serving alcohol unless they happen to be part of a hotel or an inn that has at least twenty guest rooms. If you run a stand-alone restaurant, you cannot serve alcohol to diners. Nobody seems to know the origin of this strange rule and nobody has the courage to challenge, or change it, either. There are several such incomprehensible excise rules that easily make Chennai one of the worst destinations for drinkers on this planet. For some inexplicable reason, you don't even get the regular brands that are available in the rest of the country—or even the world. But hop across to neighbouring Andhra Pradesh, Karnataka or Pondicherry, and you will feel you've entered a duty-free zone.

The car had now become a bar. Even though we badly wanted to eat now, having already had our quota of drinks, our host was in no mood to let us off easily. 'It would be a shame if I did not offer you a drink,' he said. 'Also, I hardly get to drink these days. My wife does not allow me to drink ever since I had bypass surgery. I am so glad you people are here tonight. She can't say no this time.'

The paapad and the chicken tikka disappeared in no time; the boy plied us with more. Behind the glass wall, in the restaurant, I could see the wife directing the waiters to clean up the mess left behind by the last of the guests. At the same time, she had one eye on the car parked outside: was her husband drinking too much?

By the time Saju dropped me home, I was quite drunk. But sober enough to remind myself, before I went to sleep, to wake up early so that I could frame birthday resolutions while sitting on the sands of the Marina. The Marina, after all, is not just the most important landmark of Chennai but also a temple by itself—the sea being the presiding deity, always reminding you that no matter how powerful you may think yourself to be, it considers you no different from the shell of tender coconut lying on the sands.

By the time I woke up, it was around nine. A call from Saju had woken me. He sounded angry.

'Ramesh called me just now. He said the sea is coming in. He asked me to come right away and take pictures,' Saju said. Ramesh worked in a tea-stall very close to the Marina and Saju had happened to befriend him some years ago; he knew about Saju's passion for photography.

'Then why didn't you go?' I asked him.

'All because of you! Something was wrong with the food last night. My stomach is upset. I even got ready and took out my camera, but as soon as I stepped out of home I had to go to the toilet again!'

And I thought he had called to wish me. He hung up. He must have gone back to the toilet. I tried going back to sleep. Suddenly I was reminded of my own promise to begin the day with a trip to the Marina. But it was too late now. Even if I stirred out of bed right now, it would be at least another hour before I could make it to the beach. By then the sun would be too hot. And why hurry myself up? Today all, after, was a Sunday—a holiday, my day off and, above all, my birthday. I was entitled to do things at my own pace.

But soon the calls started coming—the birthday wishes. Each caller, however, had something to say about the strange behaviour of the sea. No one was quite sure what exactly was happening: they had only heard things—things that sounded incredible—from various sources. Whatever they had heard they were now relating to me, in a very casual and dismissive manner, as if it was something meant to cause amusement—just like the story of Ganesha idols drinking milk.

The boss who had given me the brown Fab India shirt told me: 'My maid says the sea is coming to swallow us. By the way, did you feel the tremors?'

A colleague who had always been kind to me said: 'I was planning to drop by with some upma and payasam, but my driver decided to take leave today. He has heard that the sea is coming into the city. He is scared to step out.'

A columnist who lived on the East Coast Road asked: 'Can I do a story about all the fun that's going on? The sea came right up to the road! Hundreds of people have now gathered here to watch. Some tourism it is!'

Something was certainly up—something funny. I decided to check out for myself. I had a quick shower, put on the new shirt and glanced through the Sunday magazine. The cover story—titled *All Things South and Beautiful*—had been written by me; I had explained why I relocated from Delhi to Chennai and why I preferred living in the south.

As a journalist, you may be used to seeing your byline in the newsroom—either on the screen of the designer's computer while he is giving finishing touches to a page or on A3-size printouts while proofing—but a tiny current of excitement always travels down the spine when you spot your name in the finished product when it gets delivered at your doorstep. And that morning, the morning of my birthday, my byline was screaming from the front page of the Sunday magazine. I must have looked smug when I walked up to the road and hailed an autorickshaw to take me to the Marina.

It was a smooth ride, as usual, until we reached the Gemini flyover. There, the long straight road that branches off towards Marina was cordoned off by a rope. Vehicles were not allowed in. I got off the autorickshaw and decided to walk the rest of the way. There were countless people walking along with me towards the beach, and countless others coming from the opposite direction. I felt I was headed for a village fair.

But in spite of the crowds, the road seemed to have been placed on mute mode. The noise was missing, as was the enthusiasm on the people's faces—was it really a fair or the funeral of a famous public figure that I was headed to?

Even though I covered the entire distance on foot, time just flew because I kept getting calls—some were calling to wish me, others to compliment me on the cover story—and before long, I stood face to face with reality. The Marina had disappeared. It had turned into a knee-deep cesspool. And on the railing, from where one began the long walk on the sands in order to reach the sea, was perched a white Ambassador car—that sight alone was sufficient to explain what might have happened. Water had come gushing, with great force, right up to the buildings that line the beach, swallowing the entire Marina in the process and tossing around vehicles parked there.

Even then, very strangely, it didn't strike me that if the waves could toss an Ambassador in the air like a toy, what they could have done to humans. I was, in fact, quite amazed, if not amused, that waves could be powerful enough to lift even a sturdy car like the Amby. Only on the way back home, when I came across small groups of women huddled together and sobbing, did I sense that something terrible must have happened. Back home, when

I switched on the TV, I realised that the terrible thing had a name—tsunami.

Over two lakh people died and countless others went missing in thirteen countries as waves rising up to thirty feet washed away their beaches; in India, it was the coast of Tamil Nadu that was worst hit. At the Marina alone that morning, more than 150 people were washed away.

When you are barely metres from the water and when waves rise as high as a three-storey building, there's very little one can do. The sad part is when the water rose to that height, people close to the sea must have been watching in amazement, without realising that they would be washed away like tender coconuts in a matter of moments.

Until now, my birthday was known to the rest of the world as Boxing Day. Now it was going to have another name: Tsunami Day.

I spent the rest of the day taking calls from the BBC Bengali Service desk in London. That evening, my voice must have been heard eagerly by the BBC's Bengali listeners as I gave sound bites on one of the worst natural disasters in recorded history. Although, I hardly consider that to be a distinction: I am neither very proud of my voice nor of my spoken Bengali.

Meanwhile, I had found time to prepare a modest meal for my parents and also fetch them from the railway station. Over dinner, my mother recounted how a young man travelling with them lost his appetite and put away his lunch because he could not get through to his family on the phone after hearing the news of the tsunami.

I went to bed that night a reassured man. Few things can be as comforting as having your loved ones around, especially if you happen to have been living away from them. By the time I woke up the next morning, even

Chennai, like any other big city, had moved on. Tsunami was now the problem of the poor—the people who had lost their families, their homes and their boats to the sea.

The tsunami was a collective tragedy on an unmatchable scale, but every single day, the Marina plays witness to innumerable individual tragedies—people who have been ravaged by a tsunami of a personal nature and who come to its sands for relief, respite and recourse. There are times when the Marina changes their destiny, like it happened in the case of Patricia Thomas.

Patricia was only seventeen when she secretly got married to the man she fancied, believing that a Mills & Boon story was coming true—it didn't matter to her that he was thirteen years older and a Hindu. Today, at fifty-two, she can probably make millions by writing self-help books on how to survive in spite of being wedded to adversity. But Patricia doesn't need the money. She runs a chain of eateries, called Sandeepha, across the city; she earned the Best Woman Entrepreneur Award from the Federation of Indian Chambers of Commerce & Industry in 2010; and she now lives in a well-appointed duplex apartment in Velachery where you will find a Mercedes parked outside the gate.

But it's been one hellish ride for her, and a long one at that—starting from the sands of the Marina, where she once sold snacks for a living because she discovered, immediately after marriage, that the man she fell in love with was actually an incurable drug addict.

'I grew up in San Thome. My father worked in the posts and telegraph department and my mother was employed in the telephones department. I was studying in Queen Mary's College when I met the man I was going to marry.

'His family ran a restaurant on the Marina, just across the college. Since the college canteen would always be packed, I would often hop over to their restaurant. Their kitchen was visible and that was the main interest for me. I used to watch them make chhola-puri. It was something magical in those days, to watch the puris being fried.

'That is how I came to know him. I was seventeen then, he was thirty. I got married within three months of knowing him. I guess it was because of all the Mills & Boons I had read.

'My parents were very conservative, very strict, especially my father. I wasn't allowed to go out of the house. I wasn't allowed to stay out after college. My father has always been a teetotaller. He doesn't even take coffee or tea, till today. So I've been brought up in a family like that. Then I marry a person who is into bad habits, none of which I could recognise then because I used to hardly meet him for ten minutes at a time. Till today I don't know how I made such a blunder.

'I got married at the registrar's office. I was not even seventeen, so my husband's friends had to pay something. The understanding was that I would stay with my parents, finish college and only then break the news at home. But within three months, he started saying, "If you don't move in with me, I will tell your parents." His friends started telling me that if I didn't stay with him, he was going to drink even more. That's when I realised he was not okay. I had to take a call.

'I just told my parents and came out of the house. My father told me he was done with me. You see, I was the apple of his eye. He blamed my mother for whatever I did, because she was always supportive of me. My mother was the one who allowed me to go to movies with friends and gave me pocket-money. So my mother had to carry the cross on behalf of me.

'My father's brother said that since the news had spread to the streets, they should get us married the proper way. So I got married again in the church. My husband's family came to know about the marriage after the church wedding. Until then, only his friends knew. When my parents went to meet his parents they said they were not going to accept us.

'We took up a rented house. My husband was running the business on the beach. He was there all the time, and because he was there all the time he fell into bad company. That was the time these hippies were around in Madras and he got into drugs. And he got into alcohol because of his friends.

'Initially, his behaviour was fine when he was not under the influence of drugs or alcohol. But he soon started hating me because he felt I was a thorn in his flesh. Then I conceived my first child. I was not even eighteen. I had nobody around me. There was no support, no affection, no love—nothing.

'Whatever he earned he was spending on his addictions. There was no money with me at all. Until then I did not know that we needed money to run a household. Finally I told my mother that I was pregnant. She convinced my in-laws to let me move in with them. But there I could stay for only three months. It was becoming very difficult to handle him. His father, in fact, was very supportive of me. He said he had not accepted the marriage because he knew this was going to be the result.

'My mother pleaded with my father to let me move in. He said I could stay there till I delivered the baby. My husband also moved into our house, bag and baggage. My father wouldn't talk to us. He wouldn't even acknowledge that we were in the house. But I should be thankful he allowed me to be there. I was with my own people now. My mother and brother and sister stood by me like pillars.

'My son was born in 1978. From then on I decided I had to do something because I couldn't be a burden forever. Already I had created enough problems. So I told myself that either I would succumb to the problems or fight them. I decided to fight. I was not professionally qualified. I didn't know if I would get a job somewhere. My mother was trying to find a job for me, but then again I had a small son at home.

'I started making pickles and jams. My mother would take them to office and sell them to her colleagues. More orders started coming. But it wasn't sufficient. I had to look at other options. That was the time when a family friend, a doctor who was with the school for the deaf, told my father that he could help me get a kiosk at the Marina. The government allotted kiosks for such institutions.

'So I got a stall, a small box, maybe six-by-six feet. All this while, my husband had been going to his shop. Whatever money he was getting from there he spent on himself. There was nothing for me, not even for the child.

'I started the stall in 1980. I was hardly twenty. I had one girl and two boys from the school to assist me. My job was also to train them. Even though it was small, I was the boss, so it felt nice.

'But the first day was very bad. I had made samosas, cutlets and French fries. Back then no one knew what French fries were. But all I managed to sell was a cup of coffee, for fifty paise. I went back home crying. But from the next day there was no looking back.

'I have been brought up in a good family, I used to dress up well, my speaking skills were good. So, people appreciated me. Until then they had seen only cart vendors on the Marina. That is how I started getting more crowds, especially because I was particular about hygiene. I never felt ashamed of my job. That is the biggest blessing I have. Not even one day did I ask myself, "Why I was doing this?"

'But being a young woman, it was tough. There were customers who would try to act smart. Sometimes I would just break down from inside but never show it. Certain things I could not even tell my mother because she might have got scared and asked me not to go to the stall. But I usually handled such situations well. It is all about how we react to and handle people.

'That was the time when the political bandhs started happening. One day, during MGR's time, we had a complete shutdown from seven in the morning to five in the evening. People hadn't even known then what a bandh was like. Everything was shut, including cinemas. Marina was packed on that day. Customers usually order four or five coffees at a time. That day I had groups of people asking for twenty coffees, twenty-five coffees. I did tremendous business for three-four days when Pope John Paul II came to the Marina in 1986.

'After that I got an offer from the Slum Clearance Board to run their canteen. Their office is right on the Marina. I took that on. This must have been around 1988.

'Meanwhile, my husband had started coming to the kiosk ever since I set it up. He would be doped half the time. Often, he would start drinking at 6.30 or seven in the evening, and by the time I closed the kiosk, he would be totally drunk. Fortunately, my father was not home at nights. Since he worked for posts and telegraph, he was on night shifts. He would go to work at six in the evening and return at six in the morning. So for a long time he didn't even know what my husband was like. Had he known earlier, maybe things would have been different.

'By now I was making enough money to take care of my children. My daughter was also born by then. But I was still living in my parents' house. That bothered me.

'It never occurred to me that I should divorce my husband. I always thought I should get him out of his addictions. I put him up for treatment once but the doctor told me it was not going to work since he had multiple addictions. So, unless he was determined to quit, nothing was going to work. A lot of people asked me why I didn't dump him. Maybe I didn't have the time to think about it. I was so focussed on business.

'Business was good at the Slum Clearance Board canteen. That was the time all the tenements were being allotted, and the place was full with slum-dwellers. On the days of public grievance hearings, I would cater to more than a thousand people. My husband used to assist me. He handled the cash while I would be in the kitchen. He was basically from a hotel family, so I took a lot of inputs from him. I used to ask him how to do this and how to do that. I did learn a lot from him.

'So, in the mornings I would run the canteen, and in the evenings I would be at the kiosk. Then I got a chance to run the canteen of Bank of Madura on Mount Road. But it was not possible to run two canteens at the same time. Moreover, in the Bank of Madura canteen, you also had employees from neighbouring banks and *Ananda Vikatan* coming in. It was a better crowd to associate with.

I told my husband that we could take care of a canteen each, but he was not very supportive of my running a canteen individually. So I had to let go of the Slum Clearance Board canteen.

'He then started coming with me to the Bank of Madura canteen. You see, he was into severe addiction. If the movie people came to me, I could give them so many scripts. Those days I used to wear heels, wooden heels. The wood would be very heavy, so they made holes in the bottom to reduce its weight. So he used to buy strips of these tablets and insert them in my heels. I used to wonder where this man hid his stuff. Then one day I finally found him digging into my sandals. I asked him what was he doing and he said he was just cleaning them. I thought, there was no way this man was going to clean my sandals. After some time I picked up the sandals and found the soles stuffed with drugs.

'He could get violent, especially when I refused to give him money or would flush down his stuff. He would beat me. See, I've even got burn marks. He used to burn me with cigarettes.

'At the Bank of Madura, they began telling me to ask him not to come. You know, at every place I did business, I always made the contract in his name, because I felt that as a man he should be given respect. I also thought that would give him a sense of responsibility and curtail his habits. But it had the opposite effect. Whenever we had an argument, he would say the contract was in his name, and ask me to get out. The bank people started saying that if he was going to be like this, they would cancel the contract.

'Then one afternoon he hit me in public in the canteen, just because I locked up the cash. He must have felt insulted, but I had my own priorities. I had to make payments and do other things. After he hit me, I came straight out to Mount Road and took a bus to the National Institute of Port Management, which is on East Coast Road. I mean, how could I go back to the same canteen and work again after he hit me in public?

'My expenses were high by now. I had put my children in very good schools. Whatever I was earning, I was paying for their education. My only fear, as I took the bus, was, "Oh God! What if the bank people throw me out! I will be left only with the kiosk at Marina." One of my uncles had suggested that I should try my luck with the National Institute of Port Management because it was way out of town and I would not face much competition in getting the contract to run their canteen.

'I got into the bus around 2.30 pm and could reach there only by five. I tried to pull a fast one on the security guard. I told him, "Your personnel officer wanted to see me." He said, "We don't have a personnel officer, we have an administrative officer." I said, "Yeah, yeah, the administrative officer." He called up the officer on the intercom. Fortunately, the officer agreed to see me. Had he told the guard that he never asked me to come, that would have been the end.

'The administrative officer showed me the canteen and the kitchen, which was bigger than that of a five-star hotel. The moment I saw it I had a shiver running down my spine. But I was determined to do it. I had no choice. I signed the contract. This was 1991. For the first time, the contract was in my name. Making food and watching people eat it—it is a joy.

'Once I started working at the institute, my husband again started coming with me. When I got the cheque for the first week—I think it was for ₹ 80,000—he realised that the cheque was in my name. He asked me why I had made the contract in my name. I told him the institute people had done background checks with the Bank of Madura and they were very particular that the contract should be in my name. He told me if I didn't change the contract he was going to leave me. So I took a call and said, "If you want to go, please go." He went back to his parents but they did not take him in. After that I had absolutely no news of him for two years.

'Since he could get very violent if I refused to give him money—he would often say he would kill me—one of my relatives, who was a lawyer, advised that I should go for a divorce. She said if something happened to me, all my hard-earned money would go to my husband instead of the children. That got me worried and I filed for divorce. The papers were sent to his house and when he did not appear at all, the court sent someone to his house to enquire if my complaint was correct. His family said it was all correct and the divorce came through. Till today I haven't collected the judgement because I didn't require it. It was not my intention to get divorced, but I was advised to.

'Then in 1992 or '93, I got a call from a stranger who had spotted him by the road. He was very sick. I didn't want to tell my parents about it, but at the same time I could not leave him like that. I got him admitted him in a hospital. He had jaundice and typhoid together. For almost six months he was in the hospital. I used to slip out of the canteen—by then I had a car—and go all the way to the hospital and come back. Only my mother knew about this.

'When time came for his discharge, I didn't know where to take him. So I rented a house and put him there. I visited him on Saturdays and would even take my daughter to meet him. He kept the house very clean and would even prepare lunch for us. My son was in college by then and lived in its hostel.

'One day, I got a call from the landlord. He said, "The person you have kept here gets drunk every day."

'I said, "How can that be? I visit him every Saturday!"

The landlord said, "He cleans up the house before you come. Otherwise he is drinking all the time and creating a scene."

'So once I went there on a weekday. The house looked like a gangsters' den. Local autorickshaw drivers were sitting with him and drinking. I threw away the bottles. He beat me up badly. Then I told myself, "If you are not going to learn your lesson even now, even God is not going to forgive you." After that I had no clue about him for some time.

'In 2002, my son got married. He had finished his studies, first in Chennai and then in Glasgow, and had joined the merchant navy. I couldn't get in touch with my husband to inform him about the wedding because I didn't know where he was. By now I was running canteens for more institutions. My daughter was studying visual communications at MOP Vaishnav College. Monetarily, I was very comfortable now.

'Then, one day, soon after my son's wedding, I got a call around eleven in the night. I recognised my husband's voice. He was calling from somewhere in the outskirts. He said he had heard about our son's wedding. I told him I wanted to inform him but did not know of his whereabouts. Then he started asking for money. He said I was well-off now, and that I should settle him off. I told him we were divorced. He got very angry.

'That was the last conversation I had with him. My daughter was around listening, so I had to tell her everything. She did not say anything. After about a week after that, somebody called us at 11.30 at night. My daughter happened to take the call. The caller said there was a person working for him who was very sick, almost sinking, and that he had been given this number to inform. I didn't know where this place was—somewhere on the outskirts. Fortunately, my son was home, he was not sailing at the time.

'I left my daughter and daughter-in-law at home and took my son, and on the way picked up a friend of ours, and went to this place. By the time we reached he had passed away. It was a massive heart attack. I informed his home. By then his father was dead, his mother was very old; only his sisters-in-law were at home. They didn't know what to do.

'The local people, the place where he died, seemed to know him. There was also a church in the area. So we buried him in the local cemetery. My son performed the last rites. My husband was lucky that way. He got his son to do the last rites. This was in 2002. After that, my son went back sailing.

'My daughter, who was studying visual communications, passed out of college in 2004. Her exams got over on 24th April, and she got married on 29th April. The groom's family was from Chennai. They ran schools in Anna Nagar. My son had come for the wedding. After a couple of weeks—I think on 18th May—they all went together to Singapore for a holiday, my son and daughter-in-law, and my daughter and son-in-law. They were back on 27th May.

'The next day my daughter had to go to Dindigul for a wedding in her husband's family. She didn't want to go as she was very tired. But I told her that it didn't look nice, since this was the first function taking place in her new husband's family after they got married and their relatives would all be looking forward to meet her.

'She and her husband flew to Madurai to get to Dindigul, and they were supposed to fly back as well. But the landing was so bad that she called me and said, "Amma, I am not going to fly back. I will return by road." After the wedding got over, they all started for Chennai in a car—my daughter and son-in-law, and my son-in-law's elder brother and his wife, and their kid. They met with an accident near Chengelpet. It was a head-on collision. All of them died, except the child. The accident took place on 31st May—just a month after my daughter got married.

'I lost my daughter, but, look at her in-laws! They had lost both their sons and daughters-in-law. The bodies were lying on the road for three hours. Apparently, an ambulance had come by, but it did not take them to the hospital because they appeared to be dead. I mean, how do you know people are dead unless you take them to the hospital? With the insurance money I received after my daughter's death, I set up an ambulance service on the same stretch of the road where they died. An ambulance is always stationed there, and it takes accident victims to the nearest hospital—whether they have suffered a fractured or are no more.

'My daughter's death left me shattered, completely. I can't even explain. All this while I had been holding myself together only because of the children.

'By now I was associated with the Sangeetha group of restaurants. I had become the franchisee for their outlet in Spencer Plaza. After my daughter died, my son, who quit his job to be with me and help me with the business, suggested we take over the outlet and rename it after my daughter.

'That's how Sandeepha was born. My daughter's name was Pradheebha Sandra. So my son mixed and matched her name and called our new outlet Sandeepha. This was in 2005.

'Today, we have expanded across the city. My daily sales now touch two lakh rupees.

'But how can I forget the small kiosk in Marina, where I started with a sale of just fifty paise. I retained the kiosk until 2002, and guess who was running it in the later years? My father. After he retired, my mother coaxed him into sitting there. That's when he gradually began talking to me, after so many years.

'Maybe I should have retained that place. But at the time I didn't have to strength to renew the contract. There was too much happening in my life. I had to let go of it. But the Marina was my business school. It gave me my MBA.'

Chapter 9

COME DECEMBER

It is late December and I am walking through a leafy neighbourhood of Mylapore, looking for a particular auditorium. The sun is directly above my head, but there is a distinct nip in the air. The expression 'pleasant weather' may be an oxymoron for Chennai, where the climate is famously split between hot, hotter and hottest, but December is an exception. During this month, there are nights when you can do even without the fan, and it rains off and on—and it also rains music.

This is the time of the year when most cultured Chennaiites don't leave their city, and those abroad come back on vacation, because the invisible umbilical cord called

'Carnatic music' tugs at them. December, for Chennai, is a month for music.

Packing in about 1,500 concerts spread across a little over two weeks, the season typically starts mid-December, which is the beginning of the Tamil month of Margazhi. The month is considered inauspicious and must be devoted only to prayer and worship. People should not get married, purchase properties, shift homes or take up new jobs during this period. It is, therefore, only appropriate that this month should be so designated, because learning or listening to Carnatic music is a form of worship in Chennai. Accomplished yesteryear Carnatic musicians enjoy the status of saints—the elaborate patterns painted on their foreheads adding to their saintly image. They are people who can do no wrong; they are considered free of human follies. The truth could be far from that, but nobody would like to believe it or hear about it, such is the reverence they command.

Present-day Carnatic musicians may go easy on embellishing their foreheads but they have an equally firm grip on the attention of the audience. Their names might not ring a bell outside the Carnatic music circuit, but in Chennai they enjoy the status of rock stars. There is always a scramble for tickets to their shows.

This is not to say that musical concerts are restricted only to the month of Margazhi. They are a round-the-year feature in classical music-crazy Chennai. Only that, in December, the craze culminates into a carnival known variously as Music Season, Music Festival, Margazhi Festival, December Season—easily one of the biggest song and dance shows on this planet.

The concerts are all held under the banners of various sabhas, which are bodies that promote the performing arts.

Chennai has about seventy of them today. Though a sabha is democratic in structure—it has a large number of music-lovers as members who pay an annual subscription fee and elect the office-bearers—it usually relies on the patronage of some wealthy citizen or the other. Thanks to their generosity, many of the sabhas today have impressive auditoriums of their own. Many others, however, continue to hold their performances in temple courtyards, school compounds and wedding halls. But the venue hardly counts; what really matters is the stature of the sabha.

In fact, the oldest and one of the most highly esteemed sabhas in the city does not have an auditorium of its own and probably never will—for want of money. From the time it was born more than a century ago, Sri Parthasarathy Swami Sabha has led a nomadic existence, moving from one venue to another. Since the past fifteen years the concerts of this Triplicane-born sabha are being held in Mylapore—in a wedding hall called Vidhya Bharati, where I am headed this morning. Since marriages are not conducted during the month of Margazhi, the hall is rented to the sabha during the music season.

Sri Parthasarathy Swami Sabha originated in 1896 as the Sangeetha Vidwat Sabha, which was started by Triplicane resident Mani Thirumalachari, a bank employee who belonged to the prosperous Mandyam community of Iyengars. The British rule had, by then, created a wealthy class of Indians that took pride in patronising artistes, and the performing arts had begun to move out of the hallowed courtyards of temples to the courtyards of the homes of these well-to-do natives.

In 1900, Thirumalachari renamed the sabha after Parthasarathy, the presiding deity of Triplicane, and registered it as a public institution. In the initial years, the recitals were held at his home but as the audience grew, the venue kept shifting to bigger spaces. In the 1940s, the concerts began to be held at Hindu High School: it was here that the sabha saw its most glorious moments as it presented a number of iconic musicians to the public. In 1958, it obtained a piece of land on lease for twenty-five years and built an auditorium. Finally, the sabha had a place of its own! But the lease could not be renewed due to a dispute and so, in 1993, it once again became homeless.

After ninety-seven years of existence, Sri Parthasarathy Swami Sabha finally moved out of Triplicane into the Iyer territory of Mylapore—first to the Mylapore Fine Arts Society and then to Vidhya Bharati. Thirumalachari would not have been too happy with the idea of the sabha's events being conducted out of the sight of Lord Parthasarathy, but the need of the hour was such.

'When the lease ended, we did identify about ten grounds of land to build an auditorium. It was going to cost us one crore rupees,' M. Krishnamurthy, a long-time secretary of the sabha, tells me when I meet up with him in the reception area of the wedding hall. 'But by the time we were able to raise the money, the cost had shot up to two- and-a-half crore. We dropped the idea. Today, if we want to buy the same size of land in Triplicane or Mylapore, it would cost us thirty crore. Construction of the auditorium will cost another five crore. Do you think we can afford it, sir? Our sabha is, after all, run by traditional, middle-class people.'

Krishnamurthy, who is fifty-seven now and is the HR head of a pharmaceutical company, joined the sabha as a volunteer when he was in school. Back then, his job was to arrange the chairs and to usher in non-VIP ticket-holders. 'Those days, we had wooden folding chairs. It would be quite a task, folding up each chair after the concert got over. Today, the number of people interested in working for a sabha is very small. They think, "What do we get out of it?" But this is service. Nevertheless, we are identifying passionate members from the next generation to induct them in our working committee, so that they can lead the sabha for another century.'

The sabha survives today mainly on its reputation. For money, it relies mostly on donations from philanthropists, corporate sponsorship and the subscription fee paid by its members, who add up to a little over a thousand. It does not have a steady income unlike many other established sabhas which rent out their halls to supplement their finances.

'Look at the irony. When we had our own auditorium for thirty-five years, most of the other sabhas were functioning in rented properties. Today, they all have their own halls, but we are conducting our programmes in a rented building,' Krishnamurthy smiles. It is a smile of surrender.

After a moment of silence, he adds: 'Since the sabha is named after Lord Parthasarathy, the charioteer of Arjuna, I believe we are destined to move around like a chariot. That's the way I look at it.'

■ ■ ■

Inside the hall, a concert is on. The audience is made up of only twenty-nine people. The vocalist, a woman, is obviously a novice, which is explained by the late-morning slot that she has been allotted. As a musician, you know you have made it when sabhas slot you for the evening. The later in the evening, the more famous you are. It can be quite a struggle for an aspiring performer: first to land a performance in the music season and then, if deserving, to be slowly pushed ahead each year by the hands of the clock. Since I do not know the nuances of Carnatic music, I cannot say for sure whether the woman on the stage will find a better slot next year, but I have my doubts, since many in the audience are dozing. I step out of the auditorium and head for the canteen.

The music season in Chennai is a lot like Durga Puja in Kolkata, though far less boisterous and held on a much smaller scale. But the similarities are striking. The rasikas, or the lovers of music, like to sabha-hop, just like Bengalis pandal-hop. It is also during the music season that the traditional Tamil Brahmin, not very adventurous when it comes to food, loves to eat in the sabha canteen, just as the Bengali loves to eat at the stalls in various puja pandals.

And, of course, the sarees then worn are expensive. Both events are crucial to the culture of their people and an assertion of their identities. A Tamil Brahmin girl who has never been to a music class is as good as a Bengali girl who has never seen a puja pandal. The comparison may not be entirely appropriate, but not entirely inappropriate either.

In the open-air canteen, the tables are arranged as if for a wedding feast. Even the spread is elaborate. Only that, unlike in a wedding, you will have to pay here—a princely sum of seventy-five rupees, which is steep considering you get a similar spread, minus three or four items, at any of the meals-ready restaurants for half the price. The contractor running the canteen, when he learns that I am a journalist, hovers around to see that I am served well.

A middle-aged woman joins me at the table. In Chennai, you can't lay claim to an entire table in a busy eatery unless you are accompanied by enough people to occupy all the chairs. Anyone can join you and no one will feel obliged to ask, 'Do you mind if I sit here?' The purpose behind the practice, at least the way I understand it, is to make the optimum use of a table. When a table that is already in use still has some chairs vacant, why not accommodate yourself there instead of laying claim to an entire, unoccupied table? The result is that you often end up having a meal with total strangers. But no one seems to mind that. The idea is to eat, pay and get out.

Chennai is certainly not the place to linger over your meal and meditate upon each dish—for that you will have to go to one of the upscale restaurants. For the general population, eating out is a very mechanical act—it's something you want to be done with before moving on to the next chore.

During my ten years in Chennai, however, I have never had a young woman pulling up a chair at my table. It has always been men of various ages or middle-aged couples or, occasionally, like now, a middle-aged woman. She ignores my presence as she goes through the rituals of getting set for a meal, which include sprinkling water on the plantain leaf and wiping it clean with the palm of her hand and then watching the waiter decorate the leaf with small portions of the various dishes.

By the time she starts eating, I am already halfway through my lunch. I notice her looking at my food and then, suddenly, she stops eating. She frantically looks around for the waiter. In the process, our eyes meet for a moment.

'Pickle! Get me some pickle!' she shouts.

I realise that while my leaf-plate has a small lump of lemon pickle on it, hers has none. The waiter, who comes running with the pickle, gets an earful not only from the woman but also the contractor. Now that I am privy to an intimate craving of hers—the craving for pickle—the woman and I are no longer strangers.

'What do you do?' she asks me.

I tell her, and want to ask her the same question. But for some reason I presume she is a housewife, and instead ask her if the sabha canteens gave her respite from daily cooking.

'No, no, I cannot afford seventy-five rupees for lunch every day,' she says, as she drags down a small portion of vegetables from the edge of the plate and diligently mixes it with the rice to make a ball. 'I had to meet a client whose office happens to be nearby. I work with HDFC Bank. Since I was coming this way, I thought why not attend a recital and have lunch as well,' she explains without looking up from the plate. So this morning she has killed three birds with one stone. I ask her her name.

'I am Mrs Parthasarathy,' she replies. The name suits the setting. That's not even her name, but her husband's. It's the name she wants society to know her by.

■ ■ ■

In Chennai, particularly in Brahmin households, almost every child wants to be an engineer and almost every child receives training in Carnatic music—so don't be surprised if you find a celebrated vocalist holding a degree in engineering, or an engineer talking about ragas with a great degree of authority. I know at least one such engineer.

Sriram V, the heritage enthusiast who makes an appearance in the book earlier on, started training his vocal cords from the age of six but stopped when he was twelve. His father did not want him to become an artiste. So Sriram went on to join the College of Engineering, Delhi. He may be running his family business today, but Carnatic music, clearly, remains his first love, considering he has authored four books on the subject. They include the history of the formidable Music Academy, the biographies of revered vocalists Semmangudi Srinivasa Iyer and Bangalore Nagarathnamma, and, my personal favourite, *Carnatic Summer*, which looks at the lives of twenty great exponents.

One very pleasant morning I found myself sipping apple juice at Chamiers, a boutique cafeteria that, apart from serving Continental fare, sells designer clothes and jewellery and knick-knacks that make for excellent gifts. This is where Chennai's fashionable crowd likes to hang out.

I was waiting there for someone who had offered to give me juicy details about some of the well-known faces in the city. Her only condition was that I should not name her or the people she named. I had assured her that it went without saying. But she seemed to have changed her mind now because her phone uncharacteristically turned out to be switched off as I tried calling her repeatedly. I ordered the juice, just in case her phone battery was dead and she was merely caught up in traffic. After waiting for an hour, I went up to the small bookshop upstairs to kill some more time, hoping the woman—pretty and young and quite well-known herself—would still show up. There I bought Sriram's *Carnatic Summer*.

Back home, I finished the book in four hours flat. So what if I had missed knowing the salacious side of high society; this book showed me the human side of the people Madras worshipped! I got to learn, for example, how the young M.S. Subbulakshmi slipped out of her home in Madurai one night and took the train to Madras, where she knocked on the door of the much-married Sadasivam, who took her under his wing, made her a superstar and later married her.

Or how the debonair vocalist G.N. Balasubramaniam had a fetish for footwear and watches. Or how the great

Semmangudi had a running feud with fellow artistes and critics. Stories of rivalry, jealousy, love, lust and cunning emerge as you read between the lines and, why not? Even the greatest souls may have feet of clay.

Shortly after, one afternoon, I meet Sriram for lunch at the Gymkhana Club. Over mugs of draught beer, he explains to me Chennai's connection with Carnatic music:

'In 1639 when Madras was founded, Thanjavur was the heartland of culture. Till the 1850s, in order to be someone in music, you had to be from the Thanjavur belt. But, from then on, all musicians had to migrate to the big city to survive.

'The cultural development of Madras grew on very different lines compared to those of the other and older towns. Here, there were no kings. The rich businessmen, the dubashes, provided the much-needed patronage in the early years. The earliest book on Madras, the mid-eighteenth-century Sanskrit work *Sarva Deva Vilasa*, describes a soiree conducted by the dubashes for certain musicians. It was thanks to dubashes that two of the Carnatic Trinity, Muttuswami Dikshitar and Tyagaraja, visited Madras (the Carnatic Trinity is a term used to describe three great nineteenth-century Carnatic composers—Syama Sastry, Tyagaraja and Muttuswami Dikshitar. The bulk of Carnatic repertoire is their songs).

'The city played an important role in the notating of Carnatic music. The *Sangita Sarvartha Sara Sangrahamu*, the first Carnatic music book, was published here in 1857. Thirty years later, the Tachur Brothers began bringing out a series of books. In 1887, the Madras Jubilee Gayana Samaj, which can be said to be the first Sabha, began. It aimed to educate the English on Carnatic music. But it folded up in a few years.

'A major fillip came to music in 1903 when recording began. The women artistes were the first to record and from then on, Carnatic music began to be heard in homes. Song books were published and circulated and this added to the art's popularity. The freedom struggle saw Carnatic songs with it as a theme, the first such song being the 1925 elegy to Bengali freedom fighter and philanthropist Chittaranjan Das, sung by Madras Lalithangi.

'At the other end, the coronation of King George V saw several musical performances in Chennai too. From 1924, with the establishment of the Madras Presidency Radio Club, songs began to be broadcast. Then in 1931 came the Corporation Radio (from Ripon Buildings) and later, the AIR.

'It was in Chennai that music became a part of college and school curricula. One Prof. P. Sambamoorthy was the pioneer. In 1927, Queen Mary's became the first college to include music as part of its syllabus. In 1932, the music department of the Madras University began. In 1949 came the Central College of Carnatic Music.

'Sabhas began in the city from 1895. Today, the oldest is the Sri Parthasarathy Swami Sabha. In 1927, the All India Music Conference was held in Madras as part of the Indian National Congress meeting. At the conference it was decided to set up the Music Academy, which was inaugurated in 1928. A set of concerts and demonstrations was held at the Academy that year.

'In April 1929, the Academy again held a music conference during the Easter holidays when the courts were closed, because lawyers formed a large chunk of the patrons. But the response to the April conference was lukewarm, so it held one more conference during the Christmas holidays. That is how the December Music Season began.

'In 1933, the Indian Fine Arts Society also started celebrating the season and, in 1943, Tamil Isai Sangam joined in. Until the early 1980s, these were the only three sabhas that held music festivals in the month of December. All other sabhas held concerts throughout the year but they did not have anything particular in December.

'Today, of course, the season is no longer confined to the Christmas holidays, it is held throughout the month. It attracts Carnatic music-lovers from across the country and the world. Today, most musicians are globetrotters. Most tutors teach children in America over Skype. Who knows, some day Cleveland will become the Carnatic capital?'

■ ■ ■

So, what does the word 'Carnatic' mean?

No one seems to be very sure. History will tell you that a particular region in south India—represented today pretty much by the map of present-day Tamil Nadu—was called the Carnatic. But why was it called so? According to Sriram, the word derives from *karna* (the ear) and *ata* (to haunt). So, is it likely that the region got its name from the kind of music that was popular there? Or, it is that the music earned its name because of the region it was popular in?

A tradition often takes so long in evolving that dates and people involved in its genesis become as irrelevant and as indistinguishable as individual specks of sand in an hourglass. You can only piece together fragments of history and hearsay to arrive at a conclusion as to how the tradition might have come into being. No one can give you precise names or dates or reasons.

All I know is I have always run away from classical music—be it Hindustani or Carnatic. In the north, there is no need to run away because the connoisseurs of Hindustani music are outmuscled by the lovers of Hindi film music. But in the south, Carnatic music is so woven into daily life that there is no escaping it. The media coverage of Carnatic musicians or their concerts has hardly been of help: a picture of two look-alike sisters holding violins and looking lifelessly at the camera; a jargon-laden report of a concert describing how 'enchanting' the performance was; how the audience went back home 'enthralled'; the same old Bharatanatyam pose which could have been from a performance that had taken place ten years before.

Had the press shown some imagination and had the musicians themselves shown a little more flexibility in terms of their body language on stage and in experimenting with catchy rhythms, laypersons like me wouldn't have felt intimidated by the thought of sitting through a Carnatic concert.

As a layman who did not take music lessons, the onus is not on me to seek the divinity of Carnatic music, but on the performer to enchant me and make me realise how divine it is. That is the way I look at it—but then, who am I.

Things, however, have been changing.

Recently, I sat through two Carnatic concerts—one by T.M. Krishna, another by Sikkil Gurucharan. I was dragged to these concerts much against my wishes, but I sat through them voluntarily. I did not understand a thing of what they were singing, but I liked what I was hearing—there was something persuasive about their voices, as if their vocal cords were the engine of a car being subjected to the most ruthless test drive and coming out in flying colours.

Was it just their voice? I think it also had a lot to do with their style. I found these two young men singing *to* the audience. They looked the affable sort—the kind you could have a chat with after the concert, rather than stare at them from a distance in awe. Musicians like them are the products of a renaissance that swept through the Carnatic world in the past couple of decades—quite unknown to those not tuned in.

One February morning, I ring the bell at T.M. Krishna's flat in the upmarket Alwarpet area. Of course, I have made an appointment. A woman opens the door and shows me into the hall. While I wait, I find my senses assaulted by the whistle of the pressure-cooker and that delicious smell of sambar—things that always make me hungry. I could do with a plate of hot rice and some freshly-made sambar, considering that I almost always skip breakfast, but right now I can't think of eating. I am here to meet one of Chennai's best-known vocalists, and I busy myself testing the flow of ink in my fountain pen.

T.M. Krishna cuts an impressive figure as he walks into the hall. He has just had a shower. If I were a woman, I would have found him extremely attractive: sharp features, brown eyes, the curly hair just washed, the beard neatly trimmed. He is barely thirty-five. He looks rugged enough to be a rock star and not a Carnatic singer. As he settles down next to me on the sofa, I feel I am meeting an old friend and not a celebrity I've seen only on stage or in pictures in the papers.

'I primarily come from a business family and not from a family of musicians,' he begins his story. 'My grandfather ran a company called Chari and Chari Pvt. Ltd. Electrification was private in those days. The whole Guntur area in Andhra Pradesh was electrified by him. The company was in the tobacco business for some time and then, in malt, but finally settled with automobile ancillaries. My father ran the ancillaries business pretty much all his life. He was supplying to Ashok Leyland, TVS and others. So I come from a hardware company, a hardware family.

'Of course the arts, specifically Carnatic music, was very much part of the milieu. Both my grandfathers were interested in music, and my mother did do her graduation in music though she's not a professional singer. So, music has pretty much been part of the family, but primarily, we were business people.

'I was interested in economics in school and I did my graduation in economics too. My dream at that point was to go to the London School of Economics. I never thought of joining the family business.

'When I was three-and-a-half or four, my mother tried to revive her interest in music. Her teacher Seetharama Sharma—who later became my teacher—used to come home to teach her. I'm told I used to sit there, in their class, with a stick, pretending it was the tambura, and try and sing whatever they were singing. So that's how they figured that maybe I was interested in it. I was definitely not a prodigy.

'I started to learn properly when I was five-and-a-half. I had three classes a week and my teacher used to come home to teach me. Seetharama Sharma was from Andhra Pradesh, from Kuchipudi village, where every other street is full of musicians or artists. He was a tough taskmaster, very tough. I used to enjoy my classes but when you are eight or ten years old, you want to be out playing on the street. Those days we all used to play street cricket. I enjoyed singing, but not to the extent of saying that I knew it was my calling.

'Then, two things happened. One, my mother and teacher started a music school called Kalapeetham in 1985. My classes moved to this school. That's when I started learning with a group of people.

'Then there was another big change. See, in the early 1980s, everybody was predicting doomsday for Carnatic music. The main reason being that most of the stalwarts of the 1940s, 50s and 60s had passed away. And everybody was saying that since there was no young singer coming up, it was all going to die. But there was also a catch in that, because in those days it was not common to see young people performing. You had to reach the age of thirty-five or forty to be accepted as a performer.

'So, in 1985, a group of young people, who were all music students and who could perform—some of them are famous personalities today—got together and said, "Look, if nobody gives us an opportunity to perform, we'll start our own organisation." They started the Youth Association for Classical Music, or YACM. They said they would give opportunities only to people who were below thirty. This, to me, was a landmark event as far as the history of Carnatic music is concerned, because it completely transformed the colour of Carnatic music. We're all products of this organisation. I joined it in 1989, I think. I must have been thirteen then. Later, I became its president.

'At first, we used to organise concerts. Then we realised that if we wanted to get young people interested, it couldn't be just concerts, so we started creating games based on Carnatic music. Just like you have antakshari, we had something called akshara anthadi. It was the same thing, starting a song with the last consonant of another song, only the compositions were in Carnatic music. We started running fetes where every stall had competitions in Carnatic music—on ragas, on thalas, on composers. The stage used to be full of us young people participating in these competitions.

'The very important thing was that the older generation supported us like anything! The older musicians realised that this was something special happening. Every now and then we had some senior musician coming in. All these competitions used to be judged by stalwarts. They recognised that this was a movement, and that it was taking Carnatic music to another generation. This change dropped the age of performing musicians by at least two generations.

'Today, in a festival, the oldest classical musician will be fifty-two or fifty-three. This is unseen in any classical form in the world! Usually, the *youngest* would be about forty-five. Even now, in Hindustani music, it's still that way. If you look at the top artistes, the youngest will be hitting forty. Carnatic music changed because of this one organisation. Today, you have a generation after me, a generation after that, ready to take over the baton.

'I performed for the first time in 1988. I was twelve. It was at the Music Academy. You see, once the YACM movement picked up, all organisations started having youth festivals. The Academy started something called the Spirit of Youth. More opportunities started trickling in for the younger people. Still, I won't say we thought of it as a profession. A lot of musicians, even the top ones, were working at other jobs.

'I joined Vivekananda College in 1993 to study economics. But while in college, around 1994, I suddenly got a lot of recognition among my peers and among senior musicians. That's the biggest boost you can get, when your peers say, "Hey, good job done", and when your seniors say "You have a lot of talent." I think that changed my mind. I had to take a call. If I'd come from a family that was not financially well off, I would have had to take up a job, and then I don't know if I would be doing what I'm doing now. But my parents were always very cool people. They said, "Give it a shot; if it doesn't work, go back to studying."

'So in the third year of college, I decided to give music a full-fledged shot. I started singing in concerts in Coimbatore, Madurai, even in Delhi. Small organisations in Bombay had started calling me. Unlike in the West, things still work on word-of-mouth here. Meanwhile, I got married in 1997, when I was 21. My wife, Sangeetha Shivakumar, is also a musician. We met through YACM where both of us were committee members. Things kept moving in the right direction.

'I got the senior slot in the Music Academy in 2001. I think that's when I said—it looks like I've got there. By then, the youth revolution had completely taken over and corporate sponsorship had picked up. Everything had changed! The appearance of the Carnatic musician also changed. Earlier, classical musicians were always thought of as people living in a time-warp. One dhoti and one kurta and one kudumi and vibhuti, you know—very traditional, very religious, who didn't understand the reality of today. That was the mind-set, which was completely broken by our generation. Today, people realise that we are normal guys, just like them. You may see me in traditional attire on stage, but when I get off, I'm as normal as any IT guy who is thirty-five years old working for a multinational. Some people still wear vibhuti or the namam, but even those guys, offstage, will probably come and have a drink with you—you know what I mean?

'The other big change for me happened in 1996, when I started learning from Semmangudi Srinivasa Iyer. He was one of the greatest musicians this country has produced. He came to a concert of mine because he was chief guest, and as he walked out—he knew my father because of old family connections—he looked at my father and said, "Send him". He was already in his late eighties by then. So I learnt from him from 1996 till he died in 2003. Musically, it opened another canvas for me.

'Comprehension of the idiom, and how you present it—that's one aspect of being a musician. The other aspect is to have the freedom of mind to let the exploratory part of you completely burst out—within the framework you have. That's what I got from Semmangudi—the capacity to just let go and let the music flow. He never told me that, I imbibed it from him.

'Even though in his late eighties, Semmangudi was still pushing the boundaries, he was still looking for something, and that is what makes these people special. If you went to Semmangudi's house when he was alive, you would always find him singing—always. He would be on an easy chair, and behind it was a window. I used to usually go to the window before I went in so that I could hear him sing.

'Great musicians are those who have music running in their heads 24/7. There's always something new popping up. Today we have this compulsive disorder for innovation and newness. We're desperate to be different. People ask, "How am I different from the others?" I think that's a stupid question. Difference is something that comes to you; it is not something you make. People like Semmangudi did not work towards making a difference, towards innovation, or change. They simply worked and the process took them to the change. They are the greats.

'Other than Semmangudi, I've heard most other stalwarts only on tape. G.N. Balasubramaniam, T. Brinda, Musiri Subramanian Iyer, Flute Mali. Among the people I heard live, my biggest idol, when I was young, was T.V. Sankaranarayanan. He's still around and performing. He was my biggest idol. I used to haunt his concerts. I say "haunt" because I think he got a little tired of me. If he sang in twelve places I'd be there in all twelve. I liked the carefree way he used to sing. There was a great amount of romance in his music.

'Musically, I'm a traditionalist. What I do not consider important is formats of presentation. I don't believe in concert formats. I have been criticised and considered blasphemous for this. I think formats evolved only in the last hundred years when concerts became professional. I believe performance is a reflection of the art; the art is not the performance. If you start perceiving the performance as the art, then you get stuck with certain formats. My job is to understand the art, not understand performance.

'I usually practise late in the night. I'm not a morning person, though morning is supposed to be the best time to practise. My practice starts close to midnight and goes on till two or three. Even if I'm learning something new, it has to be post-midnight.

'It feels fabulous to have reached here. But in my case the greatest thing is that my wife is also a musician. Since she also performs, she understands the mechanics of what happens on stage. So there is always a reality check. There are nights when I come home and she tells me that I sang bullshit. The bubble is burst. It is a good thing, because it keeps you grounded.

'The beautiful thing about Carnatic music is that the music itself is not corporatised despite all the changes. Today, with my status, I can very easily say, "Unless you pay me 'X' amount I'm not going to be seen with you." But if I say that, I'm going to cut out all the suburban sabhas, or the smaller sabhas, or even the smaller temples, who cannot afford me. I'd be doing a disservice to the art.

'The sabha culture is what sustains the whole ethos of Carnatic music and gives every generation impetus. Unless you have sabhas in every town, every city, there won't be opportunity for younger artistes to perform. The sabha culture is holding the system together. So, one day, I will be singing at a Citibank festival in Chennai, five days later I will be singing in a small sabha in a suburb where a small hall can hold only 150 people. But it's important that both are maintained. After all, I sang in all the small sabhas when I was a nobody. All those concert experiences have given me the status I have today. One has to give back.'

Chapter

10

ALL ROADS LEAD TO CHENNAI

Then there is a new Chennai.

At seven o' clock on a muggy evening, illuminated by neon lights, Mackay's Garden is like any market square in a Bengali town that is coming alive after an afternoon nap.

Three men have just emerged on the street, freshly-bathed and wearing starched kurtas over trousers. They are being beseeched by an idling autorickshaw driver: '*Dada, ashoon! Dada, ashoon!*'—Brother, this way! This way!

A child who has just let go of his mother's hand and is sprinting ahead, is being berated by her, '*Ei, kothay jachhish, ekhane aaye bolchhi!*'—Where are you off to? Come here, I tell you!

A woman wearing the trademark pair of red and white bangles loudly complains to her husband as they head for an outing, '*Uff, aajke ja gorom!*—Phew, it's so hot today!

Hers is a typically Bengali whine.

Only, Mackay's Garden is not in Bengal, but right in the heart of Chennai, off the busy Greams Road, a short walk from the famous Apollo Hospitals. Not many in Chennai would have heard of Mackay's Garden, but to countless people living in faraway Bengal, the name is likely to ring a bell. The neighbourhood, after all, is home away from home for Bengalis when they come all the way to Chennai to seek treatment at the hospital and bide their time for admission or to convalesce here.

Until a few years ago, the joke in Apollo was that the Howrah Mail from Kolkata bound for Chennai had one bogie reserved only for patients coming to the hospital. It's no longer a joke, but serious business. Bengalis form the second-largest patient-population in Chennai's Apollo after people from Tamil Nadu. They are said to account for twenty per cent of the daily admissions. Considering that Apollo admits about eighty patients a day, nearly two dozen Bengali families must be arriving in Chennai every day—bound for Apollo alone.

Then there are those coming to the other reputed hospitals providing specialised treatments and also a patient-friendly ambience on par with Apollo. Sankara Nethralaya, the eye hospital, is one such. Here the crowds are dizzying, Bengalis forming a sizeable chunk of them, so much so the hospital has several Bengali eye-specialists on board. One doctor I once spoke to over the phone was so happy to come across a fellow Bengali living in Chennai— he must've been homesick—that he chose to have a long chat before enquiring why I had called. Before hanging up, he extracted an assurance from me that I would meet him someday.

Bengali patients bound for Chennai almost always belong to smaller towns of Bengal and rarely from Kolkata. A number of them come from Assam and from Bangladesh too. Rather strange, that they should travel all the way to Chennai rather than to nearby Kolkata, which also has several reputed hospitals including a branch each of Apollo and Sankara Nethralaya. These medical pilgrims seem to have more faith in Chennai's hospitals and doctors.

'Some time ago, a fish bone pierced my tongue,' Ananda Biswas, a resident of Nadia district in West Bengal, tells me as he waits at a travel agency—run by a Bengali—in Mackay's Garden. 'The wound developed into a permanent boil. Doctors in Kolkata could neither diagnose it nor cure it. Some said it could be cancer, others said there was nothing to worry about. Finally, I had to come here.'

Ananda, fifty years old, is now at ease after doctors at Apollo took a look at his tongue and prescribed him medicines for three months. 'In Kolkata, they make you run from pillar to post. Today, they send you to one place for a test, tomorrow to another place for another test. Here, everything is done in one go,' he tells me.

Sitting next to him is the young Suraj Biswas, Ananda's neighbour in Nadia, who nods his head in agreement: 'The service is excellent. And the hospital is spotlessly clean.' Suraj is accompanying his father who is suffering from a nervous disorder. The father has undergone a series of tests this morning and results are awaited, but Suraj is relieved that they have come to the one-stop shop when it comes to diagnosing a disease.

Outside the travel agency, I run into Ripon Dutta, a cloth merchant from Jalpaiguri. His daughter, just five, was born with a disfigured right ear, but doctors at Apollo have operated it into shape. 'From what I have seen,' he tells me, 'doctors in Kolkata keep the disease clinging to you. Here, they work towards curing it.' Strong words, but understandable, nevertheless.

Businessmen have been quick to cash in on this sentiment. Lodges have come up in Mackay's Garden; they provide kitchen space because it is difficult to imagine a Bengali, who can rarely do without mustard oil, surviving on south Indian food for even a couple of weeks. Economically, too, it makes sense to cook your own food. And you don't have to go too far to buy utensils. Right inside Mackay's Garden is Rajendra Steel Centre, its signboard painted only in the Bengali script. All the pharmacies in the area, too, include the Bengali script on their signboards. Autorickshaw-drivers speak adequate Bengali to solicit the lodgers and take them for a ride—and not always in the literal sense. Perhaps it's only a matter of time before a Kali temple comes up in the neighbourhood.

Chennai, or Madras, has always been an important pilgrimage destination in India when it comes to medical treatment. Its medical colleges, which happen to be some of the oldest in the country, have produced doctors who have gone on to be pioneers in their respective fields. Their students, and their students' students, are today scattered across the country as respectable doctors in respectable institutions. Often, when one of these finds a case a bit too complicated to handle, he refers the patient to his professor in Chennai.

Today, the quality of medical care that is provided in the city has made it the leading medical tourism hub in the country. Its hospitals not only attract a steady stream of patients from the remote corners of India but also parts of the world.

The man largely responsible for the city earning such a distinction is Dr Prathap Reddy, who founded Apollo Hospitals in 1983. He transformed the gloomy process of hospitalisation with an exercise in public relations.

Thanks to him, the patient was no longer an aggrieved soul who, apart from his ailment, had to put up with dirty beds, callous doctors, impatient nurses and an indifferent staff. Dr Reddy elevated the status of the suffering to that of a valued client, who encountered nothing but friendliness throughout the period of hospitalisation and went back home assured and, very often, cured. This also meant you often ended up paying through your nose, but patients didn't seem to mind that at all as long as they were confident of being healed.

The Apollo Effect was to soon sweep through competing hospitals. Today, most big hospitals in Chennai boast of world-class doctors, and some of these hospitals, each time a globally-renowned surgeon joins them, don't shy away from placing a front-page advertisement in newspapers to announce the new arrival—complete with a mug-shot of the star surgeon.

But the most far-reaching change brought about by the Apollo Effect, according to me, is the mushrooming of smaller hospitals and diagnostic laboratories where you don't have to pay an exorbitant sum but the quality of care is just as good.

Today, a patient in Chennai is spoilt for attention.

■ ■ ■

Far away from the dazzle of the world where the hospital industry seamlessly merges with the hospitality industry, are men and women in white coats who work with selfless dedication in the gloomy and humble precincts of government hospitals. Their praises may not be sung in high society, but countless poverty-stricken souls remain indebted to them forever for getting a new lease of life. Many such doctors, however, double as consultants in private hospitals to supplement their meagre government income. But their commitment to service is often exemplary.

One morning, not particularly in accordance to my wishes, I find myself heading for Stanley Hospital in north Chennai. A hospital, that too a government hospital, that too in north Chennai, is not a great place to spend a whole morning, that too to write about 'hand-rehabilitation', whatever that means. But the exigency is such, I can't wriggle out of the assignment. The trip, however, turns out to be great education.

'A hand injury may not be fatal,' Dr R. Krishnamoorthy, head of the hand-rehabilitation department, tells me, 'but it kills you every single day'. His department is the only one of its kind in the country in the government sector, where nearly fifty hand surgeries are performed every day. 'Most of these are emergency surgeries. The moment a patient comes in, we lose no time in moving him to the operation theatre because we want to restore the function of the hand as much as possible.'

Dr Krishnamoorthy presides over an outpatient department where patients with bandaged arms and fingers silently await their turn, even as senior surgeons, with the help of a slideshow, teach intern doctors about the importance of the hand in human anatomy. It's an importance that Dr Krishnamoorthy does not tire of underscoring.

'Medical colleges don't have too many specialists to teach students about the anatomy of the hand, even though, when a doctor passes out of college and joins service, one of the first cases he deals with is that of a hand injury. He doesn't know what to do,' he tells me.

Heart disease, cancer, diabetes are scary, of course, but how a hand injury can alter your life forever is demonstrated in its full grotesqueness by the victims awaiting their turn in the outpatient department.

Sasi, twenty-eight, was like any other able-bodied young man until a year ago. But a stove-burst has deformed his hands and rendered them useless: he now has to be fed by his mother. Similarly, Tamilvannan, barely fifteen, lost his fingers on the right hand while he was bursting crackers during a funeral procession. How, in a split of a second, his world had changed.

In the men's ward, about two dozen men lying on their beds stare at us blankly when Dr Krishnamoorthy leads me there. They are so young and healthy that for a moment you think they are film extras facing the camera for a hospital scene. But it is only when you notice their bandaged arms that you understand the silence that hangs heavily in the ward. Each one is coming to terms with the loss of a thumb or a few fingers or—in some cases—an entire hand. What's worse, because the affected part is the hand, they are reminded every waking moment about that particular accident or the act of negligence that changed their lives forever.

'Even if we are able to restore fifty to sixty per cent of their hands' functions, we consider it a success. We need high-quality expertise for hand surgery, because the procedure is very definitive and defined,' says Dr Krishnamoorthy. It takes a series of micro-vascular surgeries to restore partial functioning of the fingers, and in some cases, a toe fills in for a missing finger. 'We, of course, have to ask the patients if they want a toe removed. Most of the time they agree, because, while shoes can hide a missing toe, it is not easy to hide a missing finger,' says Dr Krishnamoorthy.

Since Stanley Hospital is government-run, patients don't have to pay a penny for the treatment, which can often last for years. 'If you calculate by the market rate, each year we spend about ₹ 30 crore on these surgeries. But it is passion that keeps us going,' says Dr Krishnamoorthy. He has been heading the department since 1990, but his name is unlikely to elicit nods of familiarity in fashionable Chennai. He is, after all, not a sought-after cardiac or orthopaedic surgeon.

Weeks later, to write another story, I happen to meet one of Chennai's most revered chest physicians who, after retiring from government service, decided to take a path few allopathic doctors would tread.

Dr C.N. Deivanayagam, whose name is met with great respect in the medical fraternity, decided to integrate modern medicine with the ancient Indian system of treatment called siddha.

Siddha, which has Tamil roots, is said to predate Ayurveda by several hundred—perhaps, thousand years—and has countless followers in south India even today. In this system, a master health check is run on a patient by simply putting a drop of sesame oil in a bowl containing his urine: the pattern that the drop of oil assumes in the pool of urine indicates the nature of the ailment.

'My goal is to break the mental block against traditional systems of medicine. Only an organised integrated system will work,' Dr Deivanayagam tells me even as he places the stethoscope against the back of a small boy. The petrified child refuses to cooperate, only to be scolded by his mother. The doctor, in turn, admonishes her: 'Let him be! I can deal with him.' Outside the door of his cramped clinic in Egmore, nearly hundred other patients are waiting.

Dr Deivanayagam, sixty-eight, is assisted at the clinic by a fellow allopath and a siddha doctor. Once he makes the diagnosis, his two assistants consult each other and write out the prescription, which often includes exercise and a change in lifestyle. The patients are required to pay only a one-time registration fee of fifty rupees.

Dr Deivanayagam's faith in siddha was firmly established back in the mid-1990s when he took charge of the Government Hospital of Thoracic Medicine in Tambaram, and found that he didn't have the drugs he desperately needed to treat AIDS patients admitted there.

'I was confronted with a large number of patients but there were no drugs to treat them. The health ministry officials told me their brief was only to prevent HIV—which meant promoting the use of condoms—but not treat it. So I used my emergency powers and gave my patients anti-retroviral drugs.

'But the drugs available were too little. That's when the siddha chaps came into the picture,' he tells me.

'I invited ninety siddha doctors to the hospital and hosted them for a day. We zeroed in on three drugs to treat the HIV patients. Suddenly we found that they were no longer dying. The siddha drugs had increased their white cell count and reduced the presence of the virus,' recalls the doctor, who passed out of the Madras Medical College in 1964 with a gold medal for being the best outgoing student.

Considering that very few doctors have a CV as impressive as his—he has been at the helm of top government-run hospitals in Chennai—Dr Deivanayagam could have easily set up a lucrative private practice post-retirement. Instead, he chose to embrace an ancient Indian system of treating diseases and integrated it with his knowledge of modern medicine in order to serve the people. 'Our motto is Return of Health. And that is possible only when the two systems are made to complement each other,' says the khadi-clad doctor as he calls the next patient over.

■ ■ ■

Until the morning of 22 May 1991, India hadn't heard of Sriperumbudur, then a nondescript town located about forty kilometres southwest of Madras on the road to Bangalore. Only the staunchest of Iyengars knew it to be the birthplace of Sri Ramanuja, the Vaishnavite saint.

But on the night of 21 May that year, Sriperumbudur had its name entered, indelibly in blood, in the annals of Indian history. The next morning, the entire nation, which was in the midst of electing a new prime minister, was gaping in horror at the new entry. The shocked country was trying to pronounce the tongue-twister of a word: Sriperumbudur.

Rajiv Gandhi almost did not make it to Sriperumbudur that night.

The King Air aircraft that had taken him for election meetings across Orissa and Andhra Pradesh developed an electrical snag in Vishakhapatnam, from where he was to fly to Madras. Rajiv, himself a pilot, tried to fix the snag but eventually gave up and decided to spend the night at Vishakhapatnam. Soon after he left the airport, the King Air engineer managed to detect the fault and rectify it.

When Rajiv Gandhi was informed over the wireless that the plane could now take off, he promptly returned to the airport.

Due to the abrupt change in plan, his personal security officer, O.P. Sagar, who was travelling in another car, got left behind in Vishakhapatnam. Sagar was to hand over his weapon to Pradeep Gupta, the sub-inspector who was going to accompany Rajiv through Tamil Nadu and who was now waiting at the Meenambakkam airport, along with a crowd of local Congress leaders, for Rajiv's arrival.

Rajiv Gandhi landed in Madras at 8.20 pm. In precisely two hours, he lay lifeless among a heap of people killed by a suicide bomber who had managed to sneak into his election meeting in Sriperumbudur. In the heap was also the body of Gupta, his loyal and weaponless security officer.

The scene of the murder is now an open-air memorial, easily identifiable because of the tricolour flying over it. The final steps taken by Rajiv Gandhi are marked by a tapering path—the narrower the path gets, the closer he was walking to death that fateful night. The very spot he was felled by the Tamil suicide bomber is marked by a stone and guarded by seven columns.

The memorial—manicured lawns, trees, the stone walls depicting India's progress in science and technology, the overwhelming silence—is pleasing to the eye as well as the ear; it is impossible to imagine that this is the same spot where a deafening blast had ripped through one night twenty years ago and where mangled bodies lay strewn amidst hysterical screams. Today, if you visit the memorial, you may even wonder: did it really happen?

Rajiv Gandhi's assassination is now a thing of past—it is just one of the many horrible things that have happened to India. If anyone still relives that tragic night every single day, it is Rajiv Gandhi's widow and two children—and the three Tamil men in Vellore jail who have been handed the death penalty for their role in the assassination. The rest of India seems to have moved on—Sriperumbudur certainly has.

From being known as the site for one of the most gruesome tragedies in recent history, it has long got rid of the taint and earned the reputation of a generous host to multinational companies wanting to set up shop in India. Each morning, shortly after dawn, dozens of buses, after snaking through the roads of Chennai, hit the highway to Sriperumbudur, carrying employees of the various manufacturing plants to their workplaces. Why just Sriperumbudur? The buses also head to the south-western suburbs of Oragadam and Maraimalai Nagar, and speed down the Old Mahabalipuram Road as well.

In these buses are people who are in the manufacturing industry. From 2000-kg cars to weightless lingerie, they make almost everything that is required by mankind today—mobile phones, laptops, flat-screen television sets, electronic components, condoms, mirrors, to name a few. If you take the automobile industry alone, just look at who all are here—Hyundai (which was the first to set up a plant near Chennai, in 1999), Ford, BMW, Renault, Nissan, Mitsubishi. Their factories on the outskirts of Chennai collectively roll out three cars every minute and a commercial vehicle every seventy-five seconds—something that has earned Chennai the sobriquet of 'Detroit of India'.

Why did the manufacturing giants and technology majors choose Chennai?

They were lured by a cocktail of factors. The state government welcomes foreign investment and the city as such is business-friendly; land is easily available and so is skilled labour; the workforce is disciplined and dedicated; costs are competitive; and, above all, Chennai is connected to the rest of the world by sea, air and land.

And when these companies first started coming in, less than a decade ago, even the cost of living in the city was relatively low—that must have served as the dash of lime to the cocktail.

Today, however, the very presence of these multinationals has hiked the cost of living in Chennai. Real-estate prices have gone through the roof, so have rentals. And as recently as in 2006, when my wife and I bought our first car, we were able to hire a driver for just ₹ 3,500; today, a driver expects nothing less than ₹ 10,000 a month. If you don't hire him, the vice-president of a multinational company will. The dynamics have changed.

Hitherto-unheard-of places such as Sriperumbudur, Oragadam and Maraimalai Nagar are today being projected by realtors as the Chennai of the future.

Some time ago, I was woken up from deep slumber by good old Dhanasekaran, the bank agent who had helped us get our car loan. Right now, he was calling on behalf of a real estate company.

'Sir, there is a two-bedroom house in Sriperumbudur, ideal for you and madam. Just twenty-five lakh,' he said.

'But why would I want to live in Sriperumbudur?' I asked him.

'Why not, sir? Please check with madam. She might be interested.'

'But why on earth would I want to live in Sriperumbudur?' I asked again.

'Please check with madam, sir. If she agrees, I can show you the site. Only twenty-five lakh, sir.'

Dhanasekaran knew very well that it is my wife who takes the decisions when it came to matters such as acquiring property, whereas I am only a vagabond who does not believe in saving or planning for the future.

'But why would I want to live in Sriperumbudur?' I asked him yet again.

'Why not, sir? Sriperumbudur is the future of Chennai. And who is asking you to live there? Just rent out the flat. You will recover your money in no time. Can I please have madam's phone number?'

He was angry with me for not grabbing the opportunity. His anger was genuine. The areas that were considered to be outskirts until yesterday are now goldmines in the making. If you happen to snail behind a bus in the heavy Chennai traffic, you will most likely find the rear of the vehicle bearing an advertisement urging you to buy property in these fast-growing satellite townships: 'European Styled Bungalow Apartments In Oragadam'; or 'NRI's Spanish City in Sriperumbudur'.

So Europe, which built Fort St George and created Madras nearly four centuries ago, has returned to create New Chennai. Places like Sriperumbudur, Oragadam and Maraimalai Nagar are the New Black Town. Then, the classified ads in the newspapers: 'Independent Villa at Sriperumbudur for just 17.95 lacs onwards. Now is the Right Time to Invest in this Location of the Future.'

As for Old Mahabalipuram Road, or OMR, until not too long ago it was literally just the road that joined Chennai with the ancient town of Mahabalipuram, barely 50 km down the coast. But today it is the lifeline of the city's IT industry and the pride of Chennai. I remember seeing the road in a potholed form not too long ago; now, of course, you have to pay toll to enter it. It is flanked by the plush, high-security offices of the IT majors—you name it and they are there—and equally plush, high-security residential complexes.

■ ■ ■

'Drive; don't fly', warns a signboard as soon as I leave the madness of Poonamallee High Road behind and emerge onto the highway to the Shenzhen of India—Sriperumbudur. I am visiting the Nokia plant this morning.

As the miles begin to melt, the landscape alternates between the suburban and the urban. One moment you see a village school, another moment a newly-built modern residential complex; one moment a wayside temple, another moment a large college. But on the whole it is barrenness that you encounter—a lot of fresh air.

The recently-built high-rises stand like concrete scarecrows on the fields. They will soon be joined by fellow high-rises and together they will change the skyline of Chennai. The city's boundaries will eventually expand and the suburban will become urban.

I know I am nearing Sriperumbudur when I see container-trucks laden with Hyundai cars hitting the highway. They are all pouring out of the Hyundai plant in Irungattukottai, once upon a time a tiny hamlet near Sriperumbudur. Some of the trucks go past us, while some we happen to trail and eventually overtake. I wonder about the ego of their drivers: they are driving a lorry that is as big as an aircraft which contains dozens of off-the-assembly-line high-speed cars, so how do they feel about being overtaken by a humble Tata Indica taxi? I decide to interview one such driver someday—how does it feel driving a lorry laden with cars? Will he himself ever be able to buy and drive one of them—given his salary?

I soon pass the Rajiv Gandhi memorial. You can't miss it because of the tricolour. I am tempted to ask the driver to stop for a few minutes but decide against it. I would rather make a halt on the way back and walk around the memorial at leisure. By now, apartment complexes—even hotels—begin springing up along the road. Back then, when Rajiv Gandhi drove to the site that fateful night, the idea of a posh hotel in Sriperumbudur must have been as fantastic as man living on Mars.

I arrive at the Nokia factory shortly before nine. To me its exterior resembles a large swanky airport, one of those that are built far away from civilisation. In fact, Bangalore airport first comes to my mind as soon as the taxi pulls in: nothing but vacant lands and greenery around, and a gentle breeze sweeping through the landscape. Bangalore, in any case, is just 300 kilometres down the highway.

Uniformed security guards are all around: they are the policemen in this island called the Nokia special economic zone, spread over 210 acres. Shortly before nine, the workers start trooping in. The guards scrutinise each identity card at the entrance. Since I don't have one, I kill considerable time waiting at the reception desk even as the receptionist tries to locate on her computer the name of the Nokia official I am supposed to meet. Worse, she has never heard of him. I try calling the official repeatedly from my phone but the call, for some reason, refuses to go through.

My Nokia man, it eventually turns out, has been waiting for me all along at another reception area. So, after many long minutes of disconnect in the factory of a company that connects people, I get to meet him and shake his hand in gratitude.

He is a kind man: he has not only agreed to show me around—in spite of the fact that he is busy because Nokia is preparing to celebrate five years in Sriperumbudur (the operations began in 2006) he had also sent a cab home to fetch me.

Adjoining the reception desk are two conference rooms, Kingfisher and Pelican. We sit in Kingfisher, where the Nokia man informs me that this is one of the largest factories in the world of the Finnish telecom giant; that the factory has already produced 400 million handsets and will soon touch the 500-million landmark—the fastest ramp-up in any of the Nokia factories; that the operations are round-the-clock except on public holidays; that the phones that are produced are from the starting level to mid-range, and are exported to seventy countries across the world including Europe, Africa, North America, West and Southeast Asia.

'It was the setting up of the Nokia SEZ that actually brought the investment train into Tamil Nadu. The single-window clearance by the state government really helped. The memorandum of understanding was signed in 2005,' he tells me.

The SEZ also houses manufacturing units of electronic component-makers such as Foxconn, Perlos, Wintek, Salcomp (which makes phone chargers) and Laird. In all, it provides employment to 30,000 people, about 8,000 of whom work for Nokia.

'Sixty to seventy per cent of our workers are women. They come from in and around Sriperumbudur, within an 80-km radius. To be hired by us, the minimum requirement is 60 per cent marks in the twelfth standard. It is not at all difficult to find such candidates here. We train them, we provide them free door-to-door transport, and there is also a subsidised canteen,' he tells me. 'Come, let me take you inside.'

At the reception, I am asked to deposit my mobile phone—a Nokia—and other electronic items I may be carrying. I hand over my iPod too. In return, I am given a special suit to wear—it's like a flimsy raincoat which is supposed to prevent the static electricity generated by the human body from tampering with the intricate process of mobile phone-manufacturing. The Nokia man puts one on too.

The shop floor turns out to be as large as an aircraft hangar with multiple parallel assembly lines. When you use gadgets such as a mobile phone or laptop, you imagine it to have been manufactured by a bunch of reclusive nerds or grey-haired techies who have no other interest whatsoever in life than creating new technology. It can be a bit disappointing to see young women and men—who could have been working in a nursing home or a supermarket—manufacturing mobile phones for you. But then, the techies have already done their bit; as for the assembling, it requires no special qualification or skill—just a first division in the Twelfth Standard and some training.

Yet it is mind-boggling how a phone comes into being. One moment you see a circuit board being sliced into small rectangles, and the very next moment, as you walk down the assembly line, you find each small rectangular piece magically metamorphosing into a mobile phone—packed and sealed!

'We can do 750K phones a day!' reads one motivational sign in the shop floor. 'Aim zero customer complaint,' says another. My favourite: 'Quality is remembered long after the price is forgotten.'

Back at the reception desk, I reclaim my Nokia phone and take the cab back to Chennai. As I roll down the window and prepare to take in the sights, my mind goes back to the very first mobile phone that I bought in 1999 from a shop in Connaught Place in Delhi. It was a Nokia 5110, the sturdiest phone I've ever come across. Back then, it was also the smallest phone that fit into your shirt pocket—though it would look like a giant if it were to be placed alongside today's models. That phone had accompanied me to Chennai when I relocated from Delhi in 2001 and stayed with me for a very long time. I had never imagined that a Nokia factory would come to my doorstep someday.

And someday soon, one wouldn't have to drive from Sriperumbudur *back to Chennai*. Sriperumbudur will be the new Chennai, the happening Chennai. The new citizens of that new city will look down upon the places we live in today, just as we today look down upon the congested George Town, once the most happening place in Madras. The question is *how* soon—hopefully not in my lifetime.

Chapter 11

MY STREET

I started working on this book in early 2010. Back then, Karunanidhi still had about a year-and-a-half ahead of him as the chief minister of Tamil Nadu and was in a tearing hurry to move the seat of the state government into his dream building. Chennai was awash with posters of him and his two powerful but feuding sons. His daughter Kanimozhi, born of his second wife, was highly active in the city's social circuit, inaugurating some event or the other every evening. The family, in spite of the internal bickering, seemed unassailable. Very few dared cross its path.

Today, in less than two years, as I write these concluding sentences, that world of Karunanidhi has turned upside down. In April 2011, his party suffered a crushing defeat in the state elections. The reins of Tamil Nadu went into the hands of—as was expected—his bitter rival Jayalalithaa who, also as expectedly, moved the secretariat back to Fort St George and ordered that Karunanidhi's dream building be converted into a hospital. Karunanidhi's sons are hardly to be seen or heard of anymore, while his daughter is lodged in Delhi's Tihar Jail on grave charges of corruption. When it rains, it pours—very few would understand the import of this expression better than Karunanidhi today.

Chennai, meanwhile, goes on. It is an unstoppable, self-propelled chariot moving on two wheels, one wheel being tradition and the other technology. It has long grown used to political power changing hands every five years and can't be bothered anymore: it has better things to do, having earned its place on the world map as one of the biggest manufacturing hubs in Asia.

April 2011 turned out to be a month of transition for me, personally.

I had arrived in Chennai in far less complicated times, when there had been only two mainstream English newspapers in the city, *The Hindu* and *The New Indian Express*. They were rivals all right, but they were at peace with each other. Reading *The Hindu* was a Madras habit and the paper therefore was way ahead in terms of circulation; but at the same time the *Express*, basking in its anti-establishment image, had a fiercely loyal, even though much smaller, readership. The two papers neither grudged each other's strengths nor celebrated each other's weaknesses. They coexisted happily, each in its cosy corner on Mount Road.

I came to Chennai in January 2001, to join the Sunday edition of the *Express*. Its offices were located at the end of a small road that branches off Mount Road at the Spencer Plaza junction. The small road is called Club House Road because once upon a long time—from 1832 until the time of Independence—it led to the original Madras Club, the first British club in the city, for long considered the best in India, and dubbed the Ace of Clubs. The sprawling club premises subsequently became the offices of the *Indian Express*.

When I joined the paper, the actual clubhouse—a handsome 200-year-old palatial structure that had withstood countless cyclones and storms—stood neglected in one corner of the compound. I wouldn't have even noticed the building if it hadn't been let out for film shootings. Every now and then, cinema crew would take positions around it, attracting the attention of the *Express* staff. Since I worked for the Sunday paper, I didn't have daily deadlines staring at me, and I would often stroll over to the building to watch the shooting. Depending on the script, it would transform into a wholesale vegetable market one day; a battlefield in Sri Lanka on another. It was in this building, whose floors I found coated with pigeon droppings, that I got to see, for the first time, how films are shot, and also came face to face with several popular Tamil film stars, and directors, including Mani Ratnam.

Then, one fine day in 2003, the structure was razed to the ground. The Ace of Clubs became dust. In July 2006, the offices of the *New Indian Express* moved out of the clubhouse premises to the western suburbs of Ambattur. Since the relocation took place on a Saturday night, I happened to be the news editor who cleared the front page for the Sunday edition—in other words, I oversaw the last edition of *Express* to ever come out of its historic Mount Road office. It was by default that I had presided over the historical moment—not that anyone, except I, paused to give it a thought. The entire machinery was too busy shifting to the new site in Ambattur. Before we headed out to drink that night after putting the paper to bed, the small team that I was part of shook hands with the various vendors who sold tea and vadas and omelettes on Club House Road. These men had made our stay on Mount Road worthwhile—not only by giving us nourishment but also by providing us with space to let off steam. We told them we wouldn't be seeing them again. They smiled back shyly and said they knew that. The next morning we all presented ourselves at Ambattur, where the new office was being consecrated.

My romance with Mount Road had ended. For five years, from January 2001 to July 2006, that was the only road that mattered to me in Chennai—every other road either branched out off, or merged into, it. Each morning, when I set out from my home in T. Nagar, and when the autorickshaw, after traversing through G.N. Chetty Road and the legendary Gemini flyover, hit Mount Road, I would be overcome by a sense of excitement. Descending from the flyover and speeding into Mount Road, I would tear through the curtains of colours that represented Chennai.

I worked out of the Ambattur office of the *Express* for two years, following which I joined the *Times of India* when it launched its Chennai edition in April 2008. At the *Times*, which had its offices on Chamiers Road, I spent three fun-filled years. By then, I had lost my emotional connect with Mount Road. Also, by then, since I was working on this book, I had begun to look closely at *The Hindu*, the paper Chennai swears by. So, even though I had no compelling reason to leave the *Times*, I decided that the time to make the pilgrimage had come. I knocked at the doors of the 'Mahavishnu of Mount Road'—as *The Hindu* is often referred to in a lighter vein in the intellectual circles of Chennai—the reason being, it is run by an Iyengar family.

And so I returned to Mount Road.

'It is the best paper to work in!' my neighbour, also an Iyengar, gushed to me one morning when I met him on the stairs and told him about the job switch. He made a ring with his thumb and forefinger and waved it at me to emphasise the word 'best'. He has never worked in a newspaper, and it is highly unlikely that he has ever known any journalist other than me, and yet he believed *The Hindu* is the place to be—such is the respect the paper commands in the city.

The Hindu is one of the very few employee-friendly papers that remain in the country today. Lunch at the canteen costs just one rupee, employees get a handsome bonus on Diwali, and a dhoti (or saree) on Pongal, and medical expenses are completely taken care of by the company.

Since the office is a no-smoking area, each afternoon, after the one-rupee lunch, I step out to the main road to light up. And each time I step out to meditate over a cigarette, I find myself staring blankly at the giant, grey building right across the road. It is Karunanidhi's dream building, whose inauguration I had attended barely a year-and-half ago and which now lies abandoned, waiting to be turned into a hospital.

Meanwhile, on the site of the old Madras Club—the 200-year-old building where I once watched many a Tamil movie being shot—stands Express Avenue, Chennai's hippest mall.

Express Avenue could have been in Singapore or Hong Kong. Everything here is on a never-before scale as far as Chennai is concerned: a luxurious cineplex which has even a smoking area where, on payment of fifty rupees, you get a cigarette of your choice and a cup of tea or coffee; a premium car park where, on payment of ₹ 150, you can leave your car right outside the stairs to the mall; a food court where you buy a smart card and use it at any of the stalls without having to reach for the wallet each time—the amount that remains unused is returned to you. Then you have the brands of clothes and cosmetics that, until a decade ago, you saw only in the glossy pages of foreign magazines.

Those who have the money come here to shop; those who don't, come to stare—it's the latest wonder of Chennai, promising escape from the daily grind. Each time I visit the mall, which is quite often, I feel smug. I have, after all, seen something that the multitude thronging the mall hasn't. I've seen the mall's past. Turn the clock back by just eight years and the thousands of pairs of feet will walk not on the polished floor of Express Avenue, but on the wooden floor, coated with pigeon droppings, of a heritage building. I have walked on that floor.

But one thing has remained unchanged since I came to Chennai over a decade ago: my address. I continue to reside in the same old building in T. Nagar—on Murugesan Street, the same street where Pugazhendi, the filmmaker who came to receive me at the station when I arrived in Chennai in 2001, wanted me to live.

Illayaraja, the celebrated music director, lives just a few houses away—a fact I never forget to let slip whenever people ask me where I live. People are invariably impressed. Illayaraja, after all, is the real Mozart of Madras—a title created by the alliteration-loving English press which it showers on the much younger and Oscar-winner A.R. Rahman. If it was Rahman's music that made me pack my bags for Chennai nearly eleven years ago, it will be Illayaraja's tunes that I would carry along if I were to ever leave the city.

Late at night, when the street goes quiet and when I do all my writing, Illayaraja's songs often waft up to my third-floor home from the transistor of the watchman. They always make me wonder about two things—how can one conceive such impossible tunes; and is the sound from the radio, by any chance, reaching the ears of the composer?

■ ■ ■

Chennai is the only metropolis in the country where every single tarred stretch—it could be even an apology for a street—has been baptised with a name. It is a practice followed meticulously right from the days of the East India Company, when a street or road would be named after its earliest or most influential resident. The British names are still very much in use; in the case of some roads, the surnames of the civil servants in question have got corrupted beyond repair over the years, most likely due to clerical negligence or ignorance. The classic example of such ignorance is the famous Greams Road, which was once known as Graeme's Road. Or, for that matter, Eldams Road, which should have been known as Yeldham's Road. Mr Graeme and Mr Yeldham must be turning in their graves.

So who was Murugesan of Murugesan Street?

I wouldn't say this was a question that haunted me. But it did occur to me from time to time that I must find out who Murugesan was, or else the experience of living on the street would be incomplete. It would be like travelling in a train without knowing its name. I searched on the internet, but found nothing. I asked some of the neighbours, but they had no clue.

Right opposite my flat stands a two-storey house which calls itself Rathna Ghar. A portion of the ground floor serves as a dental clinic. For years, I had noticed an elderly man sitting on the balcony, looking out on to the street, lost in thought. He would often sit there for hours. From a distance it was difficult to tell his age or his physical condition: all I could see was an old man, the white of his dhoti offsetting the darkness of his skin, watching the world go by.

One morning, a few years ago, after a toothache had kept me up all night, I found myself knocking at the door of Rathna Ghar. Over time I became friends with the couple who run the clinic: Dr. Ravi, who would be about my age, and his wife Dr Sunita. The elderly man turned out to be Dr Ravi's uncle—his father's elder brother. Even though I visited the clinic several times, it never occurred to me that I should meet the man whose favourite pastime seemed to be people-gazing.

Then, one afternoon not very long ago, I ran into Dr Ravi on the street. We chatted for a while, mostly lamenting to each other how the street was going to seed. Murugesan Street is no longer the road either of us once knew. It goes back to its old self only late at night until the crack of dawn. The rest of the day it shrinks to almost half its width because of the cars and bikes parked along its length. And then the noise of the increased traffic! Not to mention the din that recently tormented the neighbourhood for several weeks when two houses adjacent to Rathna Ghar were demolished to make way for the parking lot of a well-known jewellery store. These two houses were not even very old—

and I had often wished I could own one of them—but I guess their respective owners had other plans.

'How old is your house?' I asked Dr Ravi.

'Seventy-seven,' he replied.

'I see.'

'Not 1977,' he quickly corrected himself, 'but seventy-seven years old'.

'Seventy-seven years old?' I was surprised. Rathna Ghar did not look that old. 'And how old do you think my building is?' I asked him.

'The flats were built sometime in the early '80s. I remember it because, as kids, we would playfully chip in during the construction work. But the ground floor already existed; it was an independent house. My uncle will be able to give you the details.'

'How old is he?'

'He is about eight-five now. He has been living here since the 1930s.'

I knew I had to meet the uncle. But I was in no great hurry because I saw him always sitting in the balcony—it was just a question of climbing down the stairs of my home one morning and then climbing up his. Weeks passed, then months. One afternoon, from the window of my kitchen, I found a canopy erected in the garden of Rathna Ghar. Plastic chairs had been placed under it and people were trickling in. I looked at the balcony: it was vacant. My heart sank. I had lost my chance to learn about the history of my street.

It turned out that it was the uncle's son-in-law who had died. The uncle himself was doing fine. Within days, he reappeared on the balcony. I lost no time in meeting him.

■ ■ ■

'My grandfather was an engine driver with the South Indian Railway,' the uncle, M.R. Damodaran, begins his story, sitting in a hammock in the hall. 'My father, Appasamy Mudaliar, went on to join the Burma Railways. He was an accounts officer. I was born in Rangoon. I studied in St Anthony's English Boys' School. It was one of the best schools in Burma. I still have the progress reports signed by the headmaster, A.V.M. Francis—what a great man!'

Damodaran's family hailed from Chengalpet, a town adjoining Chennai. Until the early twentieth century, a substantial chunk of present-day Chennai, including the lake that became T Nagar, fell in Chengalpet, which was then a district under the Madras Presidency. When his father retired from service, the family left Rangoon for Madras.

'We set sail on *S.S. Erinpura*, and arrived in Madras on 21 November 1938. I was eleven then. Ever since then, I have been living in this house. This was built in 1933 by my grandmother and my maternal uncle. I went to Ramakrishna Mission School. I passed SSLC in 1943; after that I joined Loyola College. Then I joined the College of Engineering in Guindy and passed out as a civil engineer in 1947. I joined the Public Works Department and was posted to the Madras Corporation. Those days, once you passed out of that college, you immediately got an appointment letter.'

The College of Engineering, Guindy, now part of Anna University, is the oldest engineering college in the country and one of the oldest engineering institutions in the world, starting as the School of Survey in Fort St George in 1794.

'Those days,' continues Damodaran, 'properties used to be auctioned to the beat of a tom-tom. Whenever you heard the tom-tom, you knew a property was up for sale.

Murray and Co. were the official auctioneers. When I was in college—I think this was 1947 or '48—Sir C.V. Raman bought three bungalows in T Nagar for one lakh rupees each. We went to watch that auction for the fun of it. Those days you could just carry your moneybag and buy a piece of land.

'In 1956, Annadurai wanted to buy property in Madras. He had already identified a building on Avenue Road in Nungambakkam. It had been rented to the Indian Bank. He wanted to make sure if he was doing the right thing in buying that property, and whether it was under litigation and free from encumbrance. Since I was the junior engineer for the Nungambakkam division, some DMK leaders approached me for my opinion on the matter. But we were under strict instructions not to identify ourselves with any political group, so I told them that I would not be able to help them. Then, one Sunday morning, I was visited by the chairman of the Kancheepuram municipality, a man called C.V. Krishnaswamy. (Annadurai also hailed from Kancheepuram, known as Conjeevaram during the British days; which is why Annadurai's initials happen to be C.N. and not K.N.)

'The man pleaded with me to come along to the Nungambakkam property to take a look. I told him it was a Sunday and that there was no way I could accompany him. He said, "In that case, please speak to Annadurai. He is waiting outside." I stepped out of the house to find Annadurai waiting in his car—it was a Hindustan Landmaster. Annadurai told me, "I understand your situation. But I have to be in Trichy (Tiruchirapalli) tomorrow. Why don't you please come with us? You don't have to come in my car. You can follow us on your motorcycle." So I went along with them to take a look at the property. I told them they could buy it. Annadurai thanked me profusely for coming along and from there he left for Trichy.'

Annadurai, waiting in his car on my street—that, too, right outside my house? This is difficult to imagine now; but with the passage of time, even the most mundane of things become material for fantasy.

Another thing difficult to imagine: Damodaran riding a motorcycle in his younger days. I have, after all, always seen him as an elderly man, sitting passively in the balcony. It was impossible to associate him with action.

'What motorcycle did you have?' I ask him.

'Royal Enfield,' he tells me with a proud smile. 'MSX 2180. When I sold it twenty years after I bought it, I still made a profit of ten thousand rupees.'

Even as I listen, spellbound, to Damodaran's stories, my eyes happen to wander around and eventually fall on a teak desk sitting in a corner of the hall. It looks ancient.

'Sir, that desk, how old is it?'

'Oh, that.' He gets up from the hammock and walks towards the desk. 'Come, I will show you. This belonged to Karamatullah, ICS, who was the collector of Madras. After Partition, he left for Pakistan. Before leaving, he auctioned his belongings. I bought this desk, for fifty-five rupees.' He strokes the wood, much to my envy. Suddenly, I spot an old Parker pen on the desk.

'Isn't that a fountain pen?' I ask.

'Yes! Wait, I will show you more.' He opens a drawer and fishes out a handful—all vintage Mont Blanc, Parker and Sheaffer. I am overcome by greed, and feel relieved when he puts them back in the drawer and shuts it.

'And this chair,' continues Damodaran, 'this was gifted to me by Nagi Reddi'.

'Nagi Reddi, the filmmaker?'

'Yes. When he was getting his son and daughter married, he extended his house in Vadapalani. It was encroaching upon a road that led to a burial ground. Since I was in charge of the area, I served him notice for violating building laws. He immediately came to my office. He was a thorough gentleman. He told me, "Sir, I have never been to a government office before. Kindly guide me." I asked him to speak to the collector and got an appointment for him. The collector settled the matter; I think he decreed that the approach road to the burial ground was not usable in any case. I found Nagi Reddi to be a very nice man. When I was transferred out of the zone, I went to see him in his office. I told him, "I can never forget you. That is why I came to say goodbye." After meeting him I came home, but even before I could reach home, this chair had arrived! He later told me, "Damodaran *garu*, whenever you sit on that chair, please think of me." I still think of him, he was a great man.'

When Damodaran returns to the hammock, I ask him what changes he has seen in Murugesan Street over the decades. 'Once upon a time it was very quiet and clean. It even got an award for being the best-maintained street.'

'And who was Murugesan?' I finally ask him.

'There were two Murugesans living on this street. One was P.M. Murugesa Mudaliar, and the other was N. Murugesa Mudaliar. Both had printing presses. But P.M. Murugesa Mudaliar was older; he was also into publishing. He published Telugu books. The street is named after him.'

'Any other memories you have?'

'Have you seen Kerala Hair Dressers in Pondy Bazaar?'

'Yes, of course.'

'Once upon a time it was known as Malabar Haircutting Saloon, and it used to be on the other side of the road. The daughter of the headmaster of T. Nagar High School, who lived on a nearby street, fell in love with a barber working in that saloon. They got married. It was a big scandal. We did not approve of such a marriage, but love is blind.

'And then, in Pondy Bazaar, there used to be Bharat Café, which also delivered meals to homes. A meal cost a rupee, and the monthly charge for home delivery was also a rupee. A young lady doctor, from a Brahmin family, fell in love with the delivery boy, and they got married. The doctor's brother used to be our playmate. Today, she must be about seventy-eight, and lives somewhere in Chennai.'

'When did Illayaraja come here?'

'He came sometime in the early Eighties. He purchased the property at a throwaway price from M. Nagaraja Rao, who used to be an editor with *The Mail*. Once upon a time, Illayaraja and his brothers—five in all—used to live in a small room on Usman Road for a monthly rent of thirty rupees. Then, he became a big man.'

'What about the building I live in?' I ask Damodaran. 'How old is it?'

'Very old. It used to be a large, single-storey house, called Sundar Niketan. Krishnaswamy Sundarji, who went on to become army chief, grew up in that house. His father, P.A. Krishnaswamy, was an inspector of survey and also taught in the College of Engineering. Sundarji had two brothers and one sister. One of the brothers, Sridhar, went on to join the navy.

'We all went to Ramakrishna Mission School. We were good friends. We used to play together at Somasundaram Ground, two streets away. Then Sundarji shifted to Madras

Christian College in Tambaram. He joined the University Officer Training Corps, which is the British equivalent of the NCC. While in the Corps he went on to earn the rank of sergeant-major, because of which he got commissioned in the army straightaway as a lieutenant. This must have been around 1945.

'In 1948, when Gandhiji was assassinated, Sundarji's mother Lalitha was inconsolable. She was wailing like anything when the news came in the papers. We could all hear her crying. The family didn't stay here for long after that. They sold the house to K.V. Reddy, a famous director of Telugu films. Reddy was a highly respected man in the industry; he made films like *Patala Bhairavi*, which was a big hit in those days. But he was a very simple man. He had five daughters and three sons, and he got all of them married in his village in Andhra Pradesh. He lived and died here.

'After his death, the house was purchased by one A.C. Abraham, who was an assistant commissioner of income-tax, for one lakh rupees. Abraham did not stay here for long: he eventually sold the property to one Kesari Jain, for one lakh and fifteen thousand rupees. Jain too didn't stay for long. He sold the house for one lakh and twenty-five thousand rupees to R.R. Flats, one of the early builders in Madras. They turned it into flats by adding more floors. Come to think of it, each occupant made only a marginal profit by selling the property.'

So: the building I have lived in for the past eleven years is where India's most flamboyant, scholarly and controversial army chief spent the best part of his childhood. Not only that: it had also served as home to one of Telugu cinema's best-known directors. And I had not known any of this.

That night, as I return home after the long chat with Damodaran and pour myself a drink, I feel extraordinarily good about living in Chennai. It's a city that can be frustratingly modest about its riches. Even if you are sitting on a pot of gold you wouldn't know about it most of the time, until a casual conversation or a chance meeting with someone who knows better makes you dig for it.

■ ■ ■

One way of measuring time that has passed is to look closely at people around you. The grey hair, weightless, carries the burden of several years; wrinkles are the graffiti these years leave on your face as they subtract from your lifespan.

At the end of my street, where it meets the busy North Usman Road, sits a fruit-seller. I have been seeing him there ever since I came to Chennai. He must have been about forty then, a small, wiry man who would sit behind a cartload of apples and oranges along with his son, who wouldn't have been more than ten. For the first few years after coming to Chennai I would often buy apples from him. Then the supermarkets opened in the neighbourhood and I stopped going to him. Over time I became blind to his existence. Recently, while waiting to cross the road, I noticed him. Our eyes met, but he did not get up from the stool upon seeing me, as he used to before. His hair had turned all grey and he looked thinner. The boy, who still sat next to his father, was now a strapping young man. A decade has passed all too soon.

January 2010–October 2011

ACKNOWLEDGEMENTS

Chennai, right from the time I stepped into the city on Pongal Day in 2001, has offered me nothing but kindness. The kindness led to an emotional attachment and the attachment to this book, which intends to be evidence—hopefully lasting—that I spent the best years of my life in this city. Needless to say, during its writing, I had people lending a hand all along. I would, however, specifically like to thank the following:

Gautam Padmanabhan, CEO of Westland, for showing continued faith;

Prita Maitra, my editor at Tranquebar and co-traveller in the journey;

S. Muthiah, Sriram V, Dr Priya Selvaraj—they helped in more ways than I can explain;

Sudeep Chowdhuri, Shruthi Venkatasubramanian, Aparna Karthikeyan, Baradwaj Rangan, Sriya Narayanan, Mimi Basu, Paula Ray—each went through parts of the text and made immensely valuable suggestions;

Lt Col. Sombit Ghosh, Sashi Nair, Bhama Devi Ravi, V. Balasubramanian, Sangeetha Kandavel, D. Suresh Kumar, K. Venkataramanan, B. Sivakumar, Shalini Umachandran, Sandhya Soman, Jeeva, Julie Mariappan, Revathi Ramanan, Ramya Manoharan, Snigdha Manchanda-Binjola, Margee Dani—for being sounding boards, for giving critical inputs and for causing doors to open.

All characters featured in this book are real. The names of some of them have been changed to protect their privacy.

www.ingramcontent.com/pod-product-compliance
Lightning Source LLC
LaVergne TN
LVHW091704070526
838199LV00050B/2279